THE
COMPLETE IDIOT'S GUIDE® TO

Etiquette

Third Edition

by Mary Mitchell

ALPHA

A member of Penguin Group (USA) Inc.

This book is dedicated to Letitia Baldrige, my treasured friend, mentor, and partner in never-to-be-revealed etiquette crimes.

ALPHA BOOKS

Published by the Penguin Group

Penguin Group (USA) Inc., 375 Hudson Street, New York, New York 10014, U.S.A.

Penguin Group (Canada), 90 Eglinton Avenue East, Suite 700, Toronto, Ontario M4P 2Y3, Canada (a division of Pearson Penguin Canada Inc.)

Penguin Books Ltd, 80 Strand, London WC2R 0RL, England

Penguin Ireland, 25 St Stephen's Green, Dublin 2, Ireland (a division of Penguin Books Ltd)

Penguin Group (Australia), 250 Camberwell Road, Camberwell, Victoria 3124, Australia (a division of Pearson Australia Group Pty Ltd)

Penguin Books India Pvt Ltd, 11 Community Centre, Panchsheel Park, New Delhi—110 017, India

Penguin Group (NZ), 67 Apollo Drive, Rosedale, North Shore, Auckland 1311, New Zealand (a division of Pearson New Zealand Ltd)

Penguin Books (South Africa) (Pty) Ltd, 24 Sturdee Avenue, Rosebank, Johannesburg 2196, South Africa

Penguin Books Ltd, Registered Offices: 80 Strand, London WC2R 0RL, England

Copyright © 2004 by Mary Mitchell

International Standard Book Number: 978-1-59257-261-8
Library of Congress Catalog Card Number: 2004106746

09 08 07   10 9 8 7 6 5

Interpretation of the printing code: The rightmost number of the first series of numbers is the year of the book's printing; the rightmost number of the second series of numbers is the number of the book's printing. For example, a printing code of 04-1 shows that the first printing occurred in 2004.

Printed in the United States of America

Note: This publication contains the opinions and ideas of its author. It is intended to provide helpful and informative material on the subject matter covered. It is sold with the understanding that the author and publisher are not engaged in rendering professional services in the book. If the reader requires personal assistance or advice, a competent professional should be consulted.

The author and publisher specifically disclaim any responsibility for any liability, loss, or risk, personal or otherwise, which is incurred as a consequence, directly or indirectly, of the use and application of any of the contents of this book.

Most Alpha books are available at special quantity discounts for bulk purchases for sales promotions, premiums, fundraising, or educational use. Special books, or book excerpts, can also be created to fit specific needs.

For details, write: Special Markets, Alpha Books, 375 Hudson Street, New York, NY 10014.

Publisher: *Marie Butler-Knight*
Product Manager: *Phil Kitchel*
Senior Managing Editor: *Jennifer Chisholm*
Senior Acquisitions Editor: *Randy Ladenheim-Gil*
Development Editor: *Jennifer Moore*
Senior Production Editor: *Billy Fields*

Copy Editor: *Cari Luna*
Illustrator: *Shannon Wheeler*
Cover/Book Designer: *Trina Wurst*
Indexer: *Tonya Heard*
Layout/Proofreading: *Becky Harmon, Donna Martin*

Contents at a Glance

Contents

Foreword

Philadelphia is one of America's most dynamic cities. It has played a significant role for more than 300 years in our nation's history. Philadelphia was William Penn's Green Country Towne ... the Revolutionary City during America's struggle to freedom ... the Federal City as the first capital of the United States ... the Athens of America as the center of culture, wealth, and social graces for the emerging nation ... the hub of America's Industrial Revolution ... the Centennial City when the world took notice of America at 100 and visitors from around the globe came to Philadelphia to celebrate and experience its refined, cosmopolitan vitality and elegance ... and the Bicentennial City when America once again celebrated—this time its 200th birthday—and Philadelphia would reinvent itself as the leading urban center it is today.

Throughout its history, Philadelphia and its citizens had to call upon social skills that made others feel welcomed. Today, courtesy, graciousness, good manners, and an appreciation of others are critical attributes in the complex and diversified world we live in. Correct business etiquette is also a must to be successful. Good manners never fade—only people who do not use them do! Proper manners don't cost anything and they are accessible to all Americans. Clearly that is a hallmark of our democracy.

At the Philadelphia Convention & Visitors Bureau, our responsibilities in promoting Philadelphia nationally and around the world always include utilizing good manners with everyone we meet and deal with. After all, we are representing one of our nation's greatest brands, the symbol of freedom: Philadelphia.

Mary Mitchell, whom we are proud to claim as a Philadelphian, is—not coincidentally—a renowned authority on all things etiquette. We enthusiastically recommend her *Complete Idiot's Guide to Etiquette, Third Edition*, a dynamic, easy-to-use reference we employ to brush up or focus on our behavior and protocol issues, especially important in dealing with the global markets and diverse cultures we encounter. We know it will become an essential and enjoyable tool for you, as well.

—Jack P. Ferguson
Vice president, Convention Division
Philadelphia Convention & Visitors Bureau

Introduction

Please, thank you, excuse me, and how do you do?

Good. But not good enough these days. We live in a new society, as different from the one in which our parents grew up as the computer is different from the typewriter. And the realities of this new American society require a new approach to the old concepts of civility.

For good or ill, virtually every aspect of our new culture is influenced, if not controlled, by the world of work. We communicate in new, fast, and sometimes jarring ways. The new world of sex and dating is more open but, at the same time, more sensitive than ever before. Family relationships are often more complex, and there are new rules for relating to in-laws, stepparents and stepchildren, biological and adoptive parents, same-sex couples, and unmarried mothers.

The shrinking globe and instant communication systems mean that we are called upon more often to respond to difficult situations involving cultural clashes and racial and ethnic diversity.

It is a world keyed to speed, skills acquisition, and an "I am my resumé" mentality, where good manners, civility, and etiquette are more important than ever before.

Whether or not it's unfair, people will make character judgments about you based on how you handle social situations. This can be a crucial factor when your superiors make decisions about how far and how high you can go in an organization.

And the rules of etiquette, new and old, must be learned. You do not know these things instinctively, no matter how smart you are. Somebody has to teach you. Somebody had to teach me.

Once, these rules were learned at home, often around the dinner table. Well, families don't gather around the dinner table as regularly or as formally as they once did, and parents in the everybody-works world have little time to conduct lessons in deportment.

Even those who have had a good grounding in etiquette need some updating in this rapidly changing world, and the idea behind this book is to provide the information you need in an orderly, easy-to-find, easy-to-understand way. You will find everything you need to know about proper behavior, socially and professionally, in casual and formal circumstances, here and abroad.

Beyond Etiquette

Once, a foreign visitor at a dinner given by Pearl Mesta, "the hostess with the most-ess," drank the water in his finger bowl instead of using it to cleanse his fingers. Mesta immediately followed suit, and the other guests took their cue from her.

Using the finger bowl as intended would have been proper etiquette, but it would not have been good manners.

Good manners come from the inside and do not change. Etiquette rules come from the outside, and they are constantly changing. The rules in school are different from the rules in the office. And the rules also change with time.

Good manners are based on kindness and respect, which transcend etiquette. In every human situation, there is the correct action, the incorrect action, and the appropriate action. This book explains the rules. Only you can judge whether to adhere to them verbatim. Knowing the rules is essential because it puts you in the position of knowing when it is appropriate to break them or bend them.

Sometimes adhering strictly to rules is used as a weapon—which is the height (or depth) of bad manners. A person's feelings are always more important.

How This Book Is Organized

The book presents etiquette by category and is divided into six parts.

Part 1, "Mind, Body, Spirit." You can't learn to live peacefully and harmoniously with others if you have no sense of inner peace yourself. In today's less-secure, stressed-filled, often chaotic world, that's an increasingly difficult proposition. Part 1 describes numerous individual and collective activities that can help you find some peace for your mind and soul, as well as healthy exercise for your body, including yoga, meditation, a spa visit, workouts at the gym, and a variety of sports activities. Following rules and principles of etiquette are particularly important in these venues, so as not to intrude on others seeking the same sense of sanctuary. Communication, respect, kindness, and compassion are the watchwords, especially for the ultimate release for your spirit and body: sex.

Part 2, "Dining and Drinking." This section includes the most common dining mistakes, table settings, how to eat difficult foods, and tips that will help you approach the most daunting dining situations with confidence. It also covers the all-important business meal and the problems and pleasures of home entertaining—everything from a casual get-together to a formal dinner.

Part 3, "Home and Community." Manners for children and young people—at home, at school, and in cyberspace—are discussed here, as well as ways to navigate the perils of peer pressure, especially in an era when the concept of family values is expanding. Extended, adoptive, same-sex families are among the norm, and the rules of compassion, consideration, and respect for each other are examined in this part. Your community and the environment are also part of your extended family, and attention to day-to-day manners in this realm is also fundamental to harmonious living.

Part 4, "Business Etiquette." Business rules are different from social etiquette, as is the whole approach to the subject of manners. Part 4 deals with what to say, how to dress, and how to react to various situations in the world of work, including the new opportunities and potential pitfalls brought about by the ongoing electronic revolution.

Part 5, "Saying the Right Thing." Here we look at how to deal with conflict and criticism. We also discuss how to meet and interact with people with disabilities, obese people, and people from other cultures, as well as how to give and receive compliments. You'll also learn some tips about how to select and present gifts for various occasions.

Part 6, "Correspondence." The pen is still powerful, the age of e-mail notwithstanding. Part 6 discusses the etiquette of e-mail, the structure and style of letters and notes, appropriate stationery for different situations, invitations, and addressing people properly.

Part 7, "Travel." Hit the road, the skies, the rails, and the seas with confidence and maximum efficiency, even in these security-conscious times. Preparation is key, and Part 7 covers what to pack, what to wear, and what to expect when you get there (and how much and whom to tip all along the way). Etiquette for every hotel and how to be the perfect houseguest are also featured.

Part 8, "Wedding Bells." The traditional wedding is back in style, but the participants are often anything but traditional. Part 8 covers all the formalities—from engagement to honeymoon—with plenty of wiggle room to tweak yours into an affair to remember, minus the angst. This part walks you through showers, rings, invitations, announcements, who's who—and then down the aisle and through the reception. This part also takes the guesswork out of being a guest or a party member in a wide variety of nuptials.

Conventions Used in This Book

This book contains several special features.

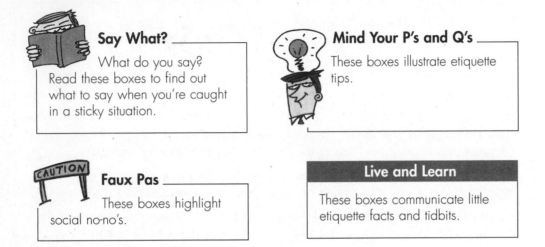

Say What?

What do you say? Read these boxes to find out what to say when you're caught in a sticky situation.

Mind Your P's and Q's

These boxes illustrate etiquette tips.

Faux Pas

These boxes highlight social no-no's.

Live and Learn

These boxes communicate little etiquette facts and tidbits.

Acknowledgments

A good editor demonstrates tenacious thinking, boundless curiosity, and a gift for clear writing, balance, and structure. Phil Beck, my personal editor, epitomizes those qualities and is a gentleman above all. His contributions to this book presented my own in their best light. I am deeply grateful.

I also very much appreciate these fine people who gave generously of their time and expertise to help make this third edition of *The Complete Idiot's Guide to Etiquette* current and authoritative: Gina Adamini, Gregory Castells, Lou DeLise, Carol Forman, Wendy Handler, Ruth Hirshey, Susan Kelly, Becky Lockridge, Lauri Maier, Alex Barke Rector, Phyllis Robinson, Reverend Betsy Salunek, Myrna Secretario, and James K. Weber, M.D.

Trademarks

All terms mentioned in this book that are known to be or are suspected of being trademarks or service marks have been appropriately capitalized. Alpha Books and Penguin Group (USA) Inc. cannot attest to the accuracy of this information. Use of a term in this book should not be regarded as affecting the validity of any trademark or service mark.

Part 1

Mind, Body, Spirit

If we do not treat ourselves and our bodies with respect and kindness, how can we truly and genuinely be respectful and kind toward anybody else (the basis of good manners)? I am convinced that we have become more rude and less considerate because we don't have enough time for ourselves.

That doesn't mean we have to pick up stakes and find a monastery in Tibet. People can and do find sanctuary in a variety of ways and not necessarily in isolation. For some, it may entail yoga, meditation, even a trip to the spa or a masseuse. Others find it in physical activities, both alone or with others—the gym, the pool, the bike and running paths, golf and other athletic pursuits. And yes, most of these activities also come with certain rules of etiquette and consideration, so we don't intrude on the sanctuary of others—including the ultimate physical and spiritual activity: sex.

The Mind-Body-Etiquette Connection

In This Chapter

- Yoga etiquette
- Meditation etiquette
- Spa etiquette
- Locker room etiquette
- Massage etiquette

Americans are flocking to gyms, salons, and spas in greater numbers than ever. We are seeking comfort and peace of mind. We are seeking a social support system to weather our anxiety-ridden, time-crunched, stressed-out lives.

More than ever, we have come to appreciate the mind/body/spirit connection and how it affects every relationship and commitment we have.

Whether we are seeking equilibrium or just to "let off a little steam" through exercise, these individual pursuits often take place in a collective, public setting. The rules of proper behavior are especially important here, to allow us all to retool, relax, and find a sense of sanctuary.

Keeping Up with the Pace of Life

Diane Sieg, R.N., C.L.C., author of *Stop Living Life Like an Emergency!*, maintains that we are "emergency living." Here are the warning signs:

You're always running late.

You've accumulated lots of clutter.

You're either in "hurry up," "catch up," or "fed up" mode.

You're always losing and forgetting things.

You have no patience.

You pride yourself on how much you get done and how fast you do it.

You often find yourself saying, "When things slow down, I'm going to … exercise, get more rest, take better care of myself."

Let's remember that for every action, there is an equal and opposite reaction. If we are going to seek more and more information, faster and faster, then we need to allow ourselves time to process it. If we don't allow ourselves time to get off "tilt," our judgment suffers, our behavior suffers, the example we set for others suffers, and we become instruments of stress and anxiety. We become less effective in whichever role we happen to be playing at any given time. There's the rub!

Live and Learn

So chill!

The mind and body are integrated and constantly talk to each other, according to a *New York Times* report on psychoneuroimmunology, the way the brain and the immune system interact. It's long been known that stress brings on an outpouring of hormones from the adrenal glands—"fight-or-flight" hormones that aid survival. But, a continuous stress-induced outpouring can inhibit the immune system, raise blood sugar and blood pressure, constrict major arteries, and interfere with digestion. That, in turn, increases the risk of hypertension, heart disease, strokes, chronic reflux disease, diarrhea or constipation, and insulin resistance—the precursor of Type 2 diabetes. Cortisol, one of the main stress hormones, fosters deposits of fat, especially around the abdomen, increasing the risk of heart disease. Excess cortisol may also contribute to being overweight and obesity.

A work/life balance—not money—is the number one concern of employees at all levels, in Canada and the United States. The ability to achieve this is the top determinant in whether they are happy on the job, and whether they stay or leave.

As Lily Tomlin advises, "For fast-acting relief, try slowing down."

Here are some ways to do that.

Yoga

Yoga helps us focus and put aside the busyness of the day that can create fractured behavior and poor judgment.

A lot of Americans are getting the yoga message—15 million, in fact. That means about 7 percent of adults practice yoga, and the numbers are growing every day. Yoga is now a part of mainstream society, and is a part of some companies' on-site health programs. In fact, doctors and researchers have cited its usefulness for relieving a number of physical conditions, including asthma, obsessive-compulsive disorder, symptoms associated with menopause, chronic pain, and arthritis.

Yoga is a "practice," not a sport. There is no competition. One teacher suggested "not measuring and comparing yourself to your last class. Instead, think about where you were six months ago." Yoga builds strength and endurance, awareness and respect, and contrary to many beginners' notions, it is not a religious practice. The chanting before and after class is a centering exercise to raise the collective energy in the room. In order to dispel fears that the yoga class has religious overtones, many classes eliminate chanting altogether.

Yoga Class Etiquette

Remove your shoes before entering the practice studio—it keeps the floor clean for others.

Arrive somewhat early to class so that you can relax from the day and give yourself a few minutes of quiet time to mentally prepare for class. Arriving late is disruptive and very bad manners. If you arrive just as the class is beginning, find a place in the back and set up your mat quickly and quietly.

If you speak to fellow classmates before class begins or after class, keep your tone of voice quiet. Others might be meditating.

Do not bring a cell phone into a yoga class.

Make sure you tell your teacher of any injuries or health conditions you might have.

Do not practice yoga on a full stomach. It will interfere with the movements and perhaps cause stomach upset.

Some yoga teachers discourage the drinking of water during class. This is said to cool the heat that builds inside the body and makes it flexible.

Bring your own yoga mat to class for hygienic reasons. Yoga is practiced in bare feet; you don't want to pick up a fungus or cold from a mat that has been used by others.

Yoga is practiced in comfortable clothes that allow for range of motion. Sleeveless tops work best. Some people prefer to wear shorts or sweatpants; others prefer stretchy "yoga pants." No need for a fashion statement in yoga; competition is the antithesis of what yoga is all about.

Personal hygiene is extremely important during yoga class because the heat that builds up intensifies body odors. Make sure you are showered and your clothing is clean and freshly laundered.

Do not wear fragrances in yoga class; the heat intensifies them and many people are allergic to perfumes.

Be mindful of your neighbors when you are practicing a pose that could interfere with their practice. Move your body so that both of you have enough room.

Practice at your own level. If you are an advanced student, don't be a showoff in beginners' class. Don't jump into an advanced class if you are a beginner—it will slow down the class and require a lot of personal attention from the instructor.

If you use the studio's mat, blanket, blocks, or straps, be sure to put them away neatly. Clean up any mess you might have made and be especially careful to wipe down any sweat.

If you must leave the class early, let your instructor know before the class begins. Leave before the final relaxation pose, Shavasana, so you don't interrupt anyone else's relaxation.

Meditation

Meditation is like flossing. We all know it's good for us. We just don't make time for it.

Meditation is an ancient practice of entering a deep, restful state of mind. It has been making its way into the mainstream. Medical studies have suggested that meditation can help reduce stress, insomnia, anxiety, and chronic pain by helping you relax and clear your mind. It can help slow your heart rate and breathing, and it relieves tense muscles.

Although we think of meditation as a prayerful, religious experience, that isn't entirely the case. Meditation is used as part of therapies for anxiety and stress-related disorders. When used in this way, it is a breath-centered, nonspiritual practice.

The goal of meditation is to be in the moment—to use concentrated breathing to empty the mind of everyday thoughts and cares. Athletes call it visualization, which is simply a positive mental rehearsal of what they are about to do. Others employ the term self-hypnosis, or self-talk, for the meditative state that clears their minds and brings to bear the best of what they have to offer the world. Whatever you want to call it, meditation has as much to do with etiquette as Tiger Woods has to do with golf. How different is visualizing a 275-yard drive across a lake to the middle of the fairway from seeing yourself heading home from a party where your confidence and self-assuredness won you new friends and admirers? Or from moving through a business lunch without a hitch? They all require the same skill sets. It's all in the mind.

Live and Learn

Steps to relax and meditate:

1. Find a quiet place where you won't be interrupted. Some soft music might be restful.
2. Find a comfortable position. Sit down with your feet on the floor; lie down on the floor; or choose to sit on a cushion.
3. Choose your focus. It might be breathing, a word, a phrase, a prayer, or simply in the moment. Gently bring your thoughts back when they wander.
4. Start gently. Don't expect yourself to be able to remain in the pose and in the moment for long periods of time. Start with 5 minutes twice a day and work up to 20-minute sessions.

The basic truth is that there is no single "right" way to meditate. Most people have to fight the voices in their heads telling them it's either a waste of time or it must be done perfectly or not at all. With persistence and practice, those voices become softer and more forgiving.

Another basic truth is that meditation does work to relieve stress, sharpen focus, and alleviate a number of physical disorders.

Spa Culture

Fitness and beauty regimens not only soothe irritated skin and sore muscles, they also psychologically and physiologically reduce stress.

Salons, spas, and gyms offer dozens of services that calm people down. They also provide a welcome escape from reality, a social environment with no strings attached.

Once thought a women-only domain, these days you're as likely to encounter men there as women. In fact, according to the International Spa Association, men now make up a quarter of American spa-goers.

Mars and Venus eye spas much differently, however. Women use spas as retreats, while men use them to cool down after sports or to compete better in business, where conveying an image of vitality provides an edge. Rather than beauty treatments, men tend to choose services that relieve tension or ease muscle strain.

Women often fly solo at spas, appreciating the solitude, relaxation, and complete lack of social pressure. Men come in groups, socialize, and rarely linger.

Spa Etiquette

When you book your appointment, ask if there are any special instructions to prepare for your service. Ask about tipping policies and procedures. Common practice is between 15 and 20 percent of the cost of a service. Most spas have envelopes at the registration desk for this purpose.

Arrive early for your appointment so you can change into your spa attire and complete any paperwork necessary. Most spas like to keep records of services performed for guests.

Keep to your plan. Each service has an allotted time frame, so be sure to allow the therapist to perform your service on schedule and don't switch services at the last minute. That could create problems with both staff and scheduling.

Give the therapist feedback as to your comfort and special troubled areas.

Relax and receive the treatments graciously and quietly. You are not expected to carry on a conversation with the therapist.

Vacate the treatment room promptly so that it can be readied for the next guest.

Share public space respectfully with other spa guests. Clean up after yourself—put used towels and robes in hampers. Don't litter the sinks and mirror area.

Faux Pas

Don't bring the kids with you to the spa. Children will find it tedious and be disruptive to other spa guests.

Locker Room Manners

If many of your friends and co-workers are members of the same health club or frequent the same spa as you, there can be some awkward situations.

You may feel perfectly comfortable in your t-shirt and shorts in the cardio and weight rooms, but find it more than a bit embarrassing to meet your same-sex colleagues in the nude in the locker room, shower, steam room, or sauna. What should you say or do?

We are all more or less self-conscious. Trying to avoid someone by timing your entrance or exit, or worse, by not showering at all, just won't work over the long haul. No one is totally happy with his or her body. And embarrassment goes two ways.

There are ways of being modest without seeming prudish. Use a towel as a cover-up. And you can simply be too polite to notice. Look directly into your colleagues' eyes and nowhere else while speaking to them, and try to go about your business matter-of-factly.

Don't engage in any conversation about your physical state—your campaign to lose or gain weight, muscle, tone, whatever. That only draws attention to your body—and your goal is to keep the attention off it.

Massage Manners

Shower before your appointment.

Arrive 5 minutes before your appointment, so that you get your full session. If it is your first time with the therapist, arrive 10 minutes early. Some therapists require that you fill out an intake form with your medical and personal history prior to your first massage, and this can take up a few minutes.

Be sure to alert your therapist of any skin conditions you may have, as well as recent surgery or any medications you may be taking.

If you have a fever, it is best not to get a massage without checking first with your therapist.

During the massage, the therapist might ask you about the level of pressure. It is perfectly acceptable to ask him or her to go deeper or to lighten up.

Suggestive or sexual language or behavior is not acceptable from either client or therapist. Either party may end the session at any time if they feel uncomfortable.

Mind Your P's and Q's

First-timers may be bit intimidated receiving a massage in the buff from a perfect stranger. Not to worry. The masseuse only exposes one area being worked on at a time, while towels cover the rest of the body. If you're still squeamish, it's perfectly okay to wear underwear or some other covering, although the therapeutic effect might not be as great.

If you must cancel an appointment, give at least 24 hours' notice. Never simply be a no-show, especially if you intend to see this therapist again.

Tip the therapist between 15 and 20 percent when the therapist is working for someone else—such as a spa, chiropractor, or fitness facility.

The Least You Need to Know

- ◆ Lots of evidence supports the idea that our minds and our bodies, and thus our behavior, are connected.

- ◆ Dealing with stressors in our work and home lives places a responsibility on us to take care of ourselves.

- ◆ Practicing yoga, meditation, and exercise helps to alleviate stress and to remain focused, so that our behavior is civilized and compassionate.

- ◆ Don't forget to tip the therapists who attend to you at spas and massage centers.

Chapter 2

Sports Etiquette

In This Chapter

- The etiquette of good sportsmanship
- Maneuvering at the gym and in the pool
- Racquet sports
- Running, biking, skiing, and blading

Sportsmanship is etiquette with an application of perspiration.

A good sport plays by the rules, gives opponents the benefit of the doubt, considers everyone's safety, dresses appropriately for the situation, and is gracious in both victory and defeat.

Parents have always found that teaching their children to behave like good sports—by being fair, trying hard to win, and always doing their best—gives them valuable, character-building tools that will help them throughout their lives.

Although the overall rules of sportsmanship apply to all athletic endeavors, each activity has its special rules of etiquette and distinct considerations. For example, some aspects of behavior on the golf course are very different from etiquette on the ski slopes. Let's look at some of these areas.

Gym Dandies

Some people seem to think it isn't necessary to exercise common sense and good manners in places where people exercise.

The opposite is true.

When the fitness-minded get single-minded about their workouts, things can get pretty grim in the gym. People can lose all consideration for—or even awareness of—those around them. Maybe it's all those mirrors.

However, the very fact that gym activities are so "me" based makes courtesy an absolute necessity to minimize distractions and to promote safety. It's a place where bad manners can cause physical injury to you or to others. For example, never join an exercise group already in session: Your arrival will be distracting to those in the group, and you may have missed important safety information given at the beginning of the workout. Here are some other considerations.

Dress Appropriately

When it comes to the gym and fashion, the key words are clean and functional. Scanty, sexy dressing is inappropriate because it is distracting and embarrassing. In addition, you shouldn't walk around in flimsy footwear or stocking feet. And watch where you're going: Walking into a metal plate or barbell can result in a broken toe or foot.

Keep It Clean

Take a towel with you, not only to wipe your own brow but also to wipe down weight machines. According to proper gym etiquette, leaving these machines wet with your perspiration is a mortal sin. However, don't leave your towels where people can walk on or trip over them, and never leave a towel on a weight machine. If you carry a water bottle or chart with you, keep them out of the way of others while you are exercising.

In the locker room, don't leave your bag or sweaty clothes on the floor, particularly in front of somebody else's locker. Clean up after yourself in the same way you would if you were using the bathroom in someone else's home.

Making the Circuit

Here are some words of advice for using free weights or weight machines, such as Nautilus:

- ◆ **Don't jump ahead.** Even if a particular machine or set of weights is next in your routine, you must still wait for your turn. If there's any doubt about the availability of the equipment, ask.

- ◆ **Don't dally.** If you're going to rest a long while between sets of reps, give up the machine—particularly if the place is crowded. Don't leave your towel on the machine in an effort to reserve the machine for yourself while you rest. If you are working out with a friend, don't stop to chat or compare notes between exercises. Keep each other's progress charts to keep the process moving.

- ◆ **Keep it quiet.** Grunts and moans are unnecessary, theatrical, distracting, and unsafe. The professionals tell me that making these noises while straining increases pressure on your respiratory system and can push your blood pressure up. And don't count out loud while you're doing reps. It can throw off others around you who are counting to themselves.

- ◆ **Unload.** Always strip plates and clear your squat bars. If you borrow those little saddle weights that go on top of the weight stacks from another machine, return them when you are finished. Never leave plates or barbells where people can trip over them.

- ◆ **Keep your chart with you.** In addition, be careful where you place your chart when you're using a machine. If hooks are provided for the chart, use them. Otherwise, put the chart on the floor.

Trainers

Working with a personal trainer involves another layer of gym etiquette. The primary rule is to respect the trainer's expertise and time. Give 24 hours' notice if you must cancel or reschedule an appointment, and be prepared to pay for the trainer's time if you don't give 24 hours' notice.

Live and Learn

Many people include a workout session when they are traveling. Here are some points to consider when you are planning to work out at a gym where you are not a regular:

- ◆ Find out about the place. Is it a straightforward workout-sports gym or an "amenities" spa with juice bar and carpeted walls?
- ◆ Ask about the guest policies. What's the fee? Do you have to be a member or be sponsored by a member?
- ◆ Find out whether the gym has a dress code.

Don't make it hard for the trainer to do the job by trying to take over or control the workout session. Sure, it's your body, but the trainer knows more about getting it in shape than you do. On the other hand, if you're ever in pain or feel uncomfortable, do let the trainer know.

The trainer's expertise is physical—not psychological—fitness and he or she shouldn't have to deal with your emotional ups and downs. Keep your dealings with him or her on a professional level and be courteous at all times. That includes waiting until your trainer is free and not interrupting if he or she is with another client.

The Pool

Generally, gym members use the pool for three purposes: lap swimming, aqua-aerobics, or just splashing around, and all of these people have an equal right to be in the pool.

Lap swimmers, of course, should stay in their lanes. If the pool is busy, you may be able to reserve a lane for a specific time. When in doubt, check. If you're going to take a break of more than a few minutes, get out of the pool.

Others using the pool, either singly or in aerobics groups, can claim a lane of their own or use an unlaned area. If you're not in a group, try to find a lane or area that is not being used by lap swimmers. Parents should instruct children not to play in the lanes lap swimmers are using.

In general, behaving cautiously is the best etiquette when it comes to swimming. If you can't swim, stay in the wading areas until you learn to swim. (Your local YMCA usually offers swim classes all year round.) Swimming provides great exercise, and more people enjoy it than any other sport.

Racquet Sports

At the exercise club or the tennis club, rules of preference or position cease to exist. Members and guests are on equal footing, whatever their status outside.

Offer to help out or even instruct beginners if they need it. It's also okay to ask others for guidance. If you're unsure about the rules of the club, ask for a briefing or check out any posted rules. The same goes for the rules of a particular game. Tennis clubs follow the rules set forth by the United States Lawn Tennis Association.

- **Dress whites.** Wearing white is usually safe for all racquet sports. Color variations are common at some places, but white is still the uniform at the stricter clubs. Find out in advance.

◆ **Behave yourself.** No matter what you see professional tennis players doing on television, having a temper tantrum—verbal or nonverbal—shows very bad form. In fact, players should be as quiet as possible while on the court. Obviously, it makes sense to exchange verbal signals with your partners when playing doubles. Beyond that, comments and exclamations are distracting to those you are playing with and to those on other courts.

◆ **Keep your chin up.** Don't make a fuss about errors or bad play, even your own. And don't dish up excuses (the weather, your partner, your health, or your shoes) for a bad game. However, there's nothing wrong with saying, "I had a really bad game today."

◆ **Even the playing field.** If you're a beginner and you'll be playing a more experienced player, let your opponent know before you get on the court. And if you're an experienced player up against a new player, your job is to give advice and encouragement, not to see how thoroughly you can destroy a novice.

◆ **No sneaky serves.** If in doubt about your opponent's state of readiness, ask whether he or she is ready.

◆ **Promptness counts.** Show up on time and leave on time, especially if you know others are waiting.

◆ **Be courteous.** If a ball comes into your court, return it during a break in the play. Don't expect others to interrupt their play to return your ball.

◆ **Stay in your own court.** And when you walk behind a court, wait for a break in the play before passing. Say, "Excuse me," on the way through.

◆ **Choose proper footwear.** The wrong shoes can damage a court.

◆ **Bring only what you need.** Don't take the pro shop with you onto the tennis court, or on any sports outing for that matter. Show up with just the equipment and accessories you know you will need. Extravagance is bad manners in most situations, and particularly in sports.

Skiing

Skiing is another sport in which the rules of etiquette are inextricably bound to safety.

Dress Appropriately

No matter how adorable (or ruggedly casual) your outfit is, you will look stupid if your attire is not appropriate to the slopes. Your clothing should not only keep you

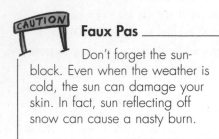

warm but also resist water and wind. The outfit must be snug while allowing you freedom of movement. Jeans are a bad idea because they don't dry out easily. They stay wet and cold and heavy.

Layering is essential. A cotton turtleneck, long underwear, sweater, ski pants, ski jacket, and a hat or cap are good choices. Wear a pair of thin socks under heavy ski socks. Goggles are more durable than sunglasses. Outer skiwear is bright and colorful so that other skiers can see you easily against the snow.

Basic Rules of Manners

Basic rules of politeness start with the T-bar or chairlift. Stay in your place in the lift line. If you're alone, offer to ride the lift with another single to avoid breaking up couples or groups. While in line, hold your skis upright in front of you to avoid whacking your neighbors. If it's your first experience with lifts, stand back and watch how the boarding procedure works before you get aboard. At the top, clear the lift area immediately so as not to cause a traffic jam.

Beginners should take some lessons before attempting the slopes. The sport only looks easy. In fact, the first experience with skis, boots, and poles can make even the most graceful individual feel like a klutz.

Experienced skiers should not boast or make remarks about the skill levels of the less experienced.

Rules of the Trails

Skiing is one of the most dangerous sports. Great care and attention to the rules are vitally important. When hitting the slopes, remember these critical points:

- ◆ Regardless of your ability, never ski alone. Anyone can fall, get a cramp, or break a piece of equipment. If you get hurt or stuck and no one is around to assist you, it's just you and the mountain and the weather—a potentially deadly combination. And if nobody knows where you are, no one can come to get you.

- ◆ Never ski on a closed trail. First, it might be closed because of dangerous conditions. Second, it might be closed in preparation for a special event. Third, the ski patrol does not watch closed trails.

◆ Ski only on trails that match your ability level. If you want the challenge of moving up to a more difficult trail, have an instructor or expert skier with you and don't try it during peak hours. Novices on expert trails endanger themselves and the more skilled skiers. Experts on novice trails panic beginners by whizzing past them. Look for these trail markers:

> Green circle for novices
>
> Blue square for intermediates
>
> Black diamond for experts

◆ The slower skier in front of you always has the right of way. If you are going to pass the slower skier, yell "track right" or "track left," depending on which side you will pass. You want to warn the other skier against turning into your path.

◆ If you're climbing on skis or on foot, stay well over to the edge of the trail. The same applies if you decide to walk down.

◆ Mountains are large. It's a good idea to select a particular spot to check in with your friends periodically rather than relying on the chance of encountering each other randomly.

Accidents

If you come upon an injured skier, remove the victim's skis, but never his or her boots. Mark the spot with crossed skis or poles. Don't attempt to move the person. You may aggravate an injury. Wait for another skier to come along before you go for help. Mark the spot well in your mind so that you will be able to lead the ski patrol to the victim.

Running

Running is the most inexpensive, effective, and convenient form of cardiovascular workout. No wonder everybody seems to be doing it these days.

However, beginners should approach the sport with some caution. Learn how to stretch properly so that you don't sprain a muscle or cause another injury that will nip your running program in the bud. Dozens of magazines for runners provide solid basic information—including the crucial consideration of getting the proper shoes.

A lot of runners start out by walking, which is itself an effective and highly recommended form of exercise.

It's a good idea to seek out designated running paths. It's a bad idea to explore unknown territory on your own. Never run in deserted or dark areas. Don't wear jewelry or carry a wallet. Let someone know where you will be running and what time you expect to return. Run somewhere with access to public telephones in case you need to make a call. You could, for instance, get a cramp and want to have someone come and pick you up.

Run against the traffic on the road. Pay attention to traffic signals. Don't expect drivers to watch out for you. Run during the day if at all possible. If you are out after sundown, wear a reflecting vest. Headphones can mask traffic noise, such as horns and sirens, and should not be played at high volumes, if at all.

Carry identification and a little change or a phone card for the telephone.

Biking

Biking is another popular sport. Before you start, familiarize yourself with the rules of the bikers' road. You can find information and safety tips at any good bicycle store, and someone at the shop might be able to put you in touch with a local biking group.

If you are interested in pursuing the sport beyond a pleasant pastime, contact the League of American Wheelmen, and obtain a copy of its magazine, *Bicycle USA* (1-800-288-BIKE).

Mind Your P's and Q's

Bike sober! You can be arrested and charged with drunk driving if you are caught operating a bicycle on a road or street while under the influence of alcohol or drugs.

On the road, your bike is a vehicle and subject to traffic regulations. Ride with the traffic, on the shoulder of the road where possible, use the proper hand signals, and give pedestrians the right of way. You must wear a helmet and, in the dark or at dusk, reflective gear. Other useful equipment includes goggles, gloves, proper shoes, and bicycle clips to keep your trousers from getting caught in the chain.

Rollerblading

Rollerblading is an increasingly popular sport. It makes traditional roller-skating seem tame.

The International In-Line Skating Association has these recommendations:

◆ **Skate with courtesy.** Stay to the right, and pass on the left. Announce your intentions by saying, "Pass on your left." Yield to pedestrians. In general, try to be a good-will ambassador for in-line skating.

- **Skate smart.** Always wear protective gear—helmet, wrist protection, and elbow and knee pads. Master the basics—moving, stopping, turning. Keep your equipment in safe condition.

- **Skate legally.** Obey all traffic regulations, especially if you're skating in the street. Check the laws in your area. Skaters have the same obligations as the operators of any wheeled vehicle.

- **Skate with awareness.** Control your speed. Watch out for road hazards. Avoid water, oil, and sand. Stay away from heavy traffic.

Other skating tips: Keep moving. If you want to chat, get out of traffic. If you take Fido with you, keep him on a leash. If you're using headphones, keep the volume low so you can hear sounds of approaching danger. Skate forward, not backward, particularly when other skaters are around. Look behind you before stopping or slowing down abruptly. Teach the kids to skate in an empty parking lot, not on the skating path. Stunts and tricks are not for the skating path.

The most crucial rules of etiquette when it comes to sports relate to safety. Physical activity, even if not particularly strenuous, always involves some risk. Consequently, following the rules is even more important than it is in social situations.

The Least You Need to Know

- Respect for others and safety are of utmost importance when participating in any sport. Always wear protective and proper clothing and use the correct equipment.

- In the gym, always return weights to their storage location, don't put charts or towels on the machines, move from one machine to another without delay, and don't try to join a group exercise session that is already in progress.

- At the pool, stay out of the way of lap swimmers.

- At the country club, wearing tennis whites is always a safe bet. Tantrums on the tennis court are strictly out of bounds.

- Run against traffic in familiar terrain. Avoid dark or deserted areas.

Chapter 3

Sex Etiquette

In This Chapter

- ◆ Making the connection
- ◆ Protecting yourself and others
- ◆ Asking for what you both want
- ◆ Performance etiquette
- ◆ Sex talk, in and out of bed

Civility and great sex go hand in hand. How, you might ask, are sex and etiquette connected? Simple. Good manners are very sexy. If you doubt this, check out the Meg Ryan flick, *Kate and Leopold*. Plot line: Boy meets girl. Boy treats girl like a treasure. At first, girl spurns boy for "edgier" mate. In the end, manners win.

Think about it. Respect is the basis for good manners. When we know we are respected and safe, we all perform better, no matter the task.

So it is with sex. Good sex. Respect is the basis for effective communication and, clearly, communication is the basis for good sex—regardless of who initiates it. Gone are the days when dainty women batted their eyelashes and held an unlit cigarette as a signal for a man to oblige. Today, women are as entitled to make the advances as men, and although this somewhat levels the playing field, the immutable fact is this: When the advance is made with good manners, respecting everyone's boundaries, the chances for success skyrocket.

In politically correct environments, men no longer automatically open doors for women, nor do they pull out chairs. And women have no right to expect such courtesies. However, when courtesies are offered, on the part of man or woman, we only can hope to be gracious and confident enough to accept them with style. Thus, it really doesn't matter who takes the flirting lead.

With this in mind, here are some suggestions to smoothly pave the way for great sex and also to ease the journey when the ride is bumpy.

The Connection

We have a number of ways for signaling to someone that we want to pursue a sexual experience. Sounds cold, yet it's very true. So the question becomes whether we do that with some style—which can be flattering even if rebuffed and might indeed be welcome—or whether we do it crudely. In the latter, it's easy for the person being approached to feel as though the approacher is completely indiscriminate. Whether it happens on the third date or the first night, the same message can be perceived in two different ways with two different outcomes.

Faux Pas

What's not appropriate is hiding the fact that you happen to be married or in a committed relationship and thus emotionally unavailable. It's also not fair to come on to another person's companion, date, or partner. You wouldn't like it done to you.

For example, "I'd really like to take this further, to have you all to myself, naked," is a lot classier than, "Let's play hide the salami." Both examples assume that each person is free to both make and accept such a pass, and both clearly communicate the message.

Turning Down Sexual Advances

All you have to say is, "No, thanks." Okay, so that doesn't always mean no forever. Your tone of voice will tell the story, and so will your body language. If you really mean, "not now, not today," your smile and direct eye contact will speak volumes. If, however, you really mean no, just keep your hands at your sides, stand up straight, make eye contact, and speak the words in the same tone that you'd say, "It's raining outside." A simple statement of fact—no apologies, no equivocating, no rebuke. Both turndowns beat righteous indignation as a response.

Protecting Yourself ... and Others

How do you know someone is "safe" from STDs? By testing for them. The conversation about testing should take place before passions are high. Let's face it, whenever it happens, you know when you're headed to bed. That's what dating and flirting are about. So don't wait until one knee is on the mattress to ask The Question. Say, in a non-judgmental way, "Naturally, I'm concerned about STDs. Have you been tested?" But remember that no one has the right to ask The Question without having been tested oneself.

If your partner refuses to be tested, it's completely mannerly to say, "Then we better back off until you are tested. I'd just feel a lot better that way."

Should your partner tell you he or she is clean and tested, but you have your doubts, think twice about having sex in the first place. Don't hesitate to back off saying, "I really don't think I am ready for this yet. I'm just too concerned about STDs and couldn't relax. It wouldn't be good for either of us."

Having said all that—and if you both decide to proceed—a woman can make wearing a condom as pleasurable an experience as possible for the man. And by offering to apply the condom, she can assure herself it is applied correctly.

Say What? _____

If the only way you'll be comfortable with your partner is through a lab test, then say so. Again, use the tone for "It's raining outside." No judgments, no rebuke, no apology. Sounds like, "I know that the only way I will be able to relax is for us both to be tested. It's not exactly a warm and fuzzy exercise in togetherness, but it would be worth it for me and I hope it would be for you, too."

Hygiene, You-Giene

Body odor. Bad breath. Aphrodisiac? No, turnoff. It's not the same as sweaty sex.

So how do you deal with the distraction? Just say, "would you like to use the shower first, or shall I?" This works well with brushing teeth, too. Again, no judgments, no rebukes, no apologies. Remember, "It's raining outside." No emotion. Statement of fact.

If you are a dewy romantic, you might try the "I'd love to take a shower together" ploy.

Remember the value of positive reinforcement. Tell your partner over and over that you adore that "squeaky clean" smell about him. You also can get more graphic by describing which parts smell especially delicious. And compliments on shampoos, colognes, perfume, and mouthwash are always welcome.

You will have to be consistent with your praise. It takes at least three weeks to create a habit.

Ready for This?

How do you ask for what pleases you? And how do you pass on what doesn't?

Pivotal here is that we are asking. We are not commanding. Granted, this is not the trash fiction approach, but this is real life.

So it might sound like, "I just love it when …." or "You drive me crazy when …." or "One of the things you do that I love most is …."

When your request is granted and your partner is giving you the best effort, don't lie there like a lox. Respond so that you encourage the effort. Say something. Make a happy sound. If there are minor adjustments, try helping to make them with your hand on your partner's and say, "try this."

Turning Off What Turns You Off

How do you decline what doesn't make you purr?

When you are in the moment, say something like, "not just now," and then move on to do something that you know your partner really likes. Or redirect your partner by saying, "I really love it when you …" So what you do here is subtly shift the roles from requestee to requestor.

When the atmosphere and mood are more conducive to conversational intimacy, perhaps happily lying in bed together, tell your partner the truth about your refusal. Again, "it's raining outside." No need to judge. Just say something like, "I'm just not comfortable with that now. I know a lot of people are, but I never have been." So, by using "I language," you are deflecting any judgment to yourself, not your partner. And you have kept the door open.

Pressure Point

Never, ever force your partner's head down in an effort to initiate oral sex. That is rude. You can't have good sex if your partner doesn't feel safe. Instead, you can gently touch your partner's head in the right direction and accept the decision your partner makes. There's nothing wrong with asking your partner directly. It's also respectful and good form to ask before performing any act yourself. Communication, physical or verbal, is a key to good sex.

Live and Learn
The rendezvous is heated. You can't wait to get your hands on each other, but something's in the way. A negligee. Panties. Bustier. Tee shirt. Tie. Boxers. Briefs. Shirt.
Are these items of clothing merely props to further the dramatic passion by being torn off each other? Maybe. Maybe not.
In either case, it's only good manners to replace the destroyed garments. That's a process that can be fun, too.

Can't Get No Satisfaction?

Everybody is wired differently. Sometimes one partner is blissfully satisfied while the other is left panting. This is not the time for the former to head to the refrigerator for a snack. Nor is it the time for blame of any kind. Instead, why not ask your partner to "do what you do so well so I can feel as good as you." It's only good manners to honor the request. After all, it's better than being blamed for leaving a job half done.

Making Improvements

So you wish your partner were a better kisser or caresser or whatever. How do you get the message across while keeping the passion intact? Clearly, criticism while in the heat of the moment is bad bed manners.

If you are in pain, of course, be firm and say, "Stop! That hurts!" If, however, we are talking about re-calibrating another's technique, say something like, "Why don't you try …", or "I love it when you …", or "I've always wondered what it would be like if you …"

Soft and Frigid

Judgment, blame, and rebuke are bad manners when we cannot perform. They only will bring a lover down, and that is the last thing we want to happen. So, when performing is not possible, say something loving like, "You look so delicious right now …. Okay if I take a rain check?" A woman might direct her partner to alternate southern accommodations and, if so, it's good manners to oblige. However, if a man has had performance issues before, it's only intelligent and caring—not to mention good manners—for his lover to reassure him of his appeal.

Women are capable of enjoying the sexual act even when they are not truly aroused. That kind of closeness and affection goes a long way to pleasure. Her partner, however, should not assume that this always is the case, and if a woman continues to be unresponsive, it's a conversation to have outside the bedroom.

Viagra Etiquette

Faux Pas

Faking it is lying. If it goes on for any length of time, it only can cause problems in the relationship. Knowing that, faking it is bad manners and bad judgment. You can say, "I didn't really get there this time, wonderful as it all was."

Tell her you take the stuff, whether it's Viagra or the other performance-enhancement drugs on the market. Before you get lusty. Language is something like, "You are very sexy and I'm looking forward to making love/having sex together. I use Viagra because it makes sex so much better."

Key Viagra point: Don't pop the pill assuming that your partner intends to head for the boudoir. It could be mighty embarrassing if such is not the case. You'll need a cape to cover things up, and gasping "down boy" just doesn't help.

I Love You? You Love Me?

Beware the trap—self-inflicted or otherwise—of panting "I love you" in the heat of the moment. It's not fair unless you do truly love the other person. One good gauge for this is whether you want to say it out of bed as well as in it.

When we hear "I love you," we filter it through our own perception glasses—love as we define it, which might be entirely apart and opposite of what the other person means. Meanwhile, we are defining our relationship one way and our partner is defining it another.

Think (and say), "You're wonderful. I'm crazy about you." These carry far less baggage.

It's bad manners to reply to "I love you" with "I love you," unless you truly mean it. Otherwise, accept the declaration neutrally and respond something like, "Well, you have good taste, but I'm not sure I deserve all that." In other words, lighten the moment.

Talking Dirty

Nothing's wrong with saying extreme things in the heat of the moment, as long as both partners understand that these actions are not expected to be performed literally by either partner. Turn-ons like that aren't meant personally or literally. So although offensive things might be said, there is no need to take offense at them. What's key is accepting that experimenting with language can be a gross-out for one while a turn-on for the other. So both partners need to feel free to express that in less passionate moments, and agree to some limits. And experimenting in the extreme with a first-time partner is a dicey risk. Only you can decide whether to take it. It's possible to go too far.

Morning, Noon, and Night

Face it, we are either morning or night people. What do you do when your partner wants to do it in the morning but you want to do it at night? Who wins? The person who is reluctant usually wins because it's bad manners to pressure anyone into sex.

Still, it's important to pay attention and fulfill a partner's requests. Maybe not every time. But surely sometimes. And the compromise might be to choose an entirely different time—a lunchtime romp, perhaps—and actually make a date. That makes everybody feel special.

Former Flames

You want to know about your partner's former lovers. Or your partner wants to know. Be too polite to remember and don't go there.

You run into an ex when you are with a new partner. Make a brief yet friendly introduction, using only names, and move on. If the person you are with interrogates, simply say it was someone you dated eons ago and leave it at that. So long ago that you cannot possibly remember any of the details.

Say What? _____

If someone intrudes on your sexual interlude, say, "I know that you will be too polite to remember this ever happened and so will I." Leave it at that. This assumes that you and your partner are not in committed relationships with anyone else at the time.

To Tell or Not to Tell …

When you believe or even know that your friend's partner is cheating, deciding whether or not to tell your friend the sad news can be a dilemma. Don't go there. It's not your place to interfere like that. Finally, never discuss the story with anyone—malicious gossip serves no one.

The Least You Need to Know

◆ If there is ever a time to do things correctly, it's when sex is involved.

◆ Conversation about STDs and protection should take place before the heat of passion.

◆ How we communicate what we want and need bears considerable forethought. "Try this" is better than "I don't like this."

◆ Don't discuss your former partners.

◆ Never engage in gossip about your sex life or anybody else's. It can come back to haunt you.

Part 2

Dining and Drinking

Although we dine less formally than ever before, knowing how to dine formally is an important foundation. Once you know and practice the rules, you are at ease about when to break them and bend them. An adage warns, "Don't dig your grave with your knife and fork," and this author adds that in every interaction we have three choices. We can do the absolutely proper thing; the absolutely improper thing; or take the absolutely appropriate course of action. This third choice usually rests somewhere between the first two—but you'll never know it without knowing all three.

The most formal dinner should not intimidate you. In fact, hosting the most elegant dinner party is well within your grasp. It's all a matter of knowing the rules, and luckily the rules are plain, no matter how fancy the meal. Other rules apply to less formal situations, from a quick meal at the office to a visit to Mickey Dee's.

Chapter 4

Table Manners: The Basics

In This Chapter

- Ten most common dining mistakes
- A little list of no-no's
- Foods from hell
- American vs. continental style

Oh, the cruelty of cutlery, the gravity of gravy, the terror in a teacup. Hey, lighten up.

Although there are very good and serious reasons for you to be concerned, even apprehensive, about the complexities of this thing called table manners, there is no reason in the world why you can't become a poised, informed, and even charming dining companion. It's mostly a matter of knowing the rules—most of which are based on plain common sense—and avoiding the most obvious mistakes.

Thou Shalt Not: The 10 Most Common Dining Mistakes

While reading this list, you may find that you've been a sinner in the past without ever realizing it. Don't worry. Redemption is at hand. And you certainly aren't alone. The sins detailed in the following list made the top 10 list only because so many people commit them so often:

1. **Cutlery.** Don't hold your fork like a cello or your knife like Lady Macbeth's dagger. Also, don't wave your cutlery triumphantly in the air to emphasize a point and don't put silverware partly on the table and partly on the plate. After you pick up a piece of cutlery, it should never touch the table again. Knives go on the plate, blade facing in and touching the inside of the plate. Only the handle should rest on the rim of the plate.

2. **Napkins.** Don't blot or rub the lower half of your face. Dab delicately. Don't flap your napkin to unfold it and don't wave it around like a flag. It belongs unfolded on your lap. If you leave the table, place your napkin on the chair and push the chair back under the table. Gently. Watch the upholstery. Don't refold your napkin at the end of the meal because an unknowing server might give it to another diner. Pick up the napkin from the center and place it loosely on the table to the left of your plate.

3. **Chewing.** Never chew with your mouth open. Also, no matter how urgently you want to inject the perfect kernel of wit and wisdom at just the right moment, don't do it with food in your mouth. And don't gulp and blurt. Finish chewing, swallow, and smile philosophically, content in the knowledge that you could have said just the right thing, but had too much class to speak with food in your mouth.

4. **Appearance.** Remember what your mother said: Sit up straight and keep your elbows off the table. If you have any doubt about where your hands belong, put them in your lap.

5. **Breaking bread.** Here is a real bread-and-butter tip. Tear bread into bite-size pieces and butter each piece just before you eat it. Don't butter the entire slice of bread or the entire roll to get it ready for occasional bites during the course of the meal.

6. **Speed.** Take it easy. Whether you're at the Ritz Carlton or Gertie's Grease Pit, gulping down food is not only unhealthy but also unattractive, and it can cross the line into rudeness when dining with others. Dining partners should have the same number of courses and start and finish each one at about the same time. Don't be huddling over your soup while others are salivating for dessert or vice versa.

7. **Don't pick!** If you have something trapped between your teeth, don't pick at it while you are at the table. If it's really driving you nuts, excuse yourself, go to the restroom, and pick to your heart's content.

8. **Lipstick etiquette.** Leaving a lipstick trail behind on stemware and flatware is bad form, especially at a business meal. If you apply lipstick in the restaurant and don't have a blotting tissue with you, make a detour to the restroom or nab a cocktail napkin from the bar on your way to the table.

9. **Smoking.** Even if you're sitting in the smoking section of the restaurant, you should never light up between courses. It affects your dining partners' taste buds and is a jarring note during any meal. Wait until the meal is over and, even then, ask if anyone minds if you smoke. If anyone does object, offer to wait or to smoke at the bar. And, please, never use a plate as an ashtray.

10. **Purses and briefcases.** Keep them off the table. And this rule goes for keys, hats, gloves, eyeglasses, eyeglass cases, and cigarette packs. In short, if it isn't part of the meal, it shouldn't be on the table.

Mind Your P's and Q's

According to G. R. M. Devereux in *Etiquette for Women*, published in 1901, after you pick up a piece of cutlery, it should never touch the table again—advice that applies today as well.

A Little List of No-No's

Having dealt with the 10 biggest mistakes, we can move on to a list of little no-no's—things not important enough to make the BIG list, but worth noting anyway. Even though common sense and a sense of courtesy may keep you from committing many of these errors, they bear repeating:

◆ Don't salt or otherwise season your food before you taste it. This behavior is particularly offensive when dining in someone's home and the cook is sitting at the table. It's also a bad idea in a restaurant, even though the chef can't be insulted because he or she is in the kitchen.

◆ Cut only enough food for the next mouthful.

◆ If someone at the table takes a pill, don't ask about it. If you must take medication at the table, don't comment about it. No explanations are necessary.

◆ Don't dunk. Doughnuts don't belong in coffee.

Say What?

You're at a fancy dinner, and you are served something unidentifiable. What do you say?

"I can't even guess what this is, but it looks wonderful. Can you clue me in?"

- Don't push your plate away and don't push your chair back when you've finished eating unless you're getting up from the table.

- Never tilt your chair.

- Always pass food to the right.

- Don't ask people where they're going if they leave the table.

- If you belch, cover your mouth with your napkin and say "Excuse me" to no one in particular.

- Never crumble crackers in your soup or blow on any liquid that is too hot. Cool yourself until it cools.

- Put butter first on your bread plate or dinner plate, not directly on the roll or other food.

Don't Panic!

Having spent so much time talking about mistakes, it's important to point out that nothing as diverse as dining with a number of other people will ever be achieved with perfect serenity. Things go wrong, and when they do, you should react calmly and, if possible, cheerfully.

Live and Learn
The custom of "breaking bread" and taking only as much as you intend to eat originated centuries ago, when people gave what was left of the communal loaf to the poor after a meal.

Let's say you knock something over, break something, or drop something. The first thing to remember is that anybody can have an accident! Stay cool. Downplay the incident as much as possible. If you spill something, blot up what you can. In a restaurant, call the incident to the server's attention—as unobtrusively as possible—and hand the server your napkin if it's wet. If the person next to you is a victim of the accident, let him or her handle the damage control. Apologize quietly and offer to pay for any dry-cleaning bills.

Foods from Hell

"How do I eat this at all—never mind gracefully?" you say to yourself as you stare at the intricately tangled spaghetti on your plate. Well, pasta isn't the only challenge when it comes to eating with elegance. The following is a list of difficult foods to eat, along with some tips on how to eat them correctly.

Before we get started, here is an important codicil to keep in mind. Remember that you can eat certain foods with your fingers, but when in doubt, use a fork or spoon. If you already have your paws on the item, go ahead and eat it. Please, please, don't say, "Hey, they invented fingers before forks. Right?"

- **Artichokes.** Eating an artichoke requires a bit of an attitude and a little digital dexterity. Pick it up with one hand, remove one leaf at a time, and dip the soft end into the accompanying sauce. Then place the whole soft end in your mouth and pull (do not yank) it through your teeth to remove the edible part. Discard the rest by placing it on the edge of the plate or on a side plate—not your bread plate!—if one is available. When you've removed most or all of the leaves, you'll reach the heart of the artichoke, which forms a firm center of meat. Use a knife to scrape the fuzzy part off and then cut the meat into bite-size pieces with the help of a knife and fork.

- **Bacon.** If the bacon is very crisp, you can eat with your fingers. Otherwise, use a knife and fork.

- **Cake.** You can eat cake with your fingers if it's in bite-size pieces. If it comes as a whole slice, if it's sticky, or if it comes with sauce or ice cream, use both a fork and spoon. Hold the spoon in your right hand to scoop up the dessert. The fork goes in your left hand, and you use it as a pusher.

- **Caviar.** To eat caviar, you first spread it on a bite-size piece of toast and then add any condiments, such as chopped onions or capers.

- **Celery, pickles, and radishes.** To eat these fresh vegetables, remove them from the serving plate with your fingers and place them on the side of your dinner plate. Take small bites, using your fingers to bring the vegetables to your mouth.

- **Chicken and other fowl.** Unless you're at a picnic, you should eat chicken and turkey with a knife and fork.

- **Corn on the cob.** Use both hands to eat an ear of corn. Butter and eat only a few rows at a time. You won't encounter this food on formal occasions in America, and you won't encounter it at all in Europe, where most people consider corn—and especially corn on the cob—to be food for livestock.

- **Crabs.** Eat crabs as you would lobster. See the following tips.

- **Lobsters.** To eat a lobster requires a host of techniques. Start by cracking the shell with a nutcracker and then extract the meat with a seafood fork (that's the tiny little thing with the three tines). If you pull out a large piece, cut it with a fork. Pull off the small claws and suck out the meat (there's not much meat in them, but what's there is sweet!) as if you were drawing liquid through a straw. Use your knife and fork to eat stuffed lobster.

◆ **Olives.** Use the same technique with olives as you did with bacon, pickles, and celery. If the olive is pitted, eat it whole. If the olive is large and unpitted, hold it in your fingers and eat it in small bites, instead of popping the whole thing in your mouth and munching. As for the pit, kiss it into the palm of your hand and then deposit it on the edge of your plate.

◆ **Pasta.** Pasta comes in many different sizes and shapes, but you can basically divide them into the long and stringy type and the short and squat type. To eat long and stringy pasta, like spaghetti or linguini, it's a good idea to avoid that business of twirling spaghetti with your fork into the bowl of a spoon. Instead, eat a few strands at a time, twirling them on your fork without the support of a spoon. Do not cut the strands with your knife. Small ziti, penne, and the like require only a fork.

◆ **Potatoes.** The technique to use on a potato depends on how it is prepared. Eat the inside of a baked potato with a fork. If you want to eat the skin, cut it into manageable pieces with a knife and fork. Don't try to convert your baked potatoes into mashed food. Cut fries in half and eat them with your fork.

Mind Your P's and Q's

"Don't, when offered a dish at a friend's table, look at it critically, turn it about with the spoon and fork, and then refuse it."

—G. R. M. Devereaux, *Etiquette for Women*, 1901

◆ **Shrimp.** If the tails are still attached, use your fingers. Eat shrimp cocktail with a seafood fork, dipping a shrimp into the sauce and popping it into your mouth in two bites if large. Better still, put them on a serving plate, spoon a little sauce on them, and then cut the shrimp with a knife and fork.

◆ **Tortillas.** If you eat tortillas with your hands, start eating them at one open end, holding the other end closed. If they're especially full and unwieldy, use a fork and knife and cut them crosswise, starting at an open end.

Fruits

The following fruits are difficult to eat:

◆ **Avocados.** If the avocado is still in its shell, use a spoon. If in pieces on a plate, use a knife and fork.

◆ **Berries.** Eat berries with a spoon if they are served with no stems attached. If served with their stems, hold the berry by the stem and eat it in one or two bites after dipping the berry into sugar or sauce.

- **Grapefruit halves.** Section grapefruit halves so that the meat is accessible without a lot of digging. Eat the sections with a spoon and never squeeze the juice.

- **Lemon wedges.** Handle lemon wedges with care. You can secure them with a fork and squeeze with the other hand or, if you pick up a wedge to squeeze between the fingers, use the other hand as a "squirt shield" so that the diner beside you doesn't get an eyeful of lemon juice.

- **Oranges and tangerines.** Either peel oranges and tangerines with a knife or with your fingers and then eat them section by section. If served on a plate, eat them with a fork.

- **Peaches.** Halve and then quarter peaches with a knife; then eat the fruits of this labor with a fork. You can either eat the skin or peel it off with a knife or your fingers.

- **Pineapple.** You eat pineapple with a spoon when served in small pieces and with a fork when sliced.

- **Watermelon.** If watermelon is served in small pieces, eat it with a spoon. Otherwise, use your fork. Put the seeds into the palm of your hand and transfer them to the side of your plate.

Continental vs. American Style

In our shrinking world, we often see people using the continental or European style of dining, as well as the more familiar (to most of us) American style. Both are perfectly correct, and neither is preferable to the other. What's important is being consistent and being correct in whichever style you choose. After it is mastered, the continental style is far more graceful and efficient, so it is well worth learning. (Children, by the way, often get the hang of this style of dining more easily than adults do.)

When knives and forks became popular in Europe in the early seventeenth century, most people probably used them in much the same way as Americans do now. Only later did the upper classes in Europe begin using what is now known as the continental style and the practice spread—but not, obviously, to America.

American style. The knife is used for cutting only. It is held in the right hand (for right-handers) while cutting, and the fork is held in the left hand to help control the object being cut. The knife is then put down on the edge

Say What?

The person sitting next to you has just commandeered your bread plate by accident. What do you say?

Nothing. Place your bread on the rim of your dinner plate.

of the plate (blade facing in), and the fork is switched to the right hand to lift the cut piece to the mouth. The tines of the fork face upward when bringing food to the mouth. Hands are in the lap when not being used.

Americans are the only people in the world who use this basically inefficient style of dining.

Continental style. The knife remains in the right hand and the fork in the left. After the food is cut, the knife is used to push it onto the fork. The prongs of the fork face downward when the cut food is lifted to the mouth unless the type of food—peas or creamed food, for example—requires a different tactic. The hands remain above the table from the wrist up when they are not in use.

Live and Learn

Small forks for eating were first used in the eleventh century in Tuscany. Prior to that and for some time after, people ate with their hands. They separated their meat by tearing it with their hands or cutting it with knives and using their fingers to pick at it. Some historians attribute the more refined use of eating utensils to Eleanor of Aquitaine, wife of Louis VII of France and Henry II of England. Eleanor is credited with initiating and encouraging many chivalrous and courtly customs.

Dining skillfully and enjoyably takes homework and practice. The good news is that it's not brain surgery, and anybody can do it. Most people take dining skills for granted until it's too late. But, just as nobody ever learned to ride a bike by reading a book, actual experience is necessary for you to become a poised, informed, and confident dining companion.

Bonne chance and *bon appétit!*

The Least You Need to Know

- Appearance is as important as performance. Sit up straight. Keep your elbows off the table. Don't wave your cutlery or flap your napkin.

- Don't hurry or dawdle. Keep pace with the others at the table.

- Never chew with your mouth open or try to speak with food in your mouth.

- If you use the wrong piece of flatware, don't panic. Continue using it. Ask the server for a replacement when you need it.

- After you pick up a piece of cutlery, it should never touch the table again. Put it on your dish, rather than leaning the used item half on and half off the plate.

5

Special Dining Situations

In This Chapter

- ◆ Bountiful banquets
- ◆ Negotiating the buffet table
- ◆ Learning the art of formal dinners
- ◆ Simple manners for fast food

Having dealt with the basics of proper dining in the previous chapter, let's investigate strategies for dealing with some special situations. These situations include banquets, at which as many as 10 people are supposed to dine comfortably at a single round table; the buffet meal and the special etiquette it requires; the dreaded formal dinner; and dining at fast food restaurants. Many of us learned basic table manners around the family dinner table, and this experience, obviously, doesn't equip us to handle these special situations (including the elaborate planning needed for business meals, examined in Chapter 7).

Braving the Baffling Banquet

You are attending an awards banquet or a wedding or the final function of a weeklong conference at the Grand Hotel in a distant city. The room is a sea of linen and candles. There are dozens of round tables, and each is supposed to seat—somehow—10 people. The place settings seem to be jammed together. One set of cutlery blends into the next. There are too many dishes and glasses, and far, far too many people at the table. Stay calm. Continue to breathe normally. You can handle this, one step at a time.

First, find your table. Then find the place card with your name on it. Never, ever, ever, rearrange place cards to suit yourself. To do so is a major breach of etiquette.

Mind Your P's and Q's ___

Here's a good way to remember what belongs to your place setting at a crowded table. The first two letters of the word *drink* are *dr*. Think "drinks right." At a crowded table, your glass will be on your right, and your bread plate on your left.

Somebody gave considerable thought to the seating, probably taking into consideration factors such as familiarity and status—within the society, family, company, or institution.

For example, it would be a bad idea to move your place card next to the host, just because you're friends. You're likely to unseat the guest of honor. (Tampering with the place cards is even ruder on private social occasions because the host has given careful thought to the seating arrangement and will not be happy if you try to second-guess him or her.)

Before you sit down at your table, introduce yourself to any dining companions you don't know and say hello to those you do. Here's an opportunity to make a positive impression on your fellow diners by taking the initiative to meet them and shake their hands. If you simply sit down, you risk having to shout your name across the centerpiece to people who, if they can hear you, won't remember what you said.

Enter your chair from the left side. Men, it is neither sexist nor theatrical for you to draw out the chair for the woman on your right. Women, accept such a gesture.

The Place Setting

Once you are seated, a bewildering display of stuff will undoubtedly confront you. What faces you is an organized table, not a malicious rebus designed to befuddle you. Think of a place setting as a chart—a chart that will guide you safely through the meal.

First, look at the silverware, also known as flatware. Start at the outside and move inward as the courses arrive. Accordingly, you can usually tell the number of courses to be served by taking a good look at the flatware. (At a very formal dinner, however, the server might replace the flatware before serving each course.)

You'll probably see the following arrangement:

- Knives and spoons are on the right.
- Forks and napkins are on the left.

◆ Glassware/crystal is on the right.

◆ Side plates, such as a salad plate or bread-and-butter plate, are on the left.

Now you are master of the universe, Arthur of the Round Table. As each course comes and goes, you will remain relaxed and confident. And, having solved the place-setting rebus, the basic rules of dealing with silverware are easy to master:

◆ After you pick up a piece of silverware, it never touches the tabletop again.

◆ You do not "tip" or lean silverware against your plate. Instead, place the knife and fork right on the plate when you're not using them. Make sure that the blade of the knife always faces you.

◆ Spoons used for coffee or tea belong on the saucer beside the cup.

> **Live and Learn**
>
> The phrase *powder room* was originally used at formal balls in England centuries ago to designate the room in which servants attended to the wigs of the guests.

Braving the Baffling Buffet

The buffet meal scene may resemble the siege of the Bastille. Somehow, ordinarily sensible people seem to think the food will be taken away before they get some or that others will take all of the food, leaving them to starve.

This irrational approach results in the two major buffet blunders: approaching the table too quickly and putting too much food on your plate.

Approach

Before piling food on your plate, look at the dining tables. If utensils and/or plates are already there, you don't need to look for them at the buffet table. Remember, if place cards are on the tables, do not shift them around to suit yourself.

Then take a look to see whether the buffet has one or two lines. If two lines are moving, you will find serving utensils on both sides of the table.

Take your place in line. Gender and status privileges do not apply in the buffet line, so don't try to get ahead of anyone and don't break up a couple or a group going through the line together.

Dishing

If one item is in short supply, go easy on it. At a restaurant or hotel, it is fine to ask to have a dish replenished. At a private party, don't ask.

Use the serving spoon or fork provided for a particular dish and put the serving piece next to the platter or chafing dish when you are finished. A hot metal spoon in a chafing dish could burn the fingers of another diner.

Don't overload your dish. Going back for seconds or thirds is perfectly acceptable. Don't take platefuls of food for the table. That defeats the whole idea of a buffet, which is offering a multitude of choices for a variety of tastes and appetites.

Serving Stations

When various dishes are served at serving stations, as at a brunch buffet, remember that the attendants are limited in what they can provide. Special requests are okay if they are easily accomplished. For example, you can ask for scrambled eggs at the omelet station, but don't ask for "over easy" if no whole eggs are in sight. And only ask for ingredients in your omelet that are in sight and readily available. Similarly, don't ask for an end cut of beef if you don't see one.

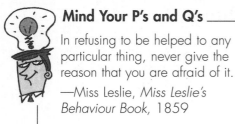

Mind Your P's and Q's

In refusing to be helped to any particular thing, never give the reason that you are afraid of it.

—Miss Leslie, *Miss Leslie's Behaviour Book,* 1859

Plates

In a restaurant, plenty of clean, freshly polished plates should be available, which means you should not have to reuse a plate. When you're going back to the buffet for seconds, don't hesitate to ask a server to replace a plate or silverware or retrieve what you need at the buffet table.

In a private home, use common sense to determine whether you should retain your plate or ask for a new one. In any case, never scrape and stack your plates when you're finished.

Sitting Down

If people invite you to join their table as you leave the buffet line, either accept graciously or find a way to decline just as graciously. For instance, you could say, "I'm sorry, but I promised Tom and his family that I'd eat with them." Even though people at your table will be sitting down to eat at different times, it's still a good idea to generally keep pace with others at the table and engage them in conversation. If you need to leave the table temporarily, be sure to place your napkin on the seat or arm of your chair.

Standing Up

If you're eating while standing up, it's even more important to avoid overloading your plate. That way you can circulate a bit. Indeed, one of the few—maybe the only—advantages of a stand-up buffet is that you can drift around and chat with a lot of people. For example, food at cocktail parties is often consumed while standing.

When you settle on a place to stand, make sure you are not blocking a path to the buffet table or anything else.

Going Uptown: Facing the Formal Dinner

Now that you've solved the mysteries of the banquet hall and the buffet table, you are ready to move on to that most daunting dining dilemma—the formal dinner. You'll be able to handle this challenge with grace and confidence if you know what to expect and how to react.

Before Sitting Down

A lipstick trail is the red badge of discourtesy. Take precautions before you reach the table. This is also the time to visit the restroom for hair repair and other finishing touches. Remember to greet everyone before sitting down. Gentlemen must rise to greet latecomers. They may also rise when ladies leave and return to the table, although today's woman should not expect this behavior. A server will draw the chair for you. Enter from your left.

Napkins

After you are seated, wait for your host to make the first napkin move. When the host places the napkin on his or her lap, the guests should follow suit. Similarly, at the end of the meal, the host should be the first to place the napkin on the table to signal that the meal is over, having made certain that everyone at the table has finished.

Large dinner napkins should remain folded in half and placed across your lap with the fold facing your waist. Never "flap" the napkin to unfold it.

If you leave the table during the meal, place the napkin on your chair. If the server does not push the chair back under the table, you should do so. The server may also refold your napkin and place it on the arm of your chair during your absence.

At the end of the meal, do not refold the napkin. Pick it up from its center and place it loosely on the table to the left of your plate.

Wine

Wine will be served during a formal dinner. If you don't want wine, place your finger-tips lightly on the rim of the glass when the server approaches to pour. (Never turn your glass upside down.) Say, "I'm not having any today" (or this evening or tonight). The *today* sends a message: You don't disapprove of wine, and the others should feel no compunction about enjoying their wine if they choose.

Wine is offered with the first course (soup) and will be poured from the right. Red wine (and brandy) glasses are held by the bowl because the warmth of the hand releases the bouquet. Red wine glasses may also be held by the stem, but white wine and champagne glasses are always held by the stem, so as not to diminish the chill.

Wait until your host has lifted his or her glass before you drink.

The Seven Courses

Once again, the number of pieces of silverware will indicate the number of courses you can expect, and the general rule is to start from the outside.

You may expect the formal dinner to consist of seven courses, in this order: soup, fish, sorbet (or other palate cleanser), a meat or fowl dish, salad (often served with cheese), dessert, and coffee.

Courses are served from the left, removed from the right. Wine is poured from the right. (It helps to know from which direction they will be coming at you.)

Live and Learn

The custom of clinking glasses was originally used to drive away evil spirits. If you want to clink, do so with the greatest care, particularly if you are using fine crystal. For the most part, it will suffice simply to raise your glass in the direction of the person being toasted. As for the toast itself, there is an old saying that you would do well to repeat to yourself if you are asked to propose a toast. "Be upstanding, be sincere, be brief, and be seated." Think of the "four Bs."

Try to finish each course at about the same time as others around you. When you are finished with a course, hoist out the "I am finished" pennant. Here's how: Visualize a clock face on your plate. Place both the knife and fork in about the 10:20 position with the points at 10 and the handles at 20. The prongs of the fork should be down, and the blade of the knife should face you. If you have been eating the course with the fork only, place it prongs up in the same position as the knife when finished. Placing flatware in the finished position facilitates the server clearing from the right. He or she can secure the handles with the thumb, thus reducing the risk of dropping them in the diner's lap.

Finished position.

Hoist out the "I am resting" pennant when you want to pause during a course and don't want the server to snatch your plate away. In this case, the knife and fork are crossed on the plate with the fork over the knife and the prongs pointing down. The knife should be in the 10:20 position, as on the face of a clock; the fork prongs should be at two o'clock, and the handle at eight o'clock, forming an inverted V. It is also correct to form the inverted V without crossing fork over knife.

Servers in fine restaurants are usually trained to recognize the I-am-finished and the I-am-resting signals. Now let's look at how to deal with each course.

Resting positions.

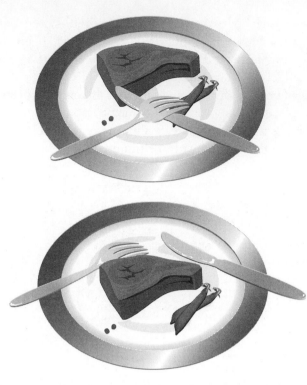

First Course: Soup

When eating soup, tilt the spoon away from you (dip the outer edge of the spoon, rather than the edge closest to you, into the soup first). This technique diminishes dribble danger and looks more appealing. Sip from the side (not the front) of the spoon, making no more noise than a spider. Yes, you may tilt the soup plate (often, inaccurately, called the soup bowl) away from you to access the last of the soup.

Leave your spoon on the soup plate. However, if the soup is served in a two-handled bowl or bouillon cup, leave the spoon on the underlying saucer.

When eating soup, tilt the spoon away from you.

Tilt the soup plate away from you to get the last bit of soup.

A two-handled soup cup.

Second Course: Fish

Watch out. In fine restaurants the fish course is often served with special fish knives and forks. In that case, hold the fish fork in your left hand, prongs down, as in the continental style of dining.

Use the fish knife to break the fish and push it onto the fork. You hold the fish knife differently than you do a dinner knife because you're not actually cutting the fish but merely breaking it apart. Hold the knife between your thumb and your index and middle fingers.

If the fish is soft and boneless, you need use only the fork. In this case, leave the fish knife on the table. Hold the fork in your right hand, prongs up. The prongs can be either up or down when the fork is resting on the plate after you're finished.

Remove fish bones with your thumb and index finger and place the bones on the side of the plate.

Say What? _____

You are halfway through your entrée, and you realize that you're using the wrong fork.

What do you say?

Nothing just then. Go ahead and finish the course with that fork. When the next course comes around, ask the server for a replacement: "May I have a new fork for this, please?"

How to hold a fish knife.

Third Course: Sorbet

Although the serving of sorbet dates back to the Roman Empire when hosts served packed snow brought down from the mountains to clear the palates of the guests, *sorbetto* did not emerge until the middle of the sixteenth century in Italy.

These days a sorbet is served only between the fish and meat courses, but it was once served to clear the palate of the distinctive flavors of each course and get it ready for the next.

If the sorbet is served with a garnish, go ahead and eat the mint leaves, fresh herbs, or flower petals.

Fourth Course: Meat and Fowl

Here you get more serious with the use of your knife than you did during the fish course. But you should still try to use it more like a surgeon than a lumberjack. Place your index finger about an inch down from the handle, on the back of the blade, to help you press down firmly. Hold the fork in your left hand, prongs down. Spear the meat and hold it firmly in place with the fork while you cut. Only cut enough food for each mouthful.

It's okay to put a small amount of potatoes and vegetables on the fork along with the meat.

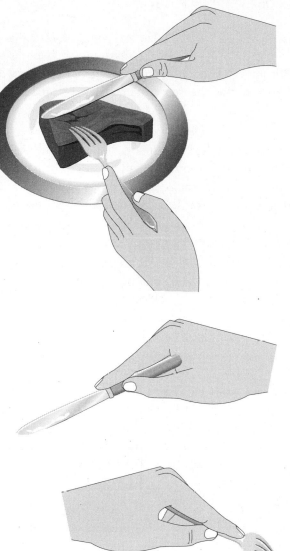

Knives and forks are held this way.

The meat knife. Place your index finger about an inch down from the handle to help you press down firmly.

Hold the fork in your left hand, prongs down.

Fifth Course: Salad

As with the fish course, you will use the salad fork and knife for this course, leaving the knife on the table if you don't need to cut anything. If cheese is served with the salad, place a small portion of cheese on your salad plate together with crackers or bread. Use the salad knife to put cheese on the crackers or bread.

Sixth Course: Dessert

When dessert is served with both fork and spoon, the fork is the pusher and the spoon is used for eating. Hold the fork in your left hand, tines down, and push the dessert onto the spoon in your right hand. Pie or cake requires only a fork. Ice cream and pudding require only a spoon. Leave the other utensil on the table.

Seventh Course: Coffee

Be careful not to overload your beverage with cream and sugar. Avoid swirling your coffee around too much, making a splash and puddle on your saucer. Don't slurp, but sip gently. If your coffee is too hot, let it sit for a while—don't blow on it. Finally, don't leave your spoon in the cup. Place it on your saucer.

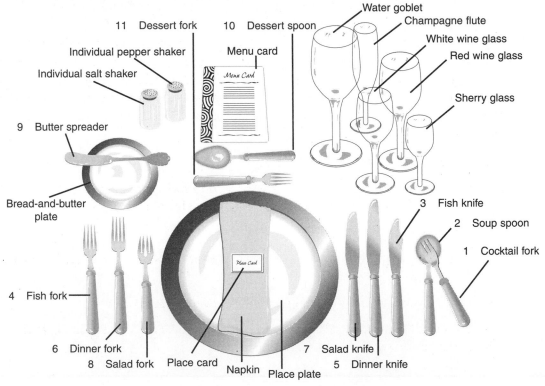

The formal place setting with cutlery, numbered in order of use.

Manners at Mickey Dee's

At the other end of the spectrum, the fast-food eatery, the company lunchroom, or eating at your desk are venues about as informal as it gets. But informal does not mean sloppy. These scenarios never will replace the traditional meal; yet, they are clearly a part of life. Here are some key points for handling them with grace:

◆ Watch that smell. Whether we are in a cubicle or on an airplane, it's rude to impose our cuisine on anybody else. High-odor foods such as fish, onions, and some lunch meats are offensive at best.

◆ Use a knife and fork even if the food doesn't strictly dictate that. For example, a drippy chicken salad sandwich is more easily managed by eating the filling with a fork until it becomes more manageable. Ditto for pizza.

◆ Keep your playing field clean. Those little packets of mustard, ketchup, sugar, and so on, are best hidden under your plate or immediately put into the bag the food came in. Nobody wants to feel they're next to someone who is starting a personal compost heap.

◆ Watch that sound. Make sure you chew with your mouth closed and don't slurp. Listening to your lunch goes a long way in killing a neighbor's appetite.

Although dining circumstances vary, you can handle them with more confidence by remembering the basics. Approach the experience with a positive attitude and a cheerful demeanor. Keep pace with the others. Watch your posture. Smile. When in doubt, do what your host does, or pick out the classiest person at the table and copy him or her. In other words: Dine among others as you would have them dine among you.

The Least You Need to Know

◆ Knives and spoons are placed on the right, and forks and napkins on the left. Liquids are on the right, and solids (such as the bread plate) are on the left.

◆ Use cutlery from the outside in.

◆ Use the side of your dinner plate for your bread if someone commandeers your bread plate.

◆ The gravest danger in buffet dining lies in overloading your dish.

◆ Never call attention to the dining mistakes of others or be overly apologetic about your own.

Chapter 6

The Anatomy of a Restaurant

In This Chapter

◆ From maître d' to busser: what role each person plays

◆ The art of toasting

◆ Using chopsticks

◆ Vegetarians

Because so many occasions for dining with others—for business or pleasure—occur in restaurants, understanding how restaurants work can help you relax and enjoy the events.

The structure of a showy Las Vegas–type dining room is different from that of a casual California-style eatery, and both are different from that of a five-star French haute cuisine establishment. Accordingly, the protocol varies with the structures.

This chapter aims to demystify the art of dining out. It decodes the tipping scene and helps you learn how to avoid getting burned while giving a toast. In addition, you'll learn how to handle chopsticks properly, as well as how to deal with the sometimes touchy subject of vegetarianism.

Cast of Characters

When you go to a restaurant, staff members actually become your employees for the duration of the meal. Smooth dining is a team game. Knowing how your team works, which function each member performs, and how each person relates to you and to the rest of the restaurant team will greatly increase your chances of having an enjoyable experience.

Mind Your P's and Q's

Tipping the maître d' is a fine but simple art. First, fold a 10- or 20-dollar bill in half, then half again, and then half again so that the amount shows on both sides. Put it into the palm of your right hand and shake hands with the maître d'. The bill will smoothly, almost magically, disappear during the handshake.

Maître d'/Host

The maître d' is often the person who seats you. He or she may also be the general manager or the owner, especially in a smaller establishment. The maître d' is in charge of all floor service, including staffing, coordinating reservations with seating, timing the flow of patrons with the pace of the kitchen staff, and handling special requests—such as presenting an engagement ring or a birthday surprise.

Captain/Head Waiter

The terms are interchangeable—captains and headwaiters—and not all restaurants have one. If one person takes your order and another serves, the first is generally your captain or headwaiter. The second person in this instance is the server, whose duties are explained shortly. The captain is the one to consult if you have a problem with the food or service.

Chef

King of the kitchen, the chef controls how food is prepared, presented, and served. Consult the chef if you have a special request concerning food. Your server can handle communicating a simple request such as serving sauce on the side. For something complicated like a sugar-free, salt-free, or wheat-free meal, you might want to make the request in advance through the maître d'.

Sommelier

Some restaurants have a sommelier, or wine steward. He or she is the one to ask which wine goes with the beef bordelaise and which with the lobster. Sometimes the sommelier will present and pour the wine as well.

Bartenders and Servers

These restaurant employees are the ones you have the most direct contact with, and they are under the supervision of the maître d' or manager in most restaurants. Servers are also called by the horrible—but gender-free and thus politically correct—term *waitron*.

Bussers

Bussers are usually the first people who come to your table, pouring water and providing bread and butter. They also clear dishes and reset tables. If something is missing at the table, such as a water glass or a piece of flatware, let the busser know.

Although the goal of all restaurant employees is to produce a gracious and satisfied customer who returns regularly, each employee is motivated by different needs. The maître d' wants everything to run smoothly, efficiently, and profitably. Servers, bartenders, and bussers are motivated by anticipated tips and recognition for a job well done.

Chefs are motivated by praise for their taste and creativity. If you visit one restaurant regularly, it pays to praise the chef when warranted. You can ask for the chef, in order to give personal congratulations, or send your message of appreciation through a server.

Tipping

Even if you use a credit card, carry some cash for tips. If you are a regular at a restaurant, or if you have gotten exceptional service and plan to return, tipping the maître d' is appropriate. A maître d' who provides you with a great table for a special event or oversees a smooth-running business meal should receive $10 to $20 in cash, depending on the size of your group and the complexity of your special requests.

A captain or waiter (the person who takes your order) should get 5 percent of the bill either in cash or specified on the bill if you use a credit card.

Your server should get at least 15 percent of your total bill, according to the level of service provided. Remember that the server usually divides your tip among the entire service team, which includes bartenders and bussers.

The sommelier should be tipped 15 percent of the wine bill if he or she performs special services (such as helping you choose the right wine for your meal).

Checkroom attendants get $1 per coat. Add another dollar for each briefcase, pair of boots, or umbrella you or your guests check.

Toasting

Toasting can make even a meal at the local diner a special occasion. It can add a festive air to a gathering and has a way of bringing everyone at the table together.

The host proposes a toast, often welcoming a guest to a meal, at the beginning of the meal. The toast may also occur in the middle of the meal, when the host raises a glass to the guest of honor on his or her right. If the host has stage fright, it is acceptable to have his or her spouse make the toast. A guest may also propose a toast, but only after the host.

Live and Learn

The toast originated during the Middle Ages, when people put a piece of scorched bread into a tankard of beer or wine because they thought it improved the flavor of the drink. The custom of putting a piece of toast in a drink is still followed in England, albeit rarely. Exactly when the custom of offering words of welcome or congratulations began to accompany the lifting of the glass is lost in the mists of history.

An example of an excellent toast was given at a dinner for Nobel Prize winners in the State Dining Room of the White House. President John F. Kennedy rose and said, "I think this is the most extraordinary collection of talent, of human knowledge, ever gathered at the White House, with the possible exception of when Thomas Jefferson dined here alone."

You don't have to be that clever. A typical welcoming toast might be "I am so pleased that you all could be here to share each other's good company and this good food. Welcome."

Mind Your P's and Q's

It has been said that toasts are like a woman's skirt. They should be long enough to cover the subject, but short enough to be amusing. That usually translates into about one minute.

Instead of offering the toast at the beginning, you might want to wait until the end. In that case, you could stand and toast the guest of honor this way, "I am so pleased that you could all be here to welcome my dear friend Florence, who's come all the way from Rome to visit."

Or "It's wonderful to have Florence with us tonight. Let's toast a rare woman who looks at every situation in life as an opportunity to give of herself, to make things better, happier, and more fun. To Florence."

Or be even more specific: "I am particularly honored to have my mother-in-law with us tonight, jogging Jo Fleischmann—triathlete, pal, coach, and mom extraordinaire. To Jo."

One-word toasts, such as the Danish *skol* and the Spanish *salud*, both of which mean "health," are pretty much universally accepted as symbols of welcome. It's a nice idea to toast people in their native tongue, but be sure to use the correct pronunciation.

Some examples follow:

- Irish: Slante (SLANT tay)

- Yiddish: L'chaim (leh KHY yim)

- German: Prosit (PRO sit)

- Japanese: Kanpai (KAHN pi)

Toasting Blunders

A wonderful toast makes gathered guests feel honored to be together and with you, whereas a bad toast just embarrasses everyone. Here are some tips to help you shine:

- Don't ever toast yourself.

- If you're the one being toasted, just listen quietly to the toast and then say a quick thank-you. Don't even put your hand on your glass, much less drink.

- Don't read your toast. If it's too long to commit to memory, it's too long. Come up with something pithier.

- Don't clink glasses. It's an old custom involving the driving away of spirits—not a happy thought at any occasion. Besides, it's bad news for glassware.

- Do keep your toast short.

- Do toast the host in return if you are the guest of honor and are being toasted. You can do this as soon as the host's toast is finished or later, during dessert. Just keep it short.

- Do not tap the rim of your glass to get everybody's attention—it's tacky.

- Do make a toast even if you're not drinking alcohol. Anything will do. It's the thought that counts.

- Do toast more than one person. For example, you might toast an entire family that has come to visit, or a whole team.

- Do not preempt. The host should be the first one to toast.

Tricky Situations

Two common and tricky situations that you might encounter when dining out are handling chopsticks and dealing with vegetarianism.

Chop Chop

In our shrinking world, you may find yourself in a situation in which politeness requires you to use chopsticks. Here is a step-by-step guide to eating with them:

1. Put the bottom chopstick in the web of your right hand between the thumb and index finger.

2. Use your two middle fingers to keep the chopstick steady. Hold it firmly but not too rigidly. This bottom chopstick will remain fairly stationary while you are eating.

3. Hold the top chopstick like a pencil between your thumb and index finger. This one does most of the moving.

You can hold the bowl or plate of food under your chin while you're eating until you feel really confident. In fact, you can continue to do so even after you have become an expert; it's proper etiquette in Asian cultures.

A good way to learn is to practice picking up popcorn with chopsticks at home.

Although it's good to know how to use chopsticks, you shouldn't hesitate to ask for a fork in most situations. In fact, the Chinese are the ones who invented the fork. (And now you know why.)

Place the bottom chopstick in the web of your right hand between the thumb and index finger.

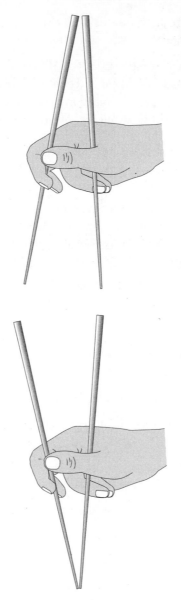

Hold the top chopstick like a pencil between your thumb and index finger.

The top chopstick does most of the moving. The bottom chopstick remains stationary.

Vegetarians

If you are a vegetarian, you have a responsibility to let your host know in advance. If one of your guests is a vegetarian, you need to ask for a little more information. Some vegetarians don't eat eggs or dairy products, for instance, whereas others do.

If you're hosting a restaurant meal, tell the maître d' that you or a guest is a vegetarian. Find out whether the restaurant offers a vegetarian menu. Ask for suggestions.

It's a good idea to ask guests whom you don't know well whether they have any special dietary considerations. If you can't accommodate them, you can say something like this: "I've planned this party around my grandmother's meat lasagna recipe, but plenty of salads and snacks will be available, or you can stop by later for dessert."

The key point is to not make a big deal out of it. A vegetarian can skip certain dishes and, if there is a question, simply say: "Everything is fine. I just don't eat meat." Comments like "I don't eat dead animals" are unnecessary, rude, and offensive.

In addition to knowing how a restaurant works, you should get to know a couple of good restaurants really well. Become a regular. Learn the names of the key staff people and engage them in conversation when convenient. After a while, you will be greeted more warmly and given special attention in these places. Also, you will feel more comfortable dining there and bringing guests.

The Least You Need to Know

- In general, tip 15 to 20 percent of the total bill in a restaurant, although 20 percent is becoming the norm.

- If you have a complaint, make it to the captain or maître d' and do so quietly.

- When toasting someone, sincerity and brevity are the best policies. The drink used needn't be alcoholic.

- Don't spend an eternity studying the menu and interrogating the server, especially if the restaurant is busy.

- Requesting a fork in a Chinese restaurant is okay if you prefer not to use chopsticks.

Chapter 7

Business Meals

In This Chapter

- ◆ Planning the meal
- ◆ Ten major no-no's
- ◆ The big day
- ◆ Wrapping up
- ◆ Eating at meetings

Business adds a new dimension to the dining experience, and dining adds a new dimension to the business experience. What happens around the dining table can form or harden opinions, dampen or heighten expectations, and remove or deepen doubts. For instance, during a lunch meeting with a colleague, you might be thinking: Can I work comfortably with this guy? Or: She should have better sense than that. Or even: If he can't organize a lunch meeting, how can he run a department?

No, a business meal is not just a meeting with food. It's a test, really. It spotlights your social skills, your ability to plan and organize, and your level of sophistication. Take these occasions very, very seriously, and prepare for them carefully.

Getting Down to the Business of Planning a Business Meal

Assume that you will be the host of a business lunch or dinner. Seeing the situation from the point of view of the host will make you a more knowledgeable and confident guest.

The host must decide, up front, that the best way to accomplish the agenda is to control the process from beginning to end. The host's job is to eliminate distractions and to keep the focus on the purpose of the meal.

Here are some guidelines to keep in mind:

♦ **Don't experiment.** Save that for when you are feeling adventurous. Instead, frequent a couple of good restaurants and become known as a "regular." Become familiar with the menu. Get to know the maître d' or manager.

♦ **Don't be a big spender.** Except for celebrations, extravagance shows bad manners and bad strategy in the business arena. Pick a quality restaurant known for its reliable service. Don't show off by consistently ordering the most expensive choices in food and wine. Your guests might feel they have to reciprocate, and they are likely to conclude that you are reckless with money—and therefore apt to be reckless in other areas.

Ten Commandments

Here's a handy list of no-no's to consult before every business meal:

♦ Thou shalt not jump straight into business talk.

♦ Thou shalt not be late.

♦ Thou shalt not table-hop.

♦ Thou shalt not talk politics, diet, or family.

♦ Thou shalt not dominate conversation.

♦ Thou shalt not dawdle over ordering or eating.

♦ Thou shalt not drink too much alcohol.

♦ Thou shalt not fight over who pays the bill.

♦ Thou shalt not neglect thy table manners.

♦ Thou shalt not forget to show appreciation.

Dress Rehearsal

Visit the restaurant a day or two before the meeting. Have a good look at the room. Is it too large? Too noisy? Look for a table in a good position and reserve it if possible. Familiarize yourself with the menu and the house specialties.

Introduce yourself to the maître d' or manager. Set up a corporate account or allow the manager to take a credit card imprint. Let the manager know that you may be ordering wine, depending upon the preference of your guests. Let him or her know what your price range is and ask for recommendations. Tip the maître d' when you leave, usually $10 or $20, depending upon the level of the restaurant.

Make the reservation in your name and your company's name. You want to emphasize that your event is a business meal. Make it quite clear that this meeting is important, that you are willing to pay for (and expect) top service, and that you—and possibly your associates—will be returning if all goes well.

Invitations

One of the most important elements of a gracious invitation to a business meal is choice: Whenever possible, offer your potential guest a chance to contribute to the time and place of the meal. Here is how a typical conversation might go when you are calling to invite someone to a business meal:

"Hello, Nick, this is Mary Mitchell. I'm calling to invite you to lunch to talk about our upcoming program. Is that something you'd like to do?"

"Sure. Sounds good."

"How about Thursday or Friday?"

"Friday would be better."

"Fine. How does Benjamin's or The Wharf sound to you?"

"Great."

"Which do you prefer?"

"The Wharf sounds good."

"Would 12:00 or 12:30 be more convenient?"

"12:30."

"Fine. I'll make the reservation. Do you prefer smoking or nonsmoking?"

"Nonsmoking, please."

"Great. I'll see you on Friday at 12:30 at The Wharf."

If you are inviting more than one guest, and Nick is the most important, provide information about the other guests after the "Sure. Sounds good" and before settling details about time and place: "I'd like also to invite Megan Newman and Nancy Love, who will be working with us on the program. Okay?"

Mind Your P's and Q's

When waiting for someone in a restaurant, stand where you can see the door without impeding traffic.

Then, when you call Megan, say: "Nick and I are having lunch Friday at The Wharf. I was hoping you and Nancy could join us."

Timing

After you establish the date of your business meal, clear your calendar. Rushing to get there on time or rushing at any point in the process can ruin your efforts to establish just the right atmosphere.

And, while allowing plenty of your time, pace the meal with respect for the schedules of your guests.

If it is a breakfast meeting, confirm the afternoon before and give your guest your home telephone number in case of an emergency. For a lunch or dinner meeting, call to confirm in the morning of that day.

If, for any reason, the meeting is cancelled, call the restaurant right away.

On the Big Day

Get to the restaurant about 15 minutes early and check your coat. If you did not tip the maître d' at the dress rehearsal, do so now. Wait for your guest near the door. If you must take your seat because there is no place to wait, leave your napkin on the table and don't eat or drink anything until your guest arrives. In other words, the table should remain pristine. Stand up when your guest arrives and remain standing until he or she is seated.

If you are waiting for more than one guest, wait near the door, if possible, for 5 or 10 minutes; then tell the maître d' you are expecting someone and ask to be seated. The ideal situation is for all of the guests to go to the table together, although this may not always be possible.

Seating

Give the preferred seat to your guest. Usually that's the one first pulled out by the maître d', but if a chair isn't pulled out, quickly decide which is the best seat (best view, most comfortable, and so on) and gesture to your guest to occupy it.

Sit at right angles to your guest if possible. If you have two guests, try to avoid sitting between them, or you will feel as if you're watching a tennis match, looking from one to the other in the course of conversation.

The host always stands when someone new joins the table and remains standing until the other person or persons is seated. If someone leaves the table, the host does not need to stand.

> **Live and Learn**
>
> The tradition of giving the most important people seats next to the chairperson goes back centuries to when the king's worst enemy was seated on his left and his closest ally on his right. This seating plan assured that the king had control of his enemy's sword hand, the right, while the king's ally (or "right-hand man") had control of the king's sword hand.

Napkins

Your napkin will be on your plate or to the left of it. As soon as you are seated, place your napkin on your lap unfolded, or half open if it's a large dinner napkin. Don't tuck the napkin into your shirt or belt. It's okay to bring the napkin up to your chest with sips of soup or sauce. If you leave the table for any reason, place the napkin on your chair and push the chair under the table. Watch the upholstery. You don't want your gravy-stained napkin to soil the upholstered seat of a chair.

> **Mind Your P's and Q's**
>
> Tip the sommelier, or wine steward, about 15 percent of the wine bill if he or she provides any service to your table.

Drinks

The server will now ask if you want anything from the bar. Decline if your guest does. Order a drink if your guest does. It doesn't have to be an alcoholic drink, and no explanations are necessary. You can remove any tinge of judgment about alcohol by using the convenient "today" tactic: "I'm not having wine today, but please do have some if you like."

Ordering

If you don't have drinks, spend 5 or 10 minutes talking before asking for menus. If you have drinks, offer your guest a refill. If the answer is no, ask for menus. If the answer is yes, ask for menus when the second round of drinks arrives.

Now it's time to order. Your dress-rehearsal exploration of the menu pays off now. Give your guests clues about your intentions by mentioning specialties and encouraging them to order appetizers. Have the server take the guests' orders first and be sure to keep pace with your guests by ordering the same number of courses, whether you want them or not.

As a guest, you should feel free to ask, "What do you recommend here?" if the host has not given clues.

Be decisive! Neither the host nor guest should spend a long time poring over the menu. Steer clear of user-unfriendly items such as spaghetti, salads, large sandwiches, or anything that will be messy or difficult to eat.

Control and Damage Control

The host's responsibility is to pay attention to the quality of the service and the food. Make sure your guests are served properly and have whatever condiments they might need.

If it looks like something is wrong, ask your guest. If it is, call the maître d' and have the item replaced. If things are going badly, keep your cool. Do not engage in a confrontation with the server or the maître d'. Tell your guest: "I'm so sorry. The restaurant seems to be having a bad day." Then deal with the manager later.

Finishing Touches

Encourage your guests to have dessert when the server returns to the table from clearing the entrees. If they do, you do. If they don't, you don't—no matter how much you have been looking forward to that chocolate torte.

Mind Your P's and Q's

If your guest orders the poached salmon hollandaise, don't order a cheeseburger.

Ask your guests if they would like coffee or tea. When it is served, ask for the check. Use this time to review your mealtime discussion: Make sure you understand what agreements have been reached and the follow-up steps you've decided upon.

Paying Up

Settle the bill quietly with a credit card or with a large bill if you are paying cash. Don't fiddle around with small bills or change.

It's fine to review the bill for accuracy. You should have a fair idea of what the total should be before it arrives. In any case, don't study the thing like the Dead Sea Scrolls. If you notice a discrepancy, deal with it after your guests leave. But please, no calculators at the table.

Nothing damages the effect of a smooth business meal as much as haggling over who should pay. Unfortunately, this situation is more apt to happen if the host is a woman and the guest is a man. If the subject arises, depersonalize it: "I invited you, and besides, XYZ company would like to take you to lunch."

Another tactic that is especially helpful is to arrange beforehand for a credit card imprint and for the addition of 18 to 20 percent for tip. This strategy avoids the presentation of a check at the table.

Mind Your P's and Q's

Smile at your colleagues. It is, after all, the ultimate gesture understood by all people, and it does relieve stress.

Before you leave the table, collect the checkroom tickets from your guests so that you can tip the attendant—at the rate of $1 per garment—on the way out.

Taking Leave

Escort your guests to the door. Shake hands and thank them for coming. Remind them about the next meeting, or if one has not yet been scheduled, say you will call them within a week. (And make sure that you do call within that time frame.)

The guest should thank the host, praise the restaurant, and within two days, send a handwritten note. If your penmanship truly resembles Chinese algebra, you may type the note, but a handwritten note is infinitely more desirable. Under no circumstances should you fax or e-mail your thanks.

Faux Pas

Whether you are dining at Joe's Chili Joint or at a black tie dinner, business cards should not surface during a meal. If asked, pass one as discreetly as possible. In fact, if the event has been billed as a social rather than business-related affair, you should be discreet about talking business at all.

Meeting Eating

When food is ordered in to be eaten at a business meeting, the overriding rule is to keep it simple.

If a knife and fork are provided, use them. However, feel free to use your fingers for foods such as pizza or sandwiches. In fact, you may be better off using your fingers than those flimsy plastic forks. Keep the area around you clean and tidy. Use plenty of napkins or, even better, those dampened, packaged wipes. Stack the plastic mustard and ketchup wrappers. Put bones and scraps on the side of your plate, not on the table. Keys, purses, and everything else not related to the work at hand or the meal should be off the table.

The Least You Need to Know

- ♦ Business dining is not about the food. It's about establishing a relationship or furthering a relationship.

- ♦ The host should give the guest choices of restaurant, time, and day.

- ♦ The host should provide cues to the guest about the menu, signaling to the guest the number of courses and the level of spending he or she is prepared for. For example, "Try the shrimp cocktail here. It's wonderful."

- ♦ When the business meal is important, don't hesitate to do a dress rehearsal so you can get the feel of the restaurant.

- ♦ Seek quality without extravagance in restaurant choice. Extravagance might be bad manners and bad strategy.

- ♦ Know your table manners, whether you are dining at a desk or at a "white tablecloth" restaurant.

Chapter 8

The Ins and Outs of Home Entertaining

In This Chapter

- ◆ Conquering party phobia
- ◆ Getting started
- ◆ The guest list and invitation
- ◆ Hired help and caterers
- ◆ The cocktail party

What a pleasure it is to be invited into someone's home for a gathering of friends. Parties are the best kind of sharing. They boost your spirits, stimulate your imagination, and make you smile. These are only a few of the many excellent reasons that people go to parties.

But now it's time to look at some of the reasons people dread the very idea of giving parties. Too many people cheat themselves out of the pleasure of bringing people together for good conversation and good food by telling themselves that they can't entertain. Fear grips their heart. They will be judged. They will be found wanting. It will be a mess. They can't possibly be ready. It is all too much, too much, too much.

But that's where you're wrong. It's like physics. For each party phobia, there's an equally compelling reason to throw a shindig:

Faux Pas

Don't try to bring together recently separated or divorced people with your other single friends solely for the purpose of introducing them. Such obvious attempts at matchmaking are embarrassing to all concerned and almost never work. Think interesting people, rather than interesting couples, and let what happens happen.

- ♦ "My house is a disaster area!" (No one will remember your house, just your hospitality.)

- ♦ "I don't have party stuff." (Friends, relatives, and ingenuity will supply anything you need.)

- ♦ "I can't cook." (That's what caterers and great gourmet takeout places are for.")

- ♦ "I can't handle a party alone!" (Join with friends or appoint a cohost to help.)

- ♦ "People will be bored to death." (Prepare topics, practice introductions, and invite a great mix of people.)

Here and in Chapter 9, we'll walk you through your fears, streamline your planning, trouble-shoot or avoid the pitfalls, and help you realize all your party- or dinner-hosting aspirations, whatever the occasion.

Live and Learn

When preparing to entertain, remind yourself repeatedly of the following truths:

- ♦ You don't have to be the next Julia Child with a house like Martha Stewart to give a successful party.

- ♦ Giving a successful party has nothing to do with how much furniture you have or how much money you are able to spend.

- ♦ You do not have to impress people with what you have, and you never have to apologize for what you do not have.

Just Do It!

The best way to get over your worries about entertaining is to just go ahead and give a party. Think about starting small. Most people are so pleased to be invited to someone's home that the magnitude of the party doesn't matter. One of my most pleasant memories is of my neighbor's annual holiday dessert get-together. Several neighborhood couples gathered at her house for after-dinner desserts, all purchased from nearby pastry shops and served with so much warmth and grace that we all felt very special.

The fire was roaring, the candles were lit, the coffee and cordials were warm. She was a working mother with more chores than time, but these small, uncomplicated gatherings were always successful.

Creating the Guest List

A party is only as good as its guests, so consider the chemistry of the group you're putting together when you make out your guest list. This exercise is entirely subjective, and every host has a private formula. But here's a list of do's and don'ts to help you learn some general rules.

Do:

♦ Think of the party as an opportunity to bring together people who don't know each other but who will probably enjoy meeting one another.

♦ Think of the party as an opportunity to bring together old friends who never seem to have enough time to visit with one another.

♦ Invite people who will appreciate the invitation and will make an effort to contribute to the success of the party.

Say What? _____

The debate between the Republican real estate broker and the new age existentialist is heating up, and you are worried that others will start taking sides.

What do you say?

Anything.

If you are giving a party, always be ready with a store of anecdotes or comments about something in the news that will change the subject. If this tactic fails, propose a toast to something or somebody.

Don't:

♦ Invite just one type of person. A room full of lawyers or doctors is almost antithetical to the very idea of a party.

♦ Throw in a person or a couple who don't really fit the group just because you owe them a dinner.

♦ Invite known adversaries on the theory that it will make the party livelier. It may make the party livelier than you had hoped.

Everybody has his or her own little tricks and preferences when it comes to making up a guest list. My personal formula, for example, always includes …

- A banker, because bankers know a little about a lot of industries and can talk about what's going on in the economy.

- A journalist, because journalists ask great questions.

- Somebody involved in politics, however tangentially.

- A restaurateur, because the entire world is interested in dining out and in food.

- Someone in marketing, because marketers usually have something interesting to say about trends and tastes and what people are buying.

The best guests are those who know how to sing for their supper. They know that guests as well as hosts have a responsibility to contribute to the party. They will encourage and add to conversation. They are positive and cheerful. You can depend on them. An interesting person who loves to talk—even if it's about himself—will amuse a handful of people and get others talking as well.

Understanding Your Motive

The host motivation for the party has a lot to do with the guest list. See if you can find a good motive for yourself:

- To pay back for invitations you've accepted in the past

- To reaffirm friendships

- To show off a new home, painting, furniture, and so on

- To honor someone

- To say "thank you" to people who've helped you with a particular project or problem

- To get to know new neighbors or colleagues

- To generate future party invitations for yourself

I know a woman who travels widely and spends at least two weeks in each destination. She gives a cocktail party the first evening she arrives. The next day she waits for invitations that will keep her busy for the rest of her visit.

Excluding Friends

Don't be afraid to tell friends that you are giving a party that doesn't include them. I was pleased to learn, for example, that I was not invited to a cocktail party given by a scientist friend for his colleagues. There would have been, necessarily, a lot of shop talk exclusive to the group and baffling to me. If shop talk is inevitable, the general rule is to invite only those who can participate and/or enjoy it.

Men and Women

Fortunately, we're beyond the days when only an equal number of men and women were invited to parties. It's too much trouble to try to strike an even balance, and you don't want people to have the feeling that they are assigned to someone. Today's career-oriented people are happier flying solo than they are being stuck with trying to amuse some unamusing fellow guest. Of course, you should always try to have a reasonable balance, but don't try to match up people.

Unfortunately, many divorced women and widows are still omitted from guest lists, even in what we like to think of as our enlightened times. It is not only kind but also fair to make an effort to include them. After all, they are no less interesting now than when they were married.

Negative Additions

What do you do about the unexpected guest or the last-minute addition?

If you can accommodate the extra person without undue disruption, do so gracefully and as cheerfully as possible.

However, there are situations in which you should refuse to accept the added guest. It may be that adding a seemingly discordant plate or flatware to your perfectly set table would just make you crazy. And you can't just fabricate a seventh Cornish hen when you have planned a party for six.

Mind Your P's and Q's

Guests especially appreciate being invited to parties at times when parties are scarce—Valentine's Day, Thanksgiving, Mother's Day. Never hesitate to entertain at unusual times—a breakfast party might be the best time to catch busy people.

The refusal should be accomplished with as much grace and good humor as possible to avoid bad feelings. One reputedly excellent hostess used to call on me regularly to attend her seated dinner parties. One day she called to invite me to dinner, and I told her that I had gotten married the month before. "That's terrible," she said. "What will I do? You can't bring your husband. It will ruin my seating arrangement."

Happily, I never heard from her again.

Invitations

If you want an immediate response and your party is of a fairly manageable size, invite guests by telephone. It's true that voice mail and answering machines may make the contact less direct than you would like, but people tend to respond more promptly to telephone messages than to written correspondence. Remember to smile when you make that call. It is true that a smile can be heard over the telephone. (If you are wondering what your voice sounds like, record it and listen.)

Remember that invitations of any kind should be welcoming and inviting. You don't necessarily have to use engraved stationery, but the invitation should convey a spirit of festivity. Even if you write a personal note, it should convey this spirit and make the person feel especially welcome.

Whether you are inviting people by telephone or by mail, be sure to communicate all of the vital elements of an invitation—who, what, when, where, why. Include a map or verbal directions to the location. It is also kind to clue people in about how to dress. If you are inviting someone you have just met or don't know well, give that person some idea about who else will be present. Some singles feel awkward going solo, so decide well in advance whether to invite them to bring a friend. If not, make sure they know there will be others in the same boat at the party. You don't have to be a matchmaker and shouldn't be tempted into those murky waters. Just prevent people from feeling like fifth wheels. Here are some examples:

♦ "I am calling to invite you to dinner next Friday, the tenth, and if you'd like to bring a friend, by all means do, although we'd be delighted to have just you."

♦ "We'd like to invite you and a friend for dinner on the tenth."

♦ "We'd like to invite you to dinner on the tenth."

As a guest, never assume an invitation means to bring a guest.

Always respond to an invitation immediately. It's fine to ask who else will be there, but not until after you've given your answer. Otherwise, your reply will seem conditional on the guest list.

Hired Hands

Try to hire one person to help if you're entertaining more than six people for dinner. Agencies can provide aspiring actors and students who are experienced at garnishing, serving, and cleanup. The help frees you to prepare the menu and be with your guests.

Above all, do not feel guilty or self-conscious about hiring help. Guests do not expect superhuman efforts on the part of their host. They expect their host to relax and enjoy the party along with them.

You may be able to hire a friend's college-age children. Some amateur cooks love to work parties and are flattered to be asked. Best of all is hiring your own children, as long as you pay them fairly. They know where things belong, and the experience helps them to become at ease at parties.

Faux Pas

When things go wrong with the hired help, never criticize them in public.

If none of these less-expensive alternatives are available, you will have to go the agency route. These workers are bonded and insured, which means that—in the unlikely event that something is stolen or broken negligently and you can prove it—the insurance company will pay to replace it.

Agencies work in two ways: The host pays the agency, which pays the workers; or the host pays the workers, who give a commission to the agency. In either case it is not necessary to tip bonded household workers, because their cost is so high to begin with. You also do not tip independent workers who are their own bosses.

Live and Learn

Here are some other recommendations to bear in mind when dealing with hired help:

- Be sure that payment terms are clear when you hire help. A disgruntled worker making a scene at the end of the evening can ruin the party.
- You are responsible for the cost of broken objects. Mistakes do happen. Do not attempt to take breakage costs out of anyone's wages.
- Be sure to reserve your outside help well in advance, especially in busy party seasons—fall, spring, the Christmas/New Year holiday period.
- A wise host reserves the help before inviting the guests.
- Make sure the help arrives well in advance of the party.

Tell the workers in advance what you expect them to wear. Generally, a woman should wear a black or white dress or black skirt with white shirt and apron. Black pants are also acceptable. Hair should be pulled away from the face. Men should wear black pants and white shirts with black ties. Teenagers can wear dark skirts or pants with light shirts. All males should wear ties.

Here are the chores you hire people to perform:

- Take coats
- Make drinks
- Serve appetizers and dinner
- Clear the table
- Clean up in the kitchen

The Caterer

A caterer can be a godsend for a large party. Costs vary widely, depending on how elaborate your menu needs are, the kind of help you need, and the time of your party. Night hours are more expensive, as are prime-time occasions, such as New Year's Eve.

Many caterers require a retainer of half the amount of the food costs. This payment is an assurance that you won't back out at the last minute.

Tip caterers' employees unless a service charge is added to the bill. Otherwise, give the headwaiter 20 percent of the total bill to divide among the workers.

If you're not familiar with the caterer's work, make sure you see his or her equipment and taste the food before you sign a contract. And make sure the contract specifies that payment of the bill will depend upon fulfilling the contract. If possible, ask if you can peek in on a party the caterer is doing. Many catered parties are so big that a brief visit can pass unnoticed.

Keep in mind that communication is vital when it comes to making catering arrangements. Whatever you leave unclear is bound to go wrong.

Buying and Serving Wine

If you're not a wine connoisseur, get advice on buying wine from either a knowledgeable liquor-store owner or a friendly restaurateur. Describe the menu and ask for moderately priced selections. One of my friends simply went to a liquor store and purchased a case of its most costly red Burgundy. The proprietor was thrilled, of course, but the value of the wine was lost on most guests. You don't need to be extravagant to be elegant. What you need is to be generous and make sure there is enough to go around.

Many parties these days do not have "hard bars," meaning they do not serve hard liquor. If you are serving only wine, plan on a bottle per person. If you are serving wine only during the meal, plan on half a bottle per person.

Serve red wine at room temperature. To allow the wine to breathe, open the bottle about 30 minutes before you serve it. Opening the wine permits the air to develop the bouquet and improve the taste of the wine.

Mind Your P's and Q's

Most hosts today use an all-purpose wineglass. If you don't, remember that the white wine goes in the small glass while the red wine goes in the large glass so that the wine will have more space to breathe and develop its bouquet. All wineglasses should hold at least 5 ounces.

Live and Learn

"For more than 100 years," says Gregory Castells, sommelier at La Bec Fin in Philadelphia, one of only a handful of five-star French restaurants in the United States, "inarguably the classic cork has been the best closure for wine." However, because of a problem in cork processing that has affected a small percentage of wines, "a new wave of wine stoppers has entered the industry. Some of these alternatives are screw top, plastic, agglomerate [composite material] and cork agglomerate with natural corks at each end.

"In higher-caliber restaurants you will rarely find wines that are closed with plastic or screw top stoppers. As of yet these types of stoppers are not socially acceptable. However, if a sommelier decides to feature wines with such screw top or plastic stoppers you can be sure that he or she believes the wine is of the highest quality.

"Personally, I like the idea of screw top closures, because this is a definitive way of keeping the freshness of the wine. Out of 700 wines featured on the list at Le Bec-Fin, only one has a screw top. This beautiful Pinot Gris from Australia has pleased some of our more traditional guests."

Chill white wines about two hours before serving them. If you must chill the wine more quickly, the best method is to immerse the bottles in a tub of water and ice cubes up to the neck. It doesn't help to put the wine in a freezer.

When the meal begins, the host should stand and walk around the table to fill each wineglass. If it's an informal party, the host can simply fill the glasses of the people closest to him and ask them to pass the other glasses down. The host's job is to make sure the glasses are replenished. Guests should not help themselves to wine or ask for more. It is fine for a host to offer the wine bottle to a guest with an empty glass and say, "Please help yourself."

Fill wineglasses about halfway so that the imbiber can appreciate the bouquet of the wine. Don't wrap your wine bottles in napkins when you serve.

Cocktail Parties

There's no better way to bring a large group of people together for informal camaraderie than the cocktail party. These American institutions have their supporters and detractors—sometimes for the exact same reason.

Surely they are a great, informal way to entertain a lot of people. By design, a cocktail party is a place to mingle—not engage in lengthy, penetrating conversation. Moreover, they provide great opportunities for people to meet one another and, having met, they always can proceed to dinner or a later engagement. However, they are far from inexpensive entertaining, since it's important to provide substantial food to accompany the alcohol served. It's also important to factor in the cost of stocking the bar and renting or purchasing the glasses, as well as the staff required to handle the kitchen chores, tend bar, and serve.

> **Live and Learn**
>
> Cocktail parties came into their own during Prohibition, when alcohol was illegal in the United States. Although the bars and saloons were shut down, "private" clubs and speakeasies sold bootleg whisky, and the underground subculture became the Roaring Twenties. The drinks party has been a social institution ever since.

Cocktail parties begin at 5:00, 5:30, or 6:00 P.M. because alcohol should not be served before 5:00 P.M. They should not last more than two hours. The most effective way to signal the end of the party is to shut down the bar no more than half an hour after the stated end. For example, if the invitation reads "from five to seven," make sure the bartenders know to close the bar by 7:30. Guests, too, should be aware of characteristics and protocol of this evolving party institution.

Levels of Cocktail Parties

When someone asks you to "come for drinks," usually by telephone or e-mail, the gathering usually is before some other event, such as a dinner out, the theater, or a sporting event. The host usually handles the serving because the group is small and informal. Most often only short prior notice is given. Expect very simple food—fresh vegetables and dips; various olives and cheeses; and nuts. Do not expect a meal. There will be wine, sometimes Champagne, and sometimes a full bar. Naturally, nonalcoholic drinks will be available as well.

When you are invited to "cocktails and hors d'oeuvres," it's a more formal occasion and the invitation generally comes by mail. The invitation will clearly spell out the time frame on the party—for example, 6:00 to 8:00 P.M. There will be an R.S.V.P. with the invitation. Most often there will be a professional staff, even when the host pitches in at peak times.

Hors d'oeuvres usually are passed, and other snacks are placed around the room. Again, this is not dinner. Expect wine and perhaps Champagne, as well as liquor and cocktails such as martinis.

However, when the invitation reads "cocktail buffet" or "cocktail supper," you won't need dinner afterward. The invitation generally will come by mail and will include a way to respond.

The drinks at a cocktail supper will be wine and liquor, although not necessarily mixed drinks. The food will be buffet-style and include some substantial items such as ham and turkey for mini-sandwiches; shrimp cocktail; various dips and spreads for vegetables and crackers; as well as nibbles such as olives and nuts.

How Important Is Quality of the Brand for Your Party?

It's important to provide quality brands of liquor and wine for your party, as a sign of respect for your guests if nothing else. There's no reason to be pretentious; extravagance can be in bad taste and a display of poor manners, since your guests might not be able to reciprocate in kind and thus be embarrassed.

How to Behave

Make sure you respond to a party invitation and then stick to your agreement. Nothing is worse than a no-show who has responded affirmatively; the opposite also is true. Never decline an invitation and then show up after all. Worse still is not bothering to respond to the invitation whatsoever. Here are some other general guidelines to help you attend a party with ease:

 ◆ Don't even think about bringing a guest unless you speak personally with your host and get permission.

 ◆ Don't even think about showing up early—not even a minute. And don't be a hanger-on at the party's end.

- Don't go to the party hungry—the alcohol will wreak havoc with an empty stomach and thus, your behavior. Have an apple or snack on the way to the party, and if you are fatigued at all, pass up the alcohol. Above all, know how much alcohol you can handle.

- Don't drink from a bottle. Even beer, unless the party is a very casual outdoor occasion, and even then, you look a lot more polished with a glass in hand.

- Don't wait for your host to introduce you to others—go for it! And be a party hero and introduce others you might know to each other.

- Don't hold your drink in your right hand; instead hold it in the left hand so your right is free to shake hands.

- Don't try to monopolize your host, the guest of honor, or just about anyone. Cocktail parties are for mingling; save intense conversations for another time and place.

- Don't hover near the food table; other guests will be hungry, too.

- Dispose of toothpicks, paper, and other rubbish in containers for that—never on the floor.

Inviting people into your home involves careful planning and considerable effort, but entertaining at home repays many times over. Having guests under your roof provides a special pleasure. And you flatter people by inviting them because you are bestowing a gift that only you have the power to give—the hospitality of your home.

The Least You Need to Know

- Beginner hosts should start with a small event and keep it simple.

- Invite a good mix of people, not just the same old crowd.

- You don't have to be a good cook—or cook at all—to give a party with food.

- Hire help if you need it, but make sure everyone understands the terms and conditions up front.

- Hosts should not spend all their time in the kitchen.

- Elaborate menus and extravagantly expensive wines often go unappreciated. Keep it simple.

- A cocktail party is an easy way to get a lot of people together, for a limited time, without extending yourself too much.

Chapter 9

The Dinner Party: Freedom of Choice

In This Chapter

- The simple menu
- The buffet
- The formal dinner
- Mixing drinks and people
- Seating

It's your party, you can fry if you want to. Or bake. Or stir-fry. Or none of the above. The important thing is that the party should reflect you.

My friends run the gamut from "hands on, everybody helps" party givers to those whose parties are almost too perfectly staged and neatly executed. If you are a casual sort of person, don't attempt to give a fancy, formal, seated dinner. It will seem inauthentic to everyone, including you. Everyone who gives a party frets over the menu, and too many hosts end up trying too hard. A cheerful, unstressed host does more for a party than a gourmet meal served with a side dish of anxiety.

The food at every type of gathering except the most formal dinner should be simple, identifiable, and attractive.

The Simple Menu

People are so busy and so health- and weight-conscious these days that most of your guests will be perfectly pleased if you count the hors d'oeuvres as the first course. You can serve hors d'oeuvres, attractively arranged on platters placed around the room for people to sample, during the cocktail hour. This setting lends itself to the great variety of prepared foods available today. Avoid user-unfriendly foods that are perilous to furniture and clothing. Everything should be simple enough to be picked up with fingers, speared with a toothpick, or spread with a knife.

Your main course can be as simple as a casserole with a salad or baked ham. It is a good idea to avoid roasts, which depend on a precise serving time and taste like shoe leather if left uneaten for too long. Don't think that you must purchase expensive food for your party. I once attended a dinner for out-of-towners given by a famous Philadelphia hostess. She served scrapple—a traditional Philadelphia breakfast dish, lentils, scrambled eggs, hash-brown potatoes, and chocolate ice cream with raspberry sherbet. She told her guests that she was treating them to "a flavor of Philadelphia." The guests loved it.

And, of course, the story of Eleanor Roosevelt serving hot dogs to the Queen of England is legendary.

You can also take advantage of the gourmet take-out shops, which will have your food ready for pickup or delivery just when you want it. If you're trying a shop for the first time, talk to the owner and taste the food in advance. These shops can be a godsend for "everybody works" households. Some such shops are happy to prepare their food in your own casseroles or serving pieces. That saves time and saves face, so it's worth inquiring about it.

Balance is important. If your main course is light, a heavier dessert works well, and vice versa. In any case, dessert is important. I have noticed that otherwise diet-conscious people quickly develop calorie amnesia when dessert arrives at someone else's table. However, when a guest doesn't eat what you are serving, don't think you have to whip up something special just for him or her.

If you like exotic foods and plan to serve them, ask your guests when you invite them if they like, say, moussaka. A guest who is too polite to refuse something he or she doesn't like after you cook it often will not hesitate to tell you candidly about his or her dislikes beforehand.

As a guest, you should let your host know if you have special dietary needs. If you are a vegetarian, have serious food allergies, keep kosher, or avoid certain foods for health reasons, make it known when you are invited. The host then can create a menu that will please everyone and still take your needs into consideration. Or the host may prepare an additional side dish for you, augment the side dishes, or just advise you to bring your own food.

Mind Your P's and Q's

Primer for the dinner party host:

- Make sure some tidbits are available as soon as guests arrive—nuts, veggies with salt and dips, mixed olives with lemon zest. They help get the mingling going.

- People naturally gravitate to cozy spaces, so don't fret if they seem to ignore the larger, open expanses. It's like returning to the womb. Arrange your entertaining space so it's broken up.

- Try to greet each guest at the door. If they arrive early, be prepared. Grit your teeth, smile, and tell them you're delighted to have them to yourself for a bit.

- Do your best to walk each guest to the door after the party. That's what being a good host is all about—making everyone feel special, even if you only have seconds to connect one-on-one.

- Feed your guests well—and yet provide balance, such as fresh berries as well as that decadent chocolate dessert.

- Make each guest feel special. Guests appreciate personal touches such as remembering their favorite foods, music, or including something from their native cuisine on your menu.

Cocktails Before Dinner

If you're invited to dinner, arrive within five minutes of the time on the invitation, no later.

The cocktail hour should be just that—one hour—preferably less, just long enough for the guests to arrive, have a drink, and become accustomed to the group. Letting the alcohol flow on endlessly is rude, unsafe, and unhealthy—and too much to drink ruins your taste for the meal.

If you're serving hard liquor, keep the choices simple. All you need are gin, vodka, bourbon, scotch, club soda or mineral water, soft drinks, fruit juice, and tonic. You can go the extra mile and provide garnishes, such as fruit, green olives, and pearl onions, but they are not necessary.

It's fine to set up a self-service bar. Remember that people are consuming less alcohol and caffeine these days, so stock some nonalcoholic drinks and caffeine-free colas.

Be a Mix Master

Arrange your furniture so small groups will gather to chat instead of forming one large ring around the center of the room. Never have all the appetizers and hors d'oeuvres on one table or tray in the center. This arrangement discourages conversation.

Lighting should be fairly bright at the beginning of the party. It looks festive, and guests like to see what's going on. Dim the lights as the evening progresses.

The host should be most visible and available at the start of a party when the guests are arriving. Put your guests at ease by taking their coats and offering them each a drink. Even if you have hired help, you should greet all your guests personally unless the party is so huge that doing so is physically impossible.

Take each guest around the room and introduce him or her to everyone. Don't ever leave a guest unless he or she is well into a conversation. Shoving a drink into a guest's hand does not assure that he or she will immediately begin to have a good time. Guests need attention.

Seating

You often need perseverance and a clear voice to get guests in to dinner, especially if you have a crowd. The host should announce with authority that dinner is ready and then take a couple of guests by the arm and lead them into the dining room. Don't worry about interrupting someone's conversation. After all, it is a dinner party. After you start the procession, drop back to the rear and round up the stragglers.

Leave drink glasses behind as you go into dinner. If the party is informal, though, and you are drinking wine, it is fine to carry your wineglass with you to the table, although you will probably find fresh glasses there.

At the Table

Never let seating happen by accident.

Every party of more than eight people should have place cards. (See "Place Cards" later in the chapter for details.)

For groups smaller than eight, the host should have a clear idea of seating and so instruct the guests.

Without assigned seats, guests often feel awkward making their way to the table, afraid to interrupt a conversation or afraid to branch out. Open seating can result in an uncomfortable scene with people trying to decide where to sit, people sitting and then moving, and impromptu field marshals trying to take over to organize the seating according to their own prejudices. Place cards, on the other hand, make people feel special, protected, looked after.

Guests should never, ever, rearrange place cards to suit themselves.

Live and Learn

Here are some additional seating tips:

- ◆ Try to pair up a talker and a listener and then sprinkle them around the table.
- ◆ Do your best to seat guests near at least one familiar person.
- ◆ Don't seat spouses or couples together.
- ◆ Consider those across the table as well as those on either side as conversation partners.
- ◆ If your group has 4, 8, or 12 persons, the host, who serves the meal, is seated at the head of the table, and the guest of honor of the same sex sits opposite. The guest of honor of the opposite sex sits to the right of the host. This plan prevents two persons of the same sex from sitting next to each other, although this practice has nowhere near the importance it once had if, in fact, it has any real importance at all.

The Meal—Beginnings and Endings

The host should be prepared to start the dinner table conversation if it doesn't start by itself. Purists say that the only music appropriate for dinner is the arpeggio of sparkling conversation. I'm not sure I agree. Soft, upbeat background music can be very pleasant and brighten the mood.

Don't hold up dinner for one or two late guests. Let them join the party whenever they arrive, at whatever point in the meal you happen to be. It is not your responsibility to turn into a short-order cook for someone who has missed a course or two.

Decide in advance what your response will be when a guest asks if he or she can help with serving or clearing the table. If you think another person in your kitchen will be in the way, or be more of an annoyance than a help, be prepared to say: "Thanks so much for the offer. I've got my own foolproof system, so why don't you just stay where you are and enjoy the conversation." (Guests: If you help to clear dishes, clear each dish separately, one in each hand. Never scrape or stack the dishes.)

Mind Your P's and Q's

It is a gracious custom to serve coffee away from the table after dessert. However, if conversation is spirited, it is usually best not to interrupt the flow by insisting on a change of venue.

The host signals the end of the meal by putting his or her napkin on the table, to the left of the plate. At this point the host leads the guests out of the dining room for more conversation. Otherwise, the guests might begin taking their leave. Although you want to keep the party going for a time after dinner, feel free to tell late-staying partiers that you are tired and must call it a night.

Guests who leave the party early should do so with as little fanfare as possible so that others don't start following suit, thereby bringing the festivities to a premature or awkward close. Do say good night to your host, however. You can avoid being persuaded to remain by simply saying thank you and good night. Send a thank-you note to your host the next day. At the very least, call.

The Buffet Dinner

Many hosts these days prefer the informality of buffet dining, and for good reasons. Compared to other types of entertaining, buffets …

- ◆ Are easier to prepare in advance.

- ◆ Require less help.

- ◆ Can accommodate more people, and stragglers seem less conspicuous.

- ◆ Usually consist of only one course and dessert.

Guests enjoy buffets because they can move around easily, meet new people, and are less likely to get stuck with a dud for the duration of the meal.

Buffet food must be easy to eat, especially if it is a standing-only party. Think about accommodating the clumsiest person you know, and you'll do fine. Make sure you cut the food into small pieces and butter the rolls in advance.

Do your best to make your buffet table a beautiful still life decorated with flowers. Place the table so that the guests have an easy time getting to it, serving themselves, and getting away from it. Sometimes two buffet tables are best for a large crowd. Another workable idea is one long table with identical dishes on either end, plates and cutlery in the center.

Don't display desserts at the same time as the main courses. If people put dessert on the plate with other food, things get mixed up and messy and the food ends up looking as though it has already been eaten. If possible, either clear the table and reset it with dessert, or serve dessert from a separate table.

For a seated buffet, serving dessert and coffee, rather than having it buffet style, is a nice touch.

Guests at a buffet must remember that they are in a private home and not at an all-you-can-eat salad bar.

The Formal Dinner

Most people set their tables rather informally these days for any number of valid reasons, the lack of time being the main one. Who has time to fuss over linens, crystal, and china, much less polish the silver?

However, if you're planning a formal dinner, do make a special effort. On these occasions attention to detail and doing things right are important.

Place Cards

When you are entertaining more than eight guests for dinner, use place cards even if you have a seating chart.

Place cards are either folded tents or single cards meant to lie flat on the table. The tent-style cards have the advantage of standing up on the table so that you can write the name on both sides. In this way, others at the table can see who's sitting where.

The most elegant and costly place cards are made of thick, white or off-white stock, with a narrow border of silver, gold, or another color. They measure about 2 by 3½ inches, and you can purchase them from a good stationer or jeweler.

Never hesitate to make your own place cards from materials readily available in your home. If they serve the purpose, use them.

Place cards can go in any of the following locations on your table:

- On top of a napkin, set in the middle of the plate
- On the table at the upper left of the place setting (above the forks)
- Leaning against the stem of a water or wine glass
- On the table, just above the middle of the plate in the place setting

Write the names in black ink. You may print them out for a business meal. The important thing is to make sure the names are readily legible and large enough to see from across the table. If possible, use calligraphy on them or have someone do it for you.

If all the guests know each other at an informal dinner, just write the first name of each person on his or her card. If two or more guests have the same first name, use first and last names on their cards. If not all of the guests know each other, use both names on all of the cards.

At a formal dinner party, such as a business dinner or official function, or any meal at which persons of rank will be present, use only surnames on the cards, for example, Mr. Fleischmann. If two Mr. Fleischmanns are at the table, use full names on their cards: Mr. Daniel Fleischmann.

Use the full titles of military officers and persons who hold or have held political or high appointed office, whether or not they still hold that office or title.

Place cards for the mayor and governor read *The Mayor* and *The Governor*. If they no longer hold those offices, the cards read *Mayor Rendell* and *Governor Ridge*.

Once an ambassador, always an ambassador. And a military officer is called by his or her retired rank forever.

Menu Cards

Menu cards can make a dinner more of an event. They also provide useful information to those concerned about diet. For example, knowing that the entrée is poached fish might give a dieter license to finish off the cream soup or look forward to enjoying the dessert with a clear conscience.

Mind Your P's and Q's

Don't forget to breathe before the party. Literally. Give yourself a few quiet minutes—five will do it. (See breathing meditation techniques in Chapter 1.) This will clear your mind and center yourself. Then you can put all your energy into your guests.

Menu cards may be printed out, done in calligraphy, or written in black ink. Lean them against a glass, rest them flat on the table to the left of the forks, or lay them centered over the plate above the dessert fork and spoon. Two guests may share one card, or each may have his or her own.

Write the date or the occasion at the top of the card. The courses follow in a vertical list. Wines may or may not be included.

Setting the Formal Table

Here's what you need:

◆ **Table decorations (centerpiece).** When it comes to table decorations, many interesting variations and options are possible. Some examples of these decorations include flowers, fruits and vegetables, collections of figurines, and candles.

◆ **Butter plate and knife.** These go to the upper left of your plate above the forks. The butter knife is placed horizontally across the top of the plate with the blade facing down. Some hosts place a few butter pats on the butter plate just before seating the guests, although it's also fine to pass a small plate containing butter pats with a butter knife for guests to help themselves.

Don't own butter plates? Don't worry. Pass around a small dish containing butter pats or balls. You can also use a dish into which you have spooned soft butter or margarine from a plastic tub, or a decorative container that disguises the plastic tub of butter or margarine by fitting around it perfectly. Pass around a butter knife or other small knife with the container so that guests can serve themselves. Guests should take from the container what they want, put it on the side of their plates, and pass the container to the next person.

Faux Pas

Don't use butter plates unless your menu includes something that includes bread and butter or some food that requires buttering, such as corn on the cob or baked potatoes.

◆ **Salad plates.** Salad plates range in diameter from about 7½ to 8½ inches. (Salad plates can also be used for dessert, to hold soup cups and saucers, or to serve small food items.) Many people don't have salad plates and simply put their salads onto dinner plates. Also, a separate salad fork is nice but not necessary. It is no great hardship to eat your salad with your dinner fork.

If, however, you are serving a separate salad and cheese course between the entrée and dessert, each guest will need a salad fork and a small knife as well. The sequence is this: The salad plates should be in front of all guests at the center of the place setting. Then pass the salad bowl, followed by a cheese tray with a cheese knife. Next pass the crackers. You can choose to follow the crackers with softened butter and a butter knife if guests have a coronary death wish.

◆ **Napkins.** These are best folded and placed in the center of the plate. However, they can also go to the left of the forks or can be folded imaginatively in the glassware. If you are an avid napkin folder, you can pick up some books on the subject and enjoy this opportunity to be creative.

◆ **Flatware.** Set the table so that people eat with utensils from the outside in. As a guest, when in doubt, this practice is always a pretty safe bet. Another idea is to single out the classiest-looking, most composed person at the table and do what that person does. If you are wrong, at least you will be in good company.

The dessert fork and spoon can go horizontally at the top of the plate, the bowl of the spoon facing left and the prongs of the fork facing right. You don't need both, but the fork often makes a useful "pusher" for the dessert. You can also serve dessert implements with the dessert.

♦ **Glassware.** "Drink right, eat left" means that glasses go on the right and bread and butter plates go on the left. In other words, if you hold the fork in your left hand, you'd drink with your right hand.

♦ **Salt and pepper shakers.** Place a pair of salt and pepper shakers at each end of the table. If you have a large supply of them, it's nice to provide a pair for each guest or a pair between two guests. Sometimes people use saltcellars, which are tiny receptacles for loose salt. These have a tiny spoon either in them or on the table next to them.

♦ **Candles.** Use candles only at an evening meal. Place them in the center of the table or elsewhere, as long as you make the arrangement visually appealing and keep candles out of your guests' sight lines.

Many people also place candy dishes on the table, and it is a nice, sweet touch. Place one at each end. You can use a small dish or bowl or even a stemmed glass. A good idea is to include small, excellent chocolates.

Live and Learn

You face a tough decision when it comes to whether to include an ashtray as part of your formal table setting. In the past it was routinely included; however, it is not necessary these days.

If you know your guests smoke and you decide to put ashtrays on the table, place a small ashtray and matches in front of each person who smokes. They should know enough to not even think about smoking until after everyone has finished dessert.

Serving the Meal

Form follows function when you are serving the meal. Before you entertain, review these principles yourself and most certainly with any people you have hired to help you:

♦ Serve guests from the left. The serving utensils should be positioned on the platter in a way that's convenient for the guest to reach them. Keep your arms close to the body to avoid banging people. The idea is to give the diner convenient access to the food.

- The woman on the host's right is served first. If the man on the hostess's right is the guest of honor, he is served first. After that, service goes around the table counterclockwise.

- If a couple are guests of honor, then the wife sitting next to the male host is served first. The service goes counterclockwise and ends with the host.

- Finished plates are removed from the right side. A good trick is to use your thumb or otherwise contrive to anchor utensils to the plate so they don't end up in people's laps. Never scrape or stack plates while removing them.

- Wine is served and removed from the right side.

After-Dinner Coffee

After-dinner coffee comes in demitasse cups and saucers with small coffee spoons. The cup, saucer, and spoon are to the right of the guest's place setting. Coffee is served from the right, as are other beverages. Then pass a tray with cream, sugar, and a sugar substitute.

Alternatively, the host can place a large tray containing the coffee service on the table and then pass filled cups to each person.

If you have serving help, you might want to serve coffee away from the dining table, or you can carry the entire coffee service into the living room to pour. In this case, each guest comes up to the host to receive his coffee.

Cordials are served with coffee. You can also ask guests whether they would care for water.

Preparing and serving a dinner for your guests can be as easy or as difficult as you desire. A good idea is to decide well in advance how much effort you are prepared to expend, make a plan, and stick to it. Whatever you decide, your guests will be appreciative.

Mind Your P's and Q's

Remember that coffee and teacups do not belong in a setting because they are correctly served after the meal.

The Least You Need to Know

♦ Build your menu around one dish. Give it variety and add a dash of flair. Make sure all the food is not of one color.

♦ Work out the seating in advance and never let guests decide for themselves where they will sit. Use place cards for parties of eight or more.

♦ Even a busy host should greet guests and spend a little time with them after they arrive.

♦ Curtail the cocktail hour and be persistent and insistent when it comes time for people to go to the dining room table. Start with brighter lights for cocktails and dim the lights later.

♦ The host makes sure that wineglasses are replenished. Guests neither refill their own glass nor ask for more.

♦ If serving a buffet meal, make sure the table is nicely decorated, easy to get to, and easy to get away from.

Part 3

Home and Community

Children learn the first and most important etiquette lessons at home. They must learn these lessons from scratch as they handle special questions about courtesy and behavior.

The classrooms in which these fundamental lessons are taught are themselves diverse and evolving. Today's "family" has many different looks. There is, of course, the traditional nuclear family—mom and dad and their children and pets. However, households have broadened and so have our concepts of "family" been redefined. Today we see households led by single or divorced parents; stepfamilies; gay partnerships; and couples that choose to adopt. The challenges these new configurations present sometimes require innovative solutions, explored here.

In a broader sense, the inhabitants of our neighborhoods and communities comprise our "extended" families. They can be dysfunctional and at cross purposes. But, much like our personal family units, we have to live with them. Communication, personal accommodation, and accountability can make this a pleasant and rewarding experience.

Chapter 10

Manners Begin at Home: The Fundamental First Steps

In This Chapter

- ◆ The basics
- ◆ Adults—ugh!
- ◆ Handling sticky situations
- ◆ Table manners
- ◆ How to answer the most frequently asked questions
- ◆ Children and correspondence

"Why do I have to learn this etiquette stuff?"

"Because I say so."

This time-honored bit of logical persuasion, like its colleague "siddown and shut up," may end an argument, but does not create a wonderful learning environment. "When I was your age …" is not much better. (These tactics also weaken your position when you tell youngsters that the best way to make their point is to not yell or interrupt or make faces, but to listen to what the other person has to say before stating their ideas or point of view.)

The unspoken but mutually agreed-upon code of conduct that is the glue of a civil society is so much a part of our daily adult experience that we may have forgotten that we had to learn it, that children have to learn it, and that we have to teach them.

No matter how cute their capers around the house might seem when they are very young, there will come a time—sooner than you may expect—when others will judge children harshly and, possibly, criticize them sternly for the sort of behavior parents may be inclined to overlook or dismiss as high spirits or "growing pains."

Thus, etiquette training begins at a very early age. We are teaching as we interact with children around the dinner table or in the playground. While we teach the rules, we also teach the reasons behind the rules, and what we're actually teaching is respect for others.

When you begin to teach children about the idea of manners and the rules of etiquette, you can expect to be challenged. The challenge will almost certainly take the form of questions, and you had better be armed with some answers.

The Most Basic Rules and Why

One of the most asked questions about etiquette is, "Why do we have these rules and what wise guy made them up?"

You can respond to this question by telling a story:

About 11,000 years ago, humans made a big change in the way they lived. They found they did not have to continually roam through the forest hunting animals and gathering nuts and berries to eat. Instead, humans learned about planting seeds and domesticating animals. They discovered that they could live in one place, and survival was not such a desperate daily struggle. They had more food, more leisure time, and a greater sense of security.

Soon after, humans began to develop ways of getting along with each other with as little fighting, anger, and confusion as possible. They even began to eat together at the communal table, and you can imagine what this would have been like without rules.

During the 11,000 years between then and now, the rules changed and evolved as ways of living and relating developed. But the reasons for these rules are as valid now as they were at the beginning.

Mind Your P's and Q's

Here are some easy ways to let people know that you have good manners:

- Say "please," "thank you," "you're welcome," and "excuse me."
- Look people in the eye when you speak to them.
- When you are introduced, stand up and say, "Nice to meet you" or "Hello" or "How do you do?"

Young people like things summarized. So you can tell them that two basic guidelines have held up through the centuries and form a dual bedrock of good manners:

◆ Be kind.

◆ Treat people with respect.

The second most asked question is, "What's in it for me?"

You can answer this question by telling your child: "Learning the rules of etiquette will give you self-confidence. If you know how to behave wherever you are, you will be more at ease, and you will be able to put those around you at ease. People will get the message that you are one together person."

You can go on to say that another reason to know the rules of etiquette is that people will treat you with respect if you treat them with respect.

Speaking of Respect

Remember that you're not dealing with a lower life form here. Children possess a basic, uncluttered wisdom. We cheat them by failing to share our losses and insecurities, our joys and triumphs. When you discover a commonality with your child, try saying something like "I know. I feel the same way when …." Children's questions may be blunt and basic, but often they want to know the same things as adults do. For example, a child may say, "Suppose I don't know anybody at the party. Who do I sit with? What do I talk about?" You know how that feels, don't you? But you might express it to another adult by saying, "Do you have any hints on how to work a room?"

Keep this point in mind the next time your child asks you a question.

Alien Nations—Relations with Adults

Kids and adults sometimes think of each other as alien species. This situation is tougher on kids than it is on adults because adults are bigger and know more. Both, however, tend to be a little uncomfortable when they meet for the first time. Adults may deal with this discomfort by saying dumb things like "Last time I saw you, you were wearing diapers." Children sometimes deal with it by sulking or being silent or trying to be invisible.

This awkwardness is generally called shyness, and almost all children are afflicted with it to some degree. You can help alleviate this painful stage by passing along some of the following tips. However, your child or any young person will be on the way to overcoming the curse of shyness if you can get these two basic ideas across:

- Everybody, regardless of age, is shy to some degree around new people or in unfamiliar surroundings.

- Stop worrying about yourself and focus on the other people.

I've included my own helpful tips and tricks for helping young people get along smoothly with adults in the following sections.

Meeting Someone New

When young people meet someone new, they should ...

- Stand up.

- Shake hands. In the Western world, shaking is an almost-universal gesture of goodwill.

- Smile.

- Look the other person in the eye and say hello. Use Mr., Miss, or Mrs. When in doubt, use Ms. (pronounced "mizz").

Breaking the Ice

Teach your child to use the following questions to easily open a conversation with someone:

- Do you live in the neighborhood?

- Do you have children?

- How did you meet my parents?

Conversational Tricks

Young people need to know some of the conversational tricks we all use without thinking. Let them know some of the basics:

- People like to talk about themselves.

- People don't mind questions, as long as the questions are not too personal (How much money do you make?) or downright rude (Why do you wear that ugly dress?).

- Many personal questions are okay to ask: Do you have any children? Do you live around here? Did I see you out running in the park the other day?

◆ Teach your youngster to become aware of the details that can spark a conversation. Remember that the idea behind all of this is not necessarily just to get your child to talk, but to also get the other person talking.

◆ If you notice skis or rollerblades lying around, for example, ask about these sports. If you just finished reading a book, ask the other person if he, too, has read it. Talk about the latest movie you've seen or one you'd both like to see.

◆ Listen carefully to the other person and don't interrupt the speaker unless something important has come up that he or she should know. Then say, "Excuse me."

◆ The truth is that when people say so-and-so is a good conversationalist, they really mean the person is a good listener.

Mind Your P's and Q's

If your child asks what is the worst "bad manners" thing a person can do, the answer is, to hurt someone's feelings.

Handling Sticky Situations

Remember how much you hated it when Aunt Myrtle kissed you? It doesn't hurt to let your child know that you hated it, too, but that you put up with it. Tell your youngster that the best strategy in handling this situation is simply to try to avoid it by sticking out his hand to shake. If that doesn't work, he can turn his head a little at the last moment so that the kiss becomes a brush on the cheek. This motion is also a way of communicating the fact that he doesn't like being kissed. But, no matter what, relatives are going to kiss kids, and it is uncool to refuse or to squirm around like an angry eel.

Also, it's okay for your child to tell you that Aunt Myrtle's gift is silly or ugly, but Aunt Myrtle must never know. Your response is that not everyone shares the same tastes and that the important thing is that Aunt Myrtle likes you and respects you enough to give you a gift. Explain to your child that he should, at the least, thank Aunt Myrtle and say, "It was really nice of you to think of me." If pressed, the child can say, "Of course, I like it. You gave it to me."

On the other hand, it's important to teach your children to speak up for themselves, in the right way. For example, youngsters are often discriminated against in stores. If they can see that they are being passed over in favor of adults, it is okay for them to politely say, "Excuse me, I think I'm next in line." If they are being ignored when no other customers are around, youngsters can say: "Could you please help me?" Teach your child to ask for assistance, rather than to try to get someone's attention by coughing, for example.

If your child asks you whether it is okay to ask an adult to stop smoking, say, "It depends." You can't ask someone to stop smoking in someone's home or in other private places where smoking is permitted. Tip: If ashtrays are available, smoking is expected and permitted. You can ask someone not to smoke in public places where smoking is prohibited, but you must do so correctly.

Here again, coughing is not an adequate way to let people know that smoke bothers you. Tell your child to say, "Would you please stop smoking?" but don't make a challenge or an accusation out of it. A good strategy is to tell the child to imagine that he or she is saying something like "It's raining outside" and say, "Would you please stop smoking?" with the same facial and vocal expression.

First Names and Introductions

Using first and last names properly is an area that most kids goof up. Tell young people that it is rude, even for adults, to call strangers by their first name. Upon meeting someone new, a youngster should call an adult Mr., Mrs., or Ms. until the adult asks to be called by his or her first name. Sometimes this happens right away, sometimes it takes a while, and sometimes it never happens.

It's very confusing when parents of your children's friends ask to be called by their first names. It might take a bit of coaching on the parent's part to give the child confidence to reply, "Thanks, Mrs. Donovan, but my parents' rule is to call adults by Mr. or Mrs."

Learning deference is a pivotal lesson for children, one that serves them well later on in life. We must remember that traditions still prevail in general, and especially in other cultures. Now that just about all of us live in multicultural surroundings, this lesson becomes more important than ever. Children addressing an adult of, say, Latino or Asian descent, by first name only makes the child appear disrespectful.

Faux Pas

Don't let your children be wallflowers! Tell them that the most important thing about introductions is to actually make them. Even if they make a few mistakes in the process, trying to meet new people is a whole lot better than just standing there.

When your child decides to introduce you to one of his friends or finally decides that it's okay for you to meet her teacher, explain the cardinal rule about introducing people: The star of the show gets top billing. In other words, mention the most important person first: "Mom, this is my friend, Marjorie Matthews."

Your child should learn to use honorifics when introducing adults to one another, including Dr., Captain, Mr., Mrs., and Ms. Here's an example: "Dr. Cooper, I'd like to introduce you to my father, Mr. Carter."

When introducing a teacher to a parent, the teacher's name is used first: "Mrs. Bornson, this is my mother, Mrs. Eastwood."

It helps to provide a little information about the people you're introducing so that they will have something to talk about: "Mom, this is my friend, Frank Hales. We're in the Glee Club together."

In introductions, dignitaries—congresspeople, clergy, elected or appointed officials, and so on—are mentioned first, to show respect for the offices these people hold. This practice does not mean that, as people, they are better or more important than anyone else.

Table Manners

When your child has that first job interview over lunch or has dinner for the first time with the parents of a romantic interest, both of you will be glad that good table manners were a matter of routine at your house.

But every meal doesn't have to be a lesson, and eating should not be a chore interrupted by frequent admonitions. Children learn best through immersion and osmosis. In other words, if you have good table manners, it goes a long way toward ensuring that your children will also.

The good news is that we are not talking about astrophysics here. Good dining etiquette requires only a simple awareness of the basics. Many of the most common manners that your child should learn—using the right cutlery, napkin etiquette, and other rules—are covered in Chapter 4.

Frequently Asked Questions

Whenever I talk with children about table manners, they are full of questions. Some are delightful, some are difficult, and all are unfailingly interesting. Here are some of the most common questions:

- ◆ What do I say if I burp?

  Say "Excuse me" to no one in particular and go on eating. Don't make a big deal out of it.

- ◆ Why do I have to act differently when people come to dinner?

  From the beginning of time, guests in one's home have been given a place of honor and other special treatment. We are on our best behavior so that guests feel comfortable, special, and welcome.

Live and Learn

When forks first appeared in Italy about 900 years ago, they were not widely accepted. People at that time still preferred to use their fingers and a knife. Forks became widely popular only about 200 years ago, but not all cultures embraced the newfangled invention.

◆ What do you do if somebody at the table is a sloppy eater?

The real question your child is asking is when to tell somebody that he or she is being rude. You can tactfully tell a good friend, out of the earshot of others, especially if you make light of it, but you can never tell a stranger. If you happen to be seated next to a slob, chalk it up to experience and set a good example yourself.

◆ Which place setting pieces are yours?

Your bread plate is always on your left, and your drink is always on your right. A good way to remember this rule is to remember that the word *drink* starts with the letters *DR* for "drinks right."

◆ What about finger foods?

When it comes to fingers, use your head.

Certainly, you eat things like ribs and tacos and corn on the cob—no matter what company you are in—with your fingers. For most foods, you will use cutlery. Some situations are not so clear-cut.

In the Middle East and parts of Africa, for example, people still eat properly with their hands. The food of those cultures is designed to be eaten that way. So the best rule is "When in Rome, do as the Romans do." Adjust to the standards and customs of the culture you are in. It might even be acceptable to eat with your feet, but only if you are dining with a family of baboons.

Mind Your P's and Q's

Here are a few helpful hints to pass on to your youngster:

◆ A conversation makes a meal more enjoyable. Join in.
◆ Don't begin to eat until everyone is seated and has been served.
◆ If you drop something during a meal at home, pick it up. At a friend's house, leave it until the meal is over and then pick it up. At a restaurant, ask the server to replace it if you wish.
◆ If you have to blow your nose, scratch, and so on, excuse yourself and leave the table.
◆ The trick to eating spaghetti is to swirl a little on your fork into a bite-size portion with no dangling ends to drip or flick sauce.

◆ Should I help to clean up?

Offer. Whether you are at a dinner party or a picnic, the offer is the important thing. Sometimes the host will not want you to help. If so, don't insist.

◆ What if I don't like what is being served?

If eating at someone else's house or with guests in your house, do not reject food outright.

Eat some of everything that is served. If you don't like a certain food, eat some and move the rest around on your plate as if you were eating it. This skill will serve you well through the years.

◆ What if you can't finish your food?

In restaurants, where you can't control the portions, there's no problem. Either leave the food or ask for a doggie bag. At someone's home, never take more than you know you can eat and always leave plenty for the others. If someone is serving you, you can always say, "Just a little, please."

◆ Should I bring a gift when I'm invited to dinner?

Yes, but something simple and small. Plants are nice because they remind people of the giver as they grow. Lovely paper napkins, small books, candy, and fine nuts are also good ideas. If you bring brownies or cookies, give them in a sealed tin and say something like "I thought you might like these for the weekend." Cut flowers are lovely, but they require the host to take time out to find a vase and arrange them. If a youngster is just "going over to Sally's house" and will eat while there as usual, a gift is not necessary.

Television and the Internet

Parents have the right and the responsibility to exercise some control over how much television children watch and what programs they see. Parental control of television is particularly important when children are young but this also applies to adolescents. Resist the temptation to use the television as a baby-sitter during the early years and prescreen as many programs as you can during the later years.

We have to accept the fact that our youngsters will be drawn to the computer screen and will want to explore the wonders of e-mail and the Internet. Unfortunately, with the advent of the Internet a culture has developed—especially among young people— that is disturbing. Advocates of this new cyberspace philosophy maintain, essentially, that the Internet, with its unlimited ability to acquire information and join the world in the discussion of ideas, is much more than a groundbreaking technological advance.

It is the driving force of a revolution of knowledge, much like the Renaissance, that holds all ideas are and should be free and in the public domain, to be shared and used, unfettered, by all.

Although the historical analogy may well be appropriate in its world-changing explosion of knowledge and ideas, it doesn't trump long-established rules of intellectual property or change the propriety and care we must take in our interactions with others—standards that existed long before the world became accessible from a little box in our homes.

It's important to impress on children that the Internet is a wonderful resource that comes with certain rules and responsibilities, not carte blanche to appropriate the ideas of others or use them in an inappropriate or cruel manner. The reason is simple, and at the heart of good manners: people can—directly or indirectly—be hurt.

With that in mind, make sure your children know the following:

♦ Good manners apply even in cyberspace.

♦ E-mail can be retrieved and traced to the sender. Pressing the Delete key doesn't make e-mail disappear forever, so be sure to review what you've written before you click the Send button.

♦ You cannot be sure that no record remains of what you download just because you move it from the hard drive to a disk. People have gone to jail on the basis of what experts have been able to retrieve from hard drives their owners thought were clear of incriminating material. So be aware that whatever you write or download in cyberspace can be read by others, and make sure that you would not be upset if it was.

♦ Some dangerous creeps live out there in cyberland. A correspondent who claims to be a 15-year-old cheerleader may be a 50-year-old pervert. People must be very wary of agreeing to meet a computer acquaintance in person, and never, ever meet such a person in a private place, such as a home or a secluded park.

♦ They will encounter some new and perhaps radical ideas on the Internet about things like drugs, sex, race, God, and Satan. Let them know that the best way to react to an idea they find intriguing or disturbing is to find out more about it and get different slants on it. Talking with parents, clergy, or someone they trust at school is always helpful.

♦ Make sure children understand never to respond to an e-mail that suggests a face-to-face meeting or asks for personal information such as telephone numbers, address, and credit card numbers. Explain the dangers of identity theft, how easily it can happen, and what the results are.

♦ When you see sites that encourage children to e-mail to it, a mental red flag should go up, and it's probably worth blocking the site.

◆ Teach children that anyone's request to engage in sex talk, or to post porno-graphic material online is dangerous. Do not be afraid to frighten your children with its dangers.

◆ Downloading copyrighted material from the Internet continues to be a hotly debated topic. Since the legal issues in many cases have yet to be resolved, apply some common sense, old-fashioned manners, ethics, and logic.

If you are incorporating information from the Internet into your work product or homework and claiming it as your own, it's stealing. Plagiarism is the "old fashioned" term. It's wrong. If the information is freely obtained, it's important to cite the source and quote accurately whenever you can.

If you are directly profiting—monetarily or in other ways—from information or material you obtain from the Internet— it's wrong. How would you feel if people took your stuff and claimed it as their own or used it without your permission in a way you wouldn't approve to enhance themselves?

Sometimes it helps to apply a "bricks and mortar" analogy. For example, if you needed a certain book, you'd either have to go to the library and borrow it or buy it from a bookstore. In some cases, you might have to contact the source— or even pay a fee or agree to certain conditions—to obtain permission to use it. As much as possible, follow the same rules and considerations you would if you had no access to cyberspace. Just because the Internet makes it easy to obtain information or take shortcuts to obtaining information does not make it okay to drop all your ethical standards.

Mind Your P's and Q's

The debate rages over music-swapping websites and the technology that facilitates and encourages it. Many of the legal and ethical issues are unresolved. How to han-dle those issues in the meantime?

Recognize that this material may well be the livelihood of someone else who is work-ing to bring his or her music to the world. Then apply a "bricks and mortar" analogy. In other words, what would you do if the Internet did not exist, or if the technology to swap and download music files did not exist?

What if the only way you could enjoy an album or a piece of music on a regular basis were to go to the store and buy it, or climb the stairs to your brother's room, or head to a nearby friend's house to listen to it? Then follow the equivalent ways of going about that online.

Buying pirated copies or swapping them with anonymous strangers around the world at the expense or without the permission of the artist would not be appropriate in the offline world. It's equally bad manners in cyberspace.

Play Dates

Because of problems created by work schedules and distance, the term *play dates* has entered our language. It simply means arranging for kids to play at one another's homes. Parents make sure that the time, place, and duration of the visits are understood all around. Arrangements for pick-up and drop-off and meals are made. Usually, parents who send their children to play dates host the next one or schedule one as soon as possible.

Children and Correspondence

Children who write notes and letters give a great deal of pleasure and have a better chance of experiencing the pleasure of receiving correspondence in return. More important, they grow up imbued with the knowledge of the power and pleasures of personal correspondence.

It is never too early to begin giving your children a respect for the written word and the ceremonies surrounding it. Even before children are old enough to write, you can make them aware that writing letters is an important activity by saying things such as "I'm writing to Aunt Nora to thank her for ...."

Thank-You Letters

The thank-you letter is probably the first kind of correspondence your child will send. Make the experience as comfortable as possible. A thank-you note from a seven-year-old does not have to be spelled and punctuated perfectly. It is all right for a note from a child to look like a note from a child. Praise any effort a child makes to correspond.

But the basic rules apply even to the very young. The note needs a salutation. Mention the specific gift or favor. Sign with *Love* or other appropriate sentiment. Later, thank-you notes can include an acknowledgment of the effort behind the gift: "You must have spent the whole day baking these cookies." You can also let the giver know how the gift will be used: "These cookies will be a big hit at my sleep-over party tomorrow."

And yes, a child must send thank-you notes for Christmas gifts unless the giver is present—and is properly thanked—when the gift is opened.

Don't allow your children to use preprinted thank-you notes. They defeat the purpose of giving personal thanks for a personal gift.

Apology Letters

Let's pretend that your child knocked a baseball through a neighbor's window. Even if the child apologized on the scene, a note of apology is called for. It should …

◆ Be prompt.

◆ Acknowledge fault and apologize.

◆ Offer to make amends.

It should also be written in ink and signed *Sincerely*. The envelope should have the sender's name and address in the upper-left corner, and the addressee's name should be preceded by an honorific such as Mr., Mrs., Ms., or Dr. (These, by the way, are the only honorifics that are abbreviated.) The letter will look something like this:

Dear Mr. Smith:

Please accept my apology for breaking your window the other day. It was careless of me, and I feel bad about it. I know all the trouble it has caused you. If you would like, I will repair the window myself. If you have made other arrangements, please send me the bill so that I can pay for the damage.

Sincerely,
Tommy Jones

Condolence Letters

A parent of your child's close friend has died. Even if your child has attended the funeral, sent flowers, visited, or telephoned, a condolence letter is a must. A commercial sympathy card will not do. Remember that condolence letters are comforting and diverting for those who have suffered a loss. Sometimes they become part of the family history to be passed down through the generations.

The letter should be written in ink with a fountain pen if possible. Try to use black ink. If the child's handwriting is hard to read, it is all right to have the letter typed and signed in ink.

The condolence letter should not be a formal, formula letter; it should be written from the heart. Your child can begin by acknowledging the friend's loss and saying that he or she feels sad about it. The condolence letter is the place to recall the special characteristics of the deceased, visits to your home, lessons learned from that person, good times shared. Such reminiscences celebrate the life of the deceased rather than being morbid and depressing about the loss.

Above all, don't spend all your time saying how upset *you* are. The person who receives it might think you are the one who should be getting the condolence letter.

RSVPs

Translation: Respond if you please. And, please, respond promptly.

A telephone number on the invitation absolves you from writing. So does "Regrets Only." However, if you were planning a party, wouldn't you like to get a note saying your guest is pleased to be invited and looks forward to coming?

If you can't attend, let the host know the reason you can't be there. If you accept, do your best to honor your commitment.

Schools no longer teach etiquette, and charm school is something rarely heard of these days. So, basically, it's up to parents to first convince their children that courtesy is crucial and, second, to teach them the rules of courtesy—also called etiquette. If parents don't do it, children must learn by offending people and suffering the consequences. We learn by watching the behavior of others.

The Least You Need to Know

- If you want children to be respectful, you must treat them respectfully.
- The two basic rules of proper behavior are to treat people with respect and to be kind.
- When meeting someone new, stand up, smile, shake hands, and say, "Hello" or "How do you do?"
- When introducing people, speak the name of the oldest or most important person first.
- Make sure children understand that even though the Internet makes obtaining information easy, that doesn't mean it's okay to use material without giving credit to the source.
- Encourage your children to write and send personal notes and letters, including thank-you notes and condolence letters.

11

Peer Pressure and Promise

In This Chapter

- ◆ School daze: cheating, bullies, teachers
- ◆ Spats
- ◆ (Oh no!) Parties
- ◆ Dating and the new rules

By all standards, children ask more questions about getting along with other children than about any other aspect of human interaction. No matter how straightforward or even trivial the questions may seem to you, remember that, to the youngster, these matters are worrisome, complicated, and urgently important.

Children absolutely need to know certain things when dealing with their peers, and learning these things from adults is a lot less painful than learning through experience. They need to know about the rules—etiquette if you will—that will help them behave appropriately in difficult situations, such as at parties (What do you wear? What do you say? What do you do?) and on dates (Who asks? Who pays? What do you wear? What do you say? What do you do?).

Youngsters also have to know that all friends have disagreements, even fights, and that doesn't mean they have to stop being friends. They have to know how to respond to bullies and to kids who cheat in school.

It's a complicated world. Children need all the information they can get. This chapter helps you give your child the answers they need.

The ABCs of School Etiquette

School comes along at the worst possible time. On top of experiencing the normal childhood fears, awkwardness, and other growing pains, children are for the first time meeting authority figures who are not their parents and peers who are not their siblings.

It's a time when a child should be armed with a code of behavior and a positive attitude about manners and respect for others. In brief, a child should know about etiquette.

Unfortunately, etiquette is not one of the subjects that administrators include in the curriculum of most schools.

Consider how life would improve for most students if elementary school provided that missing code of conduct in an orderly and systematic fashion, by an adult other than a parent, and with the use of a textbook to give the code weight and authority. The truth is, we have to make up as best we can for this lack.

Mind Your P's and Q's

If somebody drops her books and papers in the corridor, it is not geeky to stop and help, especially when everybody is hustling to get to the next class. Also, if you are going through a door and the person behind you is burdened down with books and things, hold the door to let him get through.

Bullies

Bigger, meaner kids who pick on littler, nicer kids are all too common today, as they have been in the past. Make it clear to your kids that they never have to put up with physical abuse. If they're slapped, pinched, or pushed around in any way, they must tell either you or their teachers, and then it's up to the adults to take care of the situation. (You might want to consider one of those martial-arts training programs that are so popular with children in first grade or older. The good ones emphasize self-defense as opposed to aggressive behavior, and they tend to develop self-confidence.)

Let your child know why bullies act the way they do. The main points you want to make are …

- Bullies use threats and force to try to control people by making them afraid. It is the only way they have of gaining acceptance or status.

- Bullies have no real friends.

♦ No matter what they say or do, their behavior is a reflection of their problems, not yours.

♦ Don't try to please or placate the bully or his clique. This is not the kind of group you want to be accepted by. Find others at school who feel the same way; they are the people you want for friends.

While we're on the subject of bullies, also let your children know that they do not have to share their lunch if they don't want to. Your child should simply say no, and if someone tries to get it from him or her by threats or force, the child should tell both you and his or her teacher. Some school districts around the country have established "bully hotlines" and other programs to report problems and address this issue. Inquire about it from your school district or PTA.

Last, it is not abusive, but instead considered part of the school tradition, for older students to treat younger students as second-class citizens. For example, sixth- and seventh-graders may confine fifth-graders to a certain part of the cafeteria or playground. Your child should accept this practice as cheerfully as possible and wait until she becomes a sixth-grader. It's not just older students entirely, but tradition.

Cheating

Your child tells you that somebody in class is copying answers from his test papers, and he doesn't like it. Should he tell the teacher?

The answer is, probably not.

Cheating is wrong, and he should not be a part of it. But shielding his paper should do the trick and may even send a message to the teacher without him saying a word. If that doesn't work, he should get the miscreant alone and say something like "Look, quit trying to look at my test answers. You know what you're doing is wrong. Others have noticed it, too."

In the unlikely event that these tactics fail, the teacher should be notified.

Internet plagiarism is another matter. A very serious one. When you read your child's homework and it sounds unusually authoritative, make sure you ask where he obtained such information. Praise him for his researching skills, and then point out how important it is to cite the source of the information. Explain that doing so is a demonstration of strength and character, not weakness. Remind your child that we're not supposed to know everything, and that when we can demonstrate industriousness in our search for the answers, though, it speaks well of us.

New School

If your child is about to enter a new school, you can be sure that she will experience a certain amount of anxiety about how to behave in the new surroundings. Here are some helpful tips you can pass along:

♦ Pay attention to your classmates instead of feeling uneasy because you don't know them. This way, you will discover who shares your interests about school subjects, sports, and so on.

♦ Don't be afraid to strike up a conversation: "Hi. I'm Julie Thomas, and I just started at this school. I noticed that you really seem to like math class. So do I. What other things do you like to do?"

♦ Get involved. Extracurricular activities, like sports and clubs, are an excellent way to get involved with the new school. Don't be afraid to volunteer. Many, many stars got to the top by starting as volunteers.

Relations with Teachers

If a teacher pronounces your child's name wrong, tell the child not to make a face. A youngster should never correct the teacher in front of the class. She or he should ask to see the teacher before or after class and explain how "my family" pronounces the name.

If your child gets blamed for something unfairly, it doesn't help to argue the issue in front of the class. It embarrasses everybody and only makes matters worse. Instead, discuss the situation with the teacher in private. Your intervention could and should result in a public apology in class.

Faux Pas

If your child comes to you with a complaint about his or her teacher, don't take the matter directly to the principal. Speak first with the teacher before deciding whether to take the matter further.

A birthday, Christmas, or end-of-year gift to your child's teacher must not be extravagant and should be something that everyone in the class can contribute to. No one in the class should be embarrassed about not being able to afford to contribute. Super gifts are plants or CDs or nice chocolates. An even better idea is for the class to make something for the teacher, perhaps a poster with a signed class picture. Wrap it—and don't forget to get a card that everyone can sign.

The (Oh, No!) Party

Do you remember when you were invited to your first party? If you do, you probably remember the turmoil that went with the invite: What should I wear? Suppose I don't know anybody? What will I talk about?

In regard to attire, your child can call the host and ask what he or she will be wearing. Or your child can call the parents of the host and check it out. But the attire problem is not the entire problem.

Whether your youngster wants to admit it or not, this is all about our old friend—shyness. When you talk to your child about it, you might want to call it nervousness. In addressing this subject, I often give a little talk about the Olympics. It goes like this:

> If you have ever watched the Olympics, you have seen athletes push themselves beyond what they thought were their physical limits. If you ask the athletes how they do so and how they overcome the nervousness they must feel before the competition, they will say, "Preparation." They get ready physically and mentally. They go over what they must do again and again, anticipating difficult patches and challenges, and deciding how they will deal with them. By the time the event begins, they are ready, excited, and confident.

Tell your child to deal with nervousness about the party in the same way. Also, ask your child what he expects to happen. Will there be dancing? Games? How large a crowd will there be? Tell your child to write down the answers.

Now, tell her to make a second list, a private one, of all of her best qualities. Maybe she really likes her hair or eyes. Maybe she has a great sense of humor that nobody knows about. Maybe she knows a lot about soccer or a certain kind of music. Recognizing these qualities will help her feel more confident and self-assured.

Mind Your P's and Q's

Let your child know that meeting new people isn't as hard as it looks. Most people that you meet are predisposed to like you. People generally hope that a new acquaintance will be somebody they like.

Next, tell your youngster to make a list of things he can talk about at the party. Magazines, newspapers, the radio, or television are all good sources for ideas. Now tell your child to imagine himself at the party, laughing and talking with others. Imagine walking over to somebody who looks nervous and shy and starting a conversation with that person. One thing your child might say is, "I noticed that you don't seem to know a lot of people here either. My name is …."

When you and your child are hosting the party, another set of sometimes uncomfortable considerations come up. It's not necessary to invite the entire grade, or even the entire class, to your child's party—only those with whom he or she has a relationship. At the same time, keep in mind that classes are like close-knit communities. Deliver your invitations outside of school, either by mail or phone. This can help prevent hurting the feelings of those not invited, and avoid making your own child guilty or self-conscious by not inviting everyone.

Say What?

If your child asks how to respond to a compliment, say the best and simplest response is "thank you."

Dances

It is perfectly all right for girls to ask boys to dance. If the world waited for boys to do everything, only half the job would get done. There was a time when custom dictated that boys do the asking, but those days are past, to the benefit of both boys and girls. (Girls also ask boys for dates these days.)

Spats

All children fight with their friends now and then.

Let your children know that everyone, even you, gets into arguments, and that most people feel rotten about it afterward. These fights are not the end of the world; they are not necessarily even the end of a friendship.

And part of feeling rotten after a fight is knowing that you said or did something during the fight that you regret. Let your young warrior know that there is absolutely nothing wrong with saying to the adversary: "Look, I'm sorry I hurt your feelings and made you angry." Often this step results in a similar apology from the other person, and fences get mended. The point is that disagreements should not mean disrespect. But often it does. The idea is to apologize for the effect his or her behavior had on the other person.

But when making apologies, the combatants have to be careful not to rehash the fight as if it were a movie they saw together. That's how fences get unmended very quickly.

Fights cause problems for noncombatants, as well. Suppose your youngster tells you that two "best friends" have had a fight, and each of them is telling your child about it.

Tell your child that the trick here is to listen without taking sides. The situation also presents an opportunity to act as peacemaker by telling each person separately that the other one is "really bummed out about the fight you two had."

Mind Your P's and Q's

Young people have a lot of doubts about how to behave during their first experience as a houseguest. Here are some tips:

◆ Be yourself. You were invited because the host enjoys your company.

◆ Bring a gift. Nothing big: Chocolates or a plant are fine.

◆ Leave the room you are staying in and the bathroom you use neater than you found them.

◆ Join in family activities even if you hate volleyball and find Monopoly tedious.

Clueless

Sometimes a youngster (or an adult for that matter) will be in a group that is discussing something he or she knows nothing about. Kids sometimes respond by sighing theatrically, rolling their eyes, or yawning. Let them know that this behavior is not only rude but also uncool. The thing to do is to be quiet and listen. See whether you can get a handle on what's happening. Ask questions. People love to demonstrate superior knowledge and will be glad to answer. If somebody asks your opinion, just say you don't know enough about the subject to have an opinion.

By the same token, if you happen to know a lot about something and you're talking with someone who is clueless, don't roll your eyes, sigh, and demonstrate your own impatience. It might be better to say, "When I got interested in this, I read/saw/listened to … You might like it, too." And leave it at that. Don't bore the other person with a topic that clearly does not interest anyone but you. Change the subject.

The Talk: Drugs and Other Substance Abuse

You should be talking to your children about drugs long before you have a heart-to-heart discussion of sex. It's never too early to say drugs are bad, that drugs hurt your body, and that we should feel sorry for people who use drugs.

Young people can easily get the idea that drugs, tobacco, and alcohol are part of a dark and dangerous, fascinating, and adult world. The truth of the matter—and the truth it's up to you to bring home—is that the drug scene is shabby and sordid and apt to be infested with twisted, dangerous people.

Your children should know that, sooner or later, someone will approach them with illegal drugs, maybe even offering to let them puff on a marijuana joint. He or she will tell your children that "it's no big deal" and "mild." It's up to you to let them know that no drug is mild. All drugs will alter the people who take them and diminish those people in some way. Tell your children that people who offer them drugs are merchants of death.

Throughout childhood, from kindergarten on, you can do a lot by warning children of the dangers that lie ahead. It's like the wicked witch and the poisoned apple. These warnings, however, should be accompanied by the reassurance that people can always just say no and walk away.

Say What?

What should your child say when offered alcohol or drugs? It's simple, but nuanced. Just say, "No, I'm not into that stuff." The key is how it is said, in as firm but matter-of-fact a tone as possible. Using "I" conveys that the decision is your child's alone, not one made in fear of or deference to you. At the same time, it doesn't judge or put your child in conflict with those making the offer. However, you should instruct your child to avoid those who are using drugs or alcohol.

Teenagers are most vulnerable to drugs. Their peers who do drugs often appear to be the cool ones, the brave, rebellious ones. You should always know what your teenagers are doing in their spare time. Keep them from visiting homes where you know there is drinking or drug use.

When you warn youngsters about alcohol abuse, hit them with the hard truths. People who abuse alcohol suffer brain, liver, and heart damage. They become bloated, red-faced, nutritionally starved. They end up weak, stupid, and sick.

When it comes to social drinking, warn them that even a small amount of alcohol has its effects. If your youngsters find themselves in a situation where they feel strong social pressure to drink, as at a college party, they can sip slowly, eat plenty, and drink water to minimize the effect of the alcohol.

Perhaps the strongest argument you can make about drugs, alcohol, and tobacco is the one you make by staying away from all three yourself.

Behavior Between the Sexes

Proper conduct between the sexes can be puzzling and troublesome even for those of us who have had years of practice. Imagine how difficult it must be for children and teenagers. No area of etiquette is changing faster. What was once considered polite might now be considered insulting. What was once common sense might now be irrelevant.

The old rules of chivalry dictated how men and women treated each other for centuries. They called for deference by virtue of gender, age, and social caste. These rules have been supplanted to a great degree by what may be called "corporate etiquette." In the past 30 or 40 years, women and minorities have exerted enormous influence on corporate culture, which is based on deference according to corporate rank, much like any military system.

As parents of both sexes and from all social groups entered the corporate culture, they absorbed this militarylike system of etiquette. Naturally, their children learned far more of these corporate attitudes and manners than of those based on chivalry. Thus the rules of chivalry have faded, and corporate etiquette has emerged as the dominant force governing modern interpersonal relationships in most parts of America.

The impact of all of this on relations between the sexes has been dramatic and confusing, particularly for young people. Remnants of the old rules of chivalry remain to haunt and sometimes confuse budding relationships. Young people often look to parents for some road maps through this unpredictable landscape.

When young people ask about rules in the area of relations between the sexes, they are really asking for clues to an eternal mystery. It seems to them that two distinct species are inhabiting the earth. The opposite sex acts, speaks, and dresses differently, is interested in different things, and relates to his or her same-sex friends differently.

However, some very clear rules can help young people deal with the usual and, for them, terribly, terribly important questions and situations that arise between the sexes.

Dates

Whether the guy or girl is asking someone for a date, the basics are the same. The invitation should not be entirely unexpected. There should be some positive, friendly feelings for each other. Get to know the person on a casual level before proposing a date. If the person declines, listen for verbal clues that will tell you whether you should ask for another date at another time. If you are the one saying no and you really would go if you could, say you are sorry about the conflict and hope the person will ask you again.

If you have to decline because you're not allowed to date, tell the truth and don't be embarrassed. We all have to live by rules we don't like at one time or another. Say "Thank you for asking, but my parents don't allow me to date yet." Don't make a big deal out of it. Don't act as if your parents are from the wax museum. You might even suggest other ways you can get together—school activities, sports, cultural events, and parties.

If you feel that you'd never want to date a person who asks you out, say something like "Thanks very much, I have other plans. It was really nice of you to think of me." You don't have to talk about these other plans. They could involve taking a nap or washing your hair.

When asking someone on a date, ask face-to-face or by telephone, not by e-mail or voice mail. Give plenty of advance notice, at least four days. If the invitation comes late, it could give the impression the person is being asked because somebody else couldn't make it. Also make sure that you're specific when posing the question to avoid any confusion or misinterpretation.

For example, "Would you like to go to the new Jackie Chan movie with me on Friday night?" is much clearer than "Wanna go to the movies sometime?" Make it plain that you're asking for a date for a certain place, time, and event. But don't buy the tickets in advance. That involves too much pressure. You might also clarify whether you would like to provide transportation or just meet the person there. "Would you like to go to the new *Star Trek* movie with me on Saturday afternoon? I can meet you outside the theater at 4 P.M."

 Say What?

When a youngster asks what to say if the date asks whether he or she had a good time, the best advice is to say yes, unless he or she had a perfectly awful time. If so, he or she should say so, and explain why it was so awful. That might sound like, "Well, I really didn't expect so much blood and guts in the movie and the wisecracks your friends were making made me really uncomfortable."

Decide what kind of date it will be. Remember that the idea is for both of you to have a good time. A staunch football fan might not enjoy an evening at the ballet. First dates should be easy and casual for both people. Don't make it into a big deal that causes nervousness. Keep the cost down so that reciprocating won't be difficult.

Remember that it's up to you to take care of the details. Get to the theater early and buy the tickets. Usually the person who does the asking does the paying. Don't expect your date to split expenses unless you have worked that out in advance. If you are going to share expenses, which is okay and often done, be clear about it: "I was hoping we could catch the discount early show and then go to the Pizza Kitchen. It shouldn't cost more than $10 each."

No matter what arrangements you make, never go on a date without money. It's wise to make sure you have enough to get home on your own, at the very least.

Finally, if your date is going to pick you up at home, brief your parents in advance. Greet your date at the door. Lead him to your parents and say, "Mom, Dad, this is David Smith. We got to know each other because we're in the same history class." Allow a few minutes for conversation before you leave, which will put your parents at ease and make you look self-confident. These few minutes could pay off later. Your parents will feel better about the company you're keeping and be more inclined to condone the relationship.

After the first date, the one who was invited should call or send a note saying that he or she had a good time. An e-mail is not good enough.

The Other Talk: Sex

Even before young people begin talking about dating or who is "seeing" whom, it's time to bring up the subject of sex. Don't wait for an opening or the right time. Just do it. The way you address the topic with boys and with girls will differ, but the basic message is the same. Sex is a very serious matter and can have profound, life-altering consequences. And, in the case of disease, those consequences can even be deadly.

Boys and girls should know that many thoughtful and sophisticated people believe in sexual abstinence prior to marriage. They can present some powerful moral and religious and practical arguments in favor of the idea. The same arguments hold water in the case of avoiding casual sex and waiting until a serious, committed relationship exists before having sex.

Girls need to be armed with reasons for saying no and a way to say it without using crushing, sarcastic, or insulting language. Men who have been turned down in a nice way sometimes become great friends or even husbands later on. Girls can say, "I'm not ready for that kind of relationship. I'd like to continue seeing you, but I'm not ready to have sex with you." If the other person persists, a girl can simply say that she has made up her mind to wait until marriage.

Your daughter should know that, no matter what they say, young men respect a woman with moral conviction, self-discipline, self-respect, and virtue. If the man is attracted to the woman and respects her, he will not be driven away by a polite or even flattering rejection.

Tell her that her youth is essentially over and her life is changed forever when a girl gets pregnant.

Tell your son that a "man who's a man" has self-control and moral integrity, that he respects women, and treats them as equal human beings and as emotional and intellectual partners.

Inform him that the responsibility and consequences of pregnancy are equally his and equally life-changing.

A father who wants his son to have a healthy attitude toward women does not use words like *broads*, does not snigger about sexual stereotypes of women, and does not make crude sexual jokes. He understands how compelling sexual appetites can be, but knows that self-control, common sense, and respect for others are of utmost importance.

Tell your son or daughter about what AIDS and other sexually transmitted diseases do to the body. Tell them that condoms are not a magical solution. Mistakes happen and have profound consequences.

The Big Question

The questions about dating, parties, and meeting people may eventually give way to the more serious questions: Is this the real thing? Am I in love?

Of course, you can't give this question a yes or no answer. What you can do when this question arises is talk about the elements that make relationships between people of any age work.

- ◆ **Honesty.** Can you be truthful with this person? Can you be yourself? Do you really like heavy-metal music, or are you just listening to it because your partner does? Are you going places and doing things and saying things just to please the other person, or because you want to?

- ◆ **Support.** Do you support and praise each other? Offering your support, though, doesn't mean you have to agree all the time. Players on the same sports team don't always agree on the next move, but after the decision is made, they honor and back it 100 percent.

- ◆ **Friendship.** Are you the other person's best friend? Do you show that you are listening and trying to understand his or her feelings? Never dismiss the feelings of a friend as silly or unimportant.

- ◆ **Faithfulness.** Do you stick by each other when disappointments arise? Do you try to see disappointments through the other person's eyes?

◆ **Respect for others.** Do both of you respect important people in each other's life? Maybe you would rather be bitten by a snake than visit your friend's parents, but you go anyway, you are polite, and you don't complain about the visit later, no matter how awful it was.

◆ **Fun.** Do you have fun together? Laugh a lot? Shared laughter is a sign of an easy relationship.

◆ **Giving space.** Can you accept the fact that the other person has his or her own life? Everybody needs time alone. Possessiveness is unnecessary in a healthy relationship.

It's tough enough, what with all the changes going on in their bodies and their heads, with new situations, new people, complex problems, and murky waters. Why make it tougher by telling young people that there are no rules or that rules are meant to be broken? It is a comfort and a steadying beacon for young people to know the rules and guidelines for interpersonal behavior—even if they are ignored.

The Least You Need to Know

◆ Many of the old gender-based rules concerning dating, paying, and so on no longer apply.

◆ Everybody suffers from some degree of shyness, and everybody can get past it to an acceptable extent.

◆ At school, your children don't have to put up with cheats or bullies. The best way to deal with bullies is simply to not play their game.

◆ Don't make the mistake of thinking that your child is too young to talk to about drugs. Even eight or nine years old is not too young.

◆ Keep watch on what your children see on TV or the Internet and intervene when necessary.

◆ Explain that relationships that are not based on mutual respect will never work.

Chapter 12

Family Etiquette

In This Chapter

- ◆ Teaching kids to be good partners
- ◆ In-law etiquette
- ◆ Gay and lesbian and adoptive families
- ◆ House rules for extended families

Ideally, our family life gives us roots and wings. It's where we first learn how to solve problems, how to get along with each other, and compassion.

Each household has its unique opportunities for learning to get along with each other. Some households contain the traditional "Family of Origin"—the bunch we are born into. That's where we first work out our social skills, loyalty issues, ethics, and other values. Other households are comprised of "Families of Choice"—the people we keep in the locket of our heart, those people with whom we have genuine experiences and choose to fill our days. Friends, for example, can be closer to us than siblings, for one reason or another—geography, age differences, gender differences, lifestyle compatibility—and we choose to focus our "family energy" on them.

Either way, these family structures provide the basis for how children view life and relationships.

How Children Learn to Be Good Partners

Children model what they see. When children see adults being on time for each other, respecting their privacy and property, supporting each other's talents, work, and friends, they learn important messages about living with others as they grow older. This forms the basis for how they interact with future partners, family, dorm mates, and others. Here are key points to remember. They will keep us from taking each other for granted, as well as provide role models:

◆ We all want our own way, all the time. Compromising creates civility at home. No one person ever has all the answers, so give way when your partner feels strongly about something.

◆ Praise often, in public. We need to know that our partner is unfailingly in our corner and also an admirer. If someone has spent a lot of time and effort getting dressed up for some occasion, say (within earshot of the children), "You look just great!"

◆ Be on time for each other, especially for commitments your partner feels are particularly important.

◆ When your partner is upset, sad, or has a major disappointment, make comforting your priority.

◆ Know and understand your partner's job, so that you can converse about it intelligently.

◆ For your partner's sake, be kind to his or her parents, even if you don't like them.

◆ Accept each other's friends, as you would like them to accept you. You don't have to like them.

Faux Pas

Never criticize your partner in front of anyone else.

In-Laws, Aunts, and Uncles

Extended family members provide invaluable context for children—aunts and uncles can be sounding boards for children's anxieties when they are too embarrassed or uncomfortable to ask their parents. They also can regale children with stories of their parents when they were the same ages as the children—always enlightening and often comforting to children.

"In-law stress" always will be a fact of life. We can minimize it by remembering the Golden Rule—do unto others as you'd have them do unto you. This, admittedly, is more easily said than done. In some cases, the most civilized solution is to minimize interaction while keeping in mind the interests of the children, who should not be deprived the company of their grandparents, aunts, and uncles.

Practicing these habits with relatives outside the immediate family will provide good examples for your children, especially when you do them with good humor. After all, someday they will be aunts and uncles and perhaps even in-laws:

◆ Never use the children as pawns in your own disagreements.

◆ Don't pump for information.

◆ Don't criticize them in public or in front of the children.

Mind Your P's and Q's

Make visits with your relatives something to look forward to, not a chore. Keep a lid on your own irritation of having to give up an evening or an afternoon to visit people who might not be your favorites. Instead, focus on the positive goal: "It makes Grandpa/Grandma/Aunt Lillie/Uncle Ed so happy when we visit them."

Prepare children with topics of conversation, perhaps involving family history, and encourage them to ask family members about them. Be sure the subjects are ones other family members are comfortable talking about. An interesting and appropriate example might be: "Grandpa traveled the world as a merchant marine. Ask him about it." Inappropriate: "Did you know that Uncle Mort did time for check kiting? I'll bet he has some interesting prison stories."

See them—and have your children see them—as often as possible and practical. When it's practical, invite them to events like school plays, recitals, or the kids' ball games. They might decline, but the invitation will make them feel special. Later, the event might provide good reasons for conversations and e-mails. Whenever someone invites us to something they are proud of, it makes us feel special, whether or not we are able to attend.

When they criticize or advise your children against your judgment, handle the situation in private. (See "Conflicts, Compliments, and Criticism" in Chapter 19.)

If one becomes widowed, pay more attention than usual to the remaining partner.

Do not abuse their babysitting or chauffeuring services—and be sure to let them know how much you appreciate what they do for you and the children.

When they live at a distance, keep in touch through e-mails or telephone calls, and let the children know what they've been up to—and vice versa.

Don't give advice on child rearing unless asked—and then don't expect the advice to be taken.

Keep your remarks about their house, decorating, driving, entertaining, and the like positive—or else keep your thoughts to yourself. In other words, be their cheerleaders.

Apologize when you've offended them, even if you feel you were right. It will keep the lines of communication open.

Don't lay any guilt trips. "You never call, you never write …." Instead, try something like, "It's always such a treat to hear from you … I admit I'm a bit jealous of the people who get to see/talk with you more than we do."

Remember their birthdays and special occasions with as much enthusiasm and cheer as you'd like them to remember your own.

Gay and Lesbian Couples

Gay and lesbian individuals are important members of our communities—socially, politically, economically, and culturally. As couples and heads of households, they deserve the same respect and treatment as any other couple. That means accepting their partnerships without judgment, blame, a sense of superiority, or sarcasm. We are all different and individual, and we all make choices. It's fair to say to children that others make choices that we might not make; and that is fine for them because they are living responsible lives in our neighborhood/community.

Say What?

Same-sex couples should prepare their children for some inevitable, thoughtlessly rude questions from other children and neighbors, such as "Why don't you have a daddy?" or "Where's your mommy?" The answer is simply, "I have two mommies …." Or two daddies.

Introduce the couple as, "This is Tim Shales and Pedro Santora, his partner." When you send a formal invitation to their home, send only one; not two. Both names belong on the envelope, listed alphabetically, one on top of the other, with their mutual address on the lines underneath (see Chapter 25).

Same-sex couples frequently have children, through previous marriages, artificial insemination, adoption, and surrogate motherhood. It's important that their children feel supported and accepted by the community. In fact, very often the adoptive children of same-sex couples become little ambassadors to neighbors who otherwise do not embrace their lifestyle.

It's a good idea for couples to prepare the children's teachers for potential problems. At the same time, children should know that it is appropriate to report excessive harassment and teachers should be on notice that you will not tolerate such prejudicial treatment of your child—not by other children, and especially not by the teacher or other school officials.

It's essential for straight individuals not to gossip or make mean-spirited remarks about these families. They are, after all, families, and families deserve respect. When children hear biased, negative comments about any minority that is what they learn, and what they model. Certainly parents have the right to instruct their children not to interact with the children of families whose lifestyles conflict with their own. At the same time, consider whether being so exclusionary is in the long-term best interests of both sets of children.

Along the same lines, it is not necessary to inform other parents if their children attend a function of yours that includes children of gay couples or the couples themselves.

Adoptive Parents

Adoptive parents are very special, generous individuals with a great capacity to love. Whether the parents are gay or straight, single or married, they deserve respect and kindness. Think before you speak. Thoughtlessly rude questions can invade their privacy. Never ask, "Why did you decide to adopt? How long did you try to have a child? Did you explore this or that fertility clinic/method? How much did it cost?" Even well-intentioned comments and questions can be rude—for instance, "My, you look so much alike, I'd never know you were adopted."

House Rules

However we define "family," family life expands and contracts, bringing with it reconfigured arrangements and challenges. Besides the parental partners and their young children, grown children frequently move back into their "old" homes, as do grandparents. This family potpourri provides the opportunity to share and learn, as well as short tempers, arguments, and frustration.

Agree in advance what share of household expenses or room and board the newcomer will pay to the head of the household.

In general, determine who pays for what expenses in advance and keep close track of what you owe, and pay it on time. Figure out a procedure and agree upon it—perhaps settling accounts at the beginning and the end of each month.

Before newcomers move in, it's a good idea to define for one another what household responsibilities and chores are whose. Charts posted in the kitchen help keep everyone accountable. They should list the chores and also "by when" the task should be accomplished. It's also important to deal with the noise factor—times to run the vacuum cleaner, for example.

Have a central telephone message center and take accurate messages.

Let household members know when you are having friends over, and pitch in to help housemates entertain whenever possible. Be sure to follow any "house rules" that may apply.

Be clear about kitchen privileges and shared supplies such as oil, butter, salt, pepper, coffee, etc.

Any redecorating by a newcomer should be agreed to by the head of the household before moving in, and it should apply only to personal, private living quarters. However, if there are furniture, pictures, or other items more appropriate for the common areas, it should be discussed in advance.

Agree in advance on rules of orderliness in the kitchen and laundry room—leaving it in perfect condition when you've used it, and so forth.

Everybody who lives in the house should agree to answer the door and greet others' guests cordially—don't just let the doorbell ring when the guest isn't yours. Offer the guest a place to wait and a beverage. Stand and greet people who come into the room when you are in it.

Make sure everyone agrees on sound levels for televisions, CD players, and so on, and respect "off limit" hours for having them on. If older people live in the house, make sure to respect their rest times.

No entering or snooping in others' rooms without permission. You wouldn't like it done to you. That goes for snooping through others' mail and messages, and "borrowing" items without permission.

The Least You Should Know

- ◆ Children model what they see. When they see adults acting as good partners, they learn valuable lessons about living with others.

- ◆ Extended family members—in-laws, aunts, uncles, cousins—provide invaluable context for children, and can be a pain. Follow the Golden Rule.

- ◆ Gay and lesbian and adoptive parents and their children are members of the community and should be accepted with kindness and respect.

- ◆ When families "expand"—older children move back in or grandparents are added to the household—agree ahead of time on the rules of the house.

Chapter 13

Neighborhood Etiquette

In This Chapter

- ◆ Treat neighbors and the neighborhood with respect and compassion
- ◆ Pet etiquette
- ◆ Foul weather etiquette
- ◆ Environmental manners

In a perfect world, we would like all our neighbors and enjoy spending time with them. Unfortunately, it's not a perfect world. That's why good manners are so important.

People who practice good manners respect others' privacy, property, and beliefs. We don't have to agree with our neighbors any more than they will agree with us. Yet respecting them—keeping a polite yet compassionate distance—can mean the difference between dealing with challenges constructively and creating feuds.

Won't You Be My Neighbor?

Neighborly kindnesses make our communities places where we want to spend time and feel good about our families spending time there. Here are some kindnesses, easily practiced, that help create friendly relations in the community:

Welcome newcomers to the neighborhood with a note. Bring a small gift—perhaps a plant or bunch of flowers, or homemade cookies. Corny? Perhaps. But remember how it felt when you moved into a new neighborhood yourself—and how much you appreciated feeling welcome. Offer to help them in any way you can. Invite them in for coffee and provide useful information about local shopping, entertainment, sports, schools, and so forth. If they have children, urge your children to befriend them and remind your kids how scary it can be to move into a new neighborhood.

Smile often. Neighbors on the street, cashiers at checkout counters, strangers next to you in line in stores and theaters appreciate it—and will likely pay it forward.

Teach children how to greet the neighbors cheerfully—with a smile, eye contact, and "Mr., Ms., or Mrs."

Keep your yard or common areas clean and neat.

Volunteer to watch your neighbors' house when they are out of town. That goes for apartment dwellers, too. Collect newspapers and mail (with their permission) to discourage potential intruders. Offer to water plants and feed pets.

Don't drop in unexpectedly.

Keep noise levels down, especially early in the morning and in the evening.

When you entertain, keep the hours and noise reasonable—and don't talk about your parties to neighbors who were not invited. It's not necessary to invite neighbors to all your parties—that becomes tedious for everyone. All of us have different friends and relationships built on different interests, after all. Let your neighbors know when the hours are, and make sure you end the party at that time.

When you borrow something, return it in the same or better condition as when you borrowed it. Return items promptly, and be sure to say how much you appreciated the help. Never, ever "borrow" something without permission.

Should you break something—or your child or pet break something—make sure to replace it at once. And apologize.

Make sure your garbage cans and containers are tightly closed so nothing leaks or smells.

Keep the right of way clear of vehicles, bicycles, and anything else that could block entrance to shared parking spaces or other shared space. That's not only polite, it's safe.

Say What?

The party is heading past its ending time and your guests are not showing signs of leaving. Announce to your guests, "It doesn't seem possible that it's already _____ o'clock—it's been such a good time. Now it's time to let my good neighbors get some solid shuteye, so let's say good night."

Say What? _____

Situation: Your neighbor borrows something and doesn't return it. What do you say?

Solution: When you lend anything, say, "I hope it won't be too inconvenient to get this right back to me. I need it … [say when, giving yourself some wiggle room]."

Or, after the fact, say "May I have my [hammer, book ….] back? You probably forgot you had it and I need it [today, tomorrow, right now ….]."

Situation: Your neighbor zealously solicits your signature/support for a cause you consider unworthy.

Solution: When he/she makes the pitch, say, "Thanks for thinking of me. Let me take a look at all the information and I'll think about it." Then forget about it.

Or, if pressed to make an immediate decision, say, "Thanks. It's just not something that I feel I can get behind." Period. End of story. No apology needed. No explanation needed. Say this with the same nonemotional tone as you would say, "It's raining outside."

Situation: Your neighbor's children play in your yard regularly—uninvited.

Solution: Don't go over their heads right away—talk to the offenders first. Explain what you want them to do—and not do—very specifically. That might sound like, "My hedges are damaged when people walk through them. So I need you to walk around if something drops into my yard." Give this solution time to work. If it doesn't, then speak with the parents and be equally specific. Of course, if neighborhood children deliberately deface your property and cause serious damage, it's time to call the police.

If your neighbors are older, in poor health, or infirm, volunteer to rake leaves and shovel snow.

Offer to take along an elderly neighbor or someone who does not drive the next time you go shopping.

When a neighbor is hospitalized, check with his or her family to see if visitors are welcome. If so, visit briefly and send a get-well note.

Invite someone whose family is far away to a holiday meal.

Invite someone of a different faith to share your holiday festivities.

Be aware of the power of small gestures. Let another driver have your parking spot; let someone go before you in the supermarket line when you have a large order and he or she has only an item or two. Move over on your seat in a bus when new people get on—before they ask you to. These simple acts of thoughtfulness can lift a mood and make our neighborhoods—and our neighbors—happier.

When there is a neighborhood need, be willing to address it. For example, open your house for a potluck supper and collectively take action to start a neighborhood watch (through your local police). Or plant some flowers or trees, or collect used children's books for the local daycare or preschool.

Don't forget to play—schedule neighborhood block parties. They build a sense of camaraderie and community and make it easier to deal with future challenges when they arise.

Live and Learn

Although respect and kindness for our neighbors is good for them, it also helps us. Who needs more stress from fractured relationships with people we see every day?

David J. Lieberman, Ph.D., author of *Make Peace With Anyone* (St. Martin's Press), offers this three-step plan to get along with just about anyone:

◆ Say something nice. We all love hearing compliments directly. It's even more powerful when we hear them second-hand from mutual friends.

◆ Let people help you. When someone does you a favor, his or her opinion of you improves because of a psychological phenomenon called cognitive dissonance. Basically, the other person might realize, perhaps unconsciously, that if he or she is doing something for you, it's probably because he or she likes you.

◆ Share a weakness. When people resist us for no apparent reason, they often do so because they feel threatened. Revealing something less-than-perfect about oneself makes the other person feel better about us, and about them.

Petiquette

Since we are human and therefore creatures of higher intelligence, it is up to us to control our pets—not the other way around. Especially when we live in close range of our neighbors.

It's our responsibility to ensure our pets don't roam free, pooping on neighbor's property, which is both irritating and can spread disease. Should your pet mark its spot in your neighbor's yard, clean up the mess right away.

Walking a dog unleashed is an accident waiting to happen—and illegal in many areas. Even "friendly" dogs that "won't hurt you" can turn when they encounter another frisky pet or an unfamiliar—or too familiar—human.

Don't approach a cat or a dog to pet them. You could get bitten—thousands of people have. Ask the owner before touching anyone else's pet.

Mind Your P's and Q's _____

Situation: Your neighbor's pet barks constantly while his owner is at work. You work from your home office and find the noise too distracting to work or conduct business.

Solution: Ask your neighbor, "Is there anything you can do to quiet Spot while you're at work? It's really tough to work/sleep/have guests when he is home alone."

If this doesn't solve the problem, you might have to call your local police department and register a complaint. That, however, should be the last resort. When you think the animal is being abused, call the American Humane Association or the Society for the Prevention of Cruelty to Animals.

Be considerate of your neighbors and their pets. That means being a responsible pet owner yourself. Give your animal attention; teach it manners from an early age. If you acquire a mature animal that is untrained, seek a professional trainer if you can. That is a sound investment in the safety and peace of your neighborhood.

Constant dog barking or cat meowing is like hearing someone scratch a chalkboard with their fingernails—it's grating and eventually leads to implosion or explosion. Make sure your pets are not annoying others in your absence—you can get a voice-activated cassette recorder to find out if they do make noise while you're not at home.

Mind Your P's and Q's _____

Remember that a pet is very much a family member. When a neighbor or friend's pet dies, be sure to express your condolences. A note would mean a lot to the bereaved. It could say something like, "I am so sorry that Molly is no longer with us. She always made me feel so welcome whenever I came to your door, with her wagging tail and affectionate manner. I will miss her, and I know this time must be very sad and difficult for you."

It's also a kindness to send a contribution in memory of the pet to your local animal shelter or charity.

Foul Weather Friendliness

A wonderful Asian saying tells us, "We teach what we want to learn." My most recent example occurred when I nearly blinded someone with my umbrella.

So, in the spirit of preventing mishaps for you, and as a humble reminder for myself, here are some umbrella etiquette tips:

- Carry umbrellas close to the body, point down, when they are closed.

- When unfurling an umbrella, be sure to look in all directions to avoid spearing anyone with its point or spokes.

- Hold an opened umbrella low or high enough so you don't block anyone's vision or poke someone in the eye.

- When two people are sharing an umbrella, let the taller person wield it. Worry less about chivalry in deference to safety, visibility, and comfort.

- Shake out the umbrella (being careful not to drench anyone nearby) before you enter a building. Floor puddles are messy and potentially dangerous.

- Keep umbrellas furled when not in use. Unfurled, they easily snag garments, as well as get tangled in coats in the closet.

Faux Pas

Think of your surroundings and other people when choosing the umbrella you'll wield on a rainy day. Unfurling a huge golf umbrella on a crowded street is rude and insensitive, even if you yell, "Fore!"

Live and Learn

The superstition that opening umbrellas indoors brings bad luck has some very real-world, practical origins. That folklore began in London about 300 years ago when stiff, metal-spoked umbrellas were a part of daily life.

Umbrellas served as some insurance against the unpredictability of weather there and were carried at all times. But their rigid, clumsy spring mechanisms made it dangerous to open them indoors, especially in small rooms. Many people were injured as a result, and many a fragile object was shattered.

Of course, victims of an umbrella's poke grumbled many angry words that could grow into major quarrels. In some ways, the superstition made for a safer life by deterring people from the practice. It seems to me that I grew up listening to my grandmother's warnings to that effect.

Today, we are inundated with weather reports from newspapers, radio, television, and the Internet. It's no longer so important to carry an umbrella each day. In fact, modern superstition holds that one insurance policy for a sunny day is to carry your umbrella—and that downpours are all but guaranteed when you leave the house without it.

Let It Snow, But Don't Let It Slide

It's snowing.

From the window at the back of the house, you can hear children playing, their laughter in sharp contrast to the softly falling flakes.

From the street come the sounds of grown-ups—and the impatient spinning of car wheels, the slamming of doors, and the tense, raised voices of people in a frustrated hurry. You would think their elevated temperatures and blood pressure would warm up the neighborhood. Not so.

Snowstorm rules are simply based on the Golden Rule: Do unto others as you would have them do unto you. Put yourself into the other guy's snowshoes. We would also do well to consider the lessons Mother Nature is teaching us when she covers the land with snow and ice:

- ◆ Slow down. Everybody else is pressured for time and needs to be somewhere else, too.

- ◆ Calm down. Yelling at other drivers and pedestrians serves no useful purpose. Remember those magic words: *please, thank you,* and *excuse me.* Use them often.

- ◆ You, too, can help. Now is the time to volunteer your strong back for shoveling, running errands, and generally being useful to others less mobile or agile than yourself.

- ◆ Don't be cheap. Should you be fortunate enough to have a neighbor's kid shovel your sidewalk, pay him or her well. We all need to learn about the free-enterprise system somehow.

- ◆ Compromise. It's the key to sanity. If digging a nice wide path to your door means obscuring your next-door neighbors' way to their front door, dig a narrower path so both households are served. The same principle applies to parking spaces.

- ◆ Keep your sense of humor. Snowstorms can bring out the silliness in us just as easily as our dark side.

- ◆ Let others pass you—on the sidewalk, on the street. If they're in such a hurry, don't compete.

- ◆ Offer help to someone who has difficulty walking, keeping his or her balance, or carrying packages.

Environmental Etiquette

Just as we build a sense of family through our community, concern for and awareness of our environment makes it possible for future families to enjoy the same sense of community. Little things do mean a lot; and modeling environmentally sound practices for our children is a gift for children to come.

In the here and now, abusing the environment is rude and destroys the world we live in.

Here are some environment-friendly guidelines for all of us to practice:

♦ Respect property. Don't ruin the grass or injure trees by tearing off branches and gouging them with knives. Other peoples' flowers are not yours for the picking.

♦ Keep to the sidewalk. Remember that others' yards are just that—not passways when we want to trample through, destroying flowers and lawns. Run, skate, or ride bikes somewhere else.

♦ Use trash bins. Litter doesn't belong dropped on the street or sidewalks, so if no bin is close by, hang on to trash until one is.

♦ Never throw things from car windows while on the road. Keep a receptacle in the car, use it, and empty it when you reach your destination.

♦ Pick up advertising circulars and flyers when they are delivered door-to-door and often simply ignored. Put them in the recycling bin where they belong.

♦ Recycle paper, cans, and plastic. The energy savings are impressive. Producing a recycled aluminum can uses only 5 percent of the energy required to make a new one, according to the Container Recycling Institute in Washington, D.C.

♦ Clean up after your pets.

♦ When you picnic at public parks, leave the site in cleaner shape than when you found it.

♦ Don't even think about graffiti. It defaces property that doesn't belong to us and robs our neighborhoods of beauty.

The Least You Need to Know

♦ Keeping a polite yet compassionate distance from your neighbors can mean the difference between dealing with challenges constructively and creating feuds.

♦ It's up to us to control our pets—not the other way around.

♦ Consider others when whipping out—and furling—your umbrella.

♦ Lower the temperature on your emotions and help diffuse acrimony when the snow starts to fall.

♦ The community and its environment are part of our "extended" family. Keep it as pristine as you would the house.

Part 4

Business Etiquette

The rules of business etiquette are unique, as is the entire approach to etiquette in the business world. And you must understand this special way of thinking about relationships and behavior and how it applies to your dealings with your superiors, your colleagues, and your subordinates.

Knowing the accepted ways of doing things—what to say, how to dress, and how to react in various situations—is vitally important and becomes even more important the higher you rise in the ranks. And technologies like cell phones, teleconferencing, and e-mail require people to learn new rules of civility.

Chapter 14

Getting Started:
The Corporate Culture

In This Chapter

- ◆ What is the corporate culture?
- ◆ The job interview
- ◆ The pressing issue of dressing
- ◆ The do's and don'ts of compliments

If you think it would be nice but not necessary to know the rules of corporate etiquette, consider that studies by Harvard University, the Carnegie Foundation, and the Stanford Research Institute have concluded that success in getting, keeping, and advancing in a job depends 85 percent on people skills and only 15 percent on technical knowledge and skills. Qualifications are one thing and, of course, important. Still, most decisions come down to the person—to the relationship we have with individuals.

Mastering the rules of business etiquette, then, can help your career. The first thing you should know is that these rules do not have the same foundation as those you may have learned as a child. Your childhood rules evolved from the code of chivalry, which called for deference to others on the basis of gender and/or age. However, relationships in the business world (or corporate culture) have always been based primarily on rank, much like any military system. Rank, or the degree of power vested in different individuals, gives a business organization the structure it needs to function effectively.

How you behave toward a peer or toward someone of another status varies with the kind of business and the style of the individual business. Corporate and social behavior in a bank, for instance, tends to be more formal than it would be in an advertising agency. And behavior in a newspaper city room makes an advertising office seem severely structured.

Don't worry if you're confused. Some basic rules will help you adjust to various business and professional situations. And behavior that is grounded in good manners—which means having respect for others and concern for their feelings—will allow colleagues to forgive (but maybe not forget) many inadvertent breaches of business or corporate etiquette.

Business Booboos

Surviving and thriving in the workplace isn't always easy—and may be especially difficult for those who lack finesse and grace. Here are 10 rather basic behavioral mistakes to guard against.

- **Expressing negative attitudes.** If you are feeling and thinking negatively, your mindset will find expression in surliness, bad temper, and general unpleasantness.

- **Wearing inappropriate clothing.** Although we like to think that we judge others by their behavior and not their appearance, it remains true that we base our opinions of others, to a large degree, on what we see.

- **Failing to make introductions.** Allowing someone to stand around without introducing him or her can make everyone present feel uncomfortable.

Faux Pas

When dressing for success, stay away from 100 percent polyester. It's called a miracle fabric because it's a miracle that anyone wears it. Polyester and wool or cotton blends are much more serviceable and usually look better.

- **Disregarding social courtesies.** Forgetting to say please, thank you, and excuse me, and failing to perform other common civilities makes colleagues and superiors doubt your judgment.

- **Criticizing others in public.** Generally, the criticizer comes off looking worse than the person being criticized.

- **Taking messages carelessly.**

- **Making people wait.**

◆ **Pronouncing names wrong or forgetting names altogether.**

◆ **Using vulgar and inappropriate
language.**

◆ **Giving someone the runaround,** which
means things like ducking responsibility
and giving vague or conflicting answers.

It might be a good idea to keep this list handy
and refer to it often.

> **CAUTION** **Faux Pas** _____
>
> The old gender rules
> have been pretty much discarded
> within the corporate culture.
> Gallantry, which is being overso-
> licitous toward women simply
> because they are women, for
> example, will get you nowhere,
> except perhaps into hot water.

The Job Interview

Believe it or not, you need to know the basics of workplace etiquette right from the
start—at the job interview. Sure, you're anxious, but here is a situation in which how
you look and everything you say and do—that is, your overall demeanor—may have a
critical impact on your future. You have to be on your best behavior.

And the person opposite you seems to have all the advantages. Recruiters and inter-
viewers usually take courses to help them develop sophisticated screening methods.
The interviewer has the home-turf advantage, and you do not. You are being mea-
sured against standards and guidelines that are clear as a bell to the interviewer, but
not to you.

But you also have some important advantages of your own, including …

◆ The company or organization needs someone, or it wouldn't be interviewing
people.

◆ The company or organization is hoping you are the person for the job.

These two facts are key. But you also have to be prepared by dressing appropriately,
preparing a list of the points you want to make, and having a pretty good idea of what
will happen and how to respond. By doing so, the situation won't seem nearly as one-
sided.

Be Prepared

Find out everything you can about the company before your interview. Read any reports,
reference books, or brochures you can find, and check out the company website, if

one exists. Also, try to contact somebody you know who works at the company, preferably a friend, acquaintance, or someone who attended the same college as you did.

Some of the things you should find out about the company you are interviewing with are …

- The correct pronunciation and spelling of its name.

- The business of the company: what it produces or what services it provides.

- Whether it's a national or international company, as opposed to regional or local.

- The size of the company.

- Its attitude toward women and minorities. Most companies have a stated policy on diversity and it can be found on its website.

- How long the company has been in business.

- Its general reputation.

- The reputation the company has for working conditions and environment.

Before your interview, you should also find out everything you can about yourself. Take a long, honest look at yourself and be prepared to talk about your traits. One way to help with this process is to make a list of important points about yourself, including …

- Your level of education.

- How much and what kind of volunteer work you've done.

- Any honors and awards that you've received.

- Your interests and hobbies.

- Why you want to work for this company.

- The abilities you can bring to the company.

The Interview

In general, you should dress conservatively for interviews. However, dress can vary dramatically from company to company. Khakis and Docksiders might be the standard at one place, whereas wingtips and double-breasted suits are typical of another. When in doubt, don't hesitate to ask an employee or someone in the human resources department about appropriate interview attire.

Upon arriving for your interview, enter the room, smile, and make eye contact with your interviewer. Then wait until he or she asks you to sit before taking a seat. During the meeting, don't fidget or handle things on the other person's desk. Also, listen carefully to what you are being asked and don't treat any question as unimportant. If a question is difficult, pause before answering. Compose yourself. At the end of the meeting, thank the interviewer cordially and follow up with a note.

Bear in mind that your first interview with a company will probably be a "screening interview." The purpose of this interview is to screen out applicants. For instance, companies want to know whether you're willing to relocate, have sufficient language skills, and fill other requirements or prerequisites.

The interview will be held at the company site, a hotel suite, an airport lounge, or even by telephone. You *must* arrive on time (but no more than a few minutes early). If you are being interviewed by telephone, make sure that you have your materials on hand. If you don't, get the name and telephone number of the interviewer and call back promptly. Whether you're being interviewed on site or by telephone, don't volunteer information you haven't been asked for.

Live and Learn
Remember that the interviewer wants to know more than your past employment record or your grades and courses in school. He or she wants to get a feeling for your personality, your trainability, your potential for success. So, you shouldn't dwell too long on your past experiences or make repeated references to past achievements. The interviewer heard you the first time.

The Next Step

After the screening interview (and perhaps other preliminary interviews), you'll have a meeting with the hiring manager. This person makes the final decision, and this interview is the most unpredictable. The interviewer usually has no formal training in interviewing, may ask the wrong questions, and may be vague. The hiring manager is casting around for enough information to make the decision. The manager may be looking for that undefined "certain something."

"So, tell me about yourself." When an interview poses this challenge, reply by being enthusiastic but honest and polite. Make eye contact. Talk about your strongest skills and your greatest areas of knowledge. Use positive, active language such as "I enjoy detail work. I am committed to excellence."

In general, it is a good idea to think of a job interview as an opportunity, not as a test.

Business Attire

Never, ever underestimate the critical importance of attire within the corporate culture. What you wear says a lot about you, and you can damage or even destroy your chances of success in business by dressing inappropriately.

What do your clothes say about you? Do they say you have good sense and good taste? Do they say you have self-respect and that you have respect for those you deal with every day? People, particularly your superiors, are apt to conclude that the quality of your work will match the quality of your appearance.

Live and Learn

Although business casual dress is widely practiced, classic business dress is gaining in respect and popularity. The fact remains that we perform better "in uniform," so it's a good idea to dress up a notch rather than dress down.

Corporate America is gradually accepting body piercings and tattoos, but very gradually. If you want a tattoo and piercings to express yourself, consider getting them on places that can be easily covered. Only you can decide whether to risk exposing them in your work culture. Check with human resources to find out if there are any company policies on the matters.

Hint, Hint

If your organization has a dress code, observe both the letter and the spirit of the code right off the bat. Don't assume that a white shirt and striped tie will fit into any office situation.

If the organization does not have a dress code, you can't go wrong by studying how the senior managers dress. And don't be afraid to ask questions. It only means you care enough to get things right. Say to your boss: "I'm a little puzzled by the variety of styles I see here. What kind of dress best represents the company?" Avoid extreme fashions. Don't buy things just because the fashion gurus say so. Think about what is good for you and your career rather than what is in vogue.

Think Before Buying

When you decide to add to your closet, think in terms of your entire wardrobe. Many variables affect what you should choose for your wardrobe and what you should wear on given occasions. Here are some of the variables you would be wise to consider:

♦ **Regional variations.** Take climate and geography into account. An outfit that looks terrific in Vermont might look odd in Atlanta. The attire of a Wall Street broker will probably look downright funeral in Los Angeles. And colors! What might look fine in the easy sunshine of San Diego would have a jarring effect on Philadelphia bankers.

♦ **Business environment.** Think about the type of company you work for and the kind of work you do. If you're going to be tramping around a construction site with a hard hat on your head, you should not have high heels on your feet.

♦ **Type of position.** Consider what you want your outfit to say about you. If you want it to say, "Your investment will be safe with us," don't dress in a way that says, "We're a friendly bunch of folks here."

Details

When it comes to dressing, your accessories are every bit as important as the basic outfit. Pay careful attention to details such as shoes and jewelry. Sometimes the little things are what people notice most and remember longest. One jarring detail, such as scuffed shoes or a missing button, can ruin the impression made by a carefully selected outfit. Take the following into account:

♦ **Jewelry.** It shouldn't be obtrusive, and it shouldn't jangle. Avoid wearing big rings on your right hand so that you won't have to worry about them getting in the way when you shake hands. Wear a watch, even if your internal clock functions well. Business in the United States runs according to schedules and deadlines, and promptness counts.

♦ **Furs.** Don't wear furs in the business world. They signal pretentiousness more than they signal success and may actually offend some people.

♦ **Shoes.** If you're not careful, your shoes can shoot you in the foot. To give them a quick shine, use fabric softener sheets, which you can easily keep in your desk or briefcase. If you wear sneakers for your commute, change both your shoes and socks or hose when you get to the office. Feet tend to perspire a lot in sneakers, and socks absorb odors.

♦ **Briefcases.** Keep your briefcase polished and clean. It should not be overly large nor should it be overstuffed. If it's beat-up, get a new one.

Business Appointments and Functions

When attending a business appointment, take off your topcoat, and if someone offers to hang it up, surrender it gladly. If not, ask where you can put it, along with umbrella and galoshes on bad weather days. If there is no place to hang your coat, drape it on the back of your chair. But don't wear your coat inside and don't carry it around.

When you're in someone else's office, keep your suit jacket on. If someone suggests that you remove it, you may, or you may decide not to. Taking off your jacket is sort of invasive: It looks as if you're moving in. And if you do take it off, don't roll up your sleeves. You are a guest in that office, and you should behave accordingly even if you are working there for a short time.

Don't scatter things around. Keep files on your lap. Put your briefcase or handbag on the floor or keep it on your lap. Don't put things or touch things on the other person's desk.

Invitations to special business functions often specify the appropriate dress for the occasion in the lower-right corner. If you have any doubts about what to wear, you can call the host or hostess.

Here are the definitions of two types of business functions as described on invitations:

◆ Black tie formal means different things in different parts of the country. Black is always correct for men. White jackets are not. Women don't have to wear gloves and never should shake hands in them.

◆ Informal or semiformal is slightly less dressy than black tie. Men should wear a dark business suit, a white shirt, and a dark silk tie with a quiet pattern. Women should wear a dressy suit in an evening fabric, a short cocktail dress, or a long skirt and blouse.

The most important thing to remember about business etiquette is that so much of it is based on rank. If you remember this, common sense and a cool head should get you through most situations.

Faux Pas

Skirts and trousers should not be so tight that they convey a message of sexiness. Miniskirts and exposed cleavage are not appropriate business attire for women, just as tight "muscle" shirts or shirts that expose the chest are inappropriate for men.

Faux Pas

Don't give false compliments and don't tell polite lies to people at social functions. For example, "You look fabulous" can sound hollow when a person says it too often. "It's been a long time since I've seen you" can be better than an insincere "It's great to see you." People will detect your insincerity, no matter how good an actor you think you are.

The Least You Need to Know

♦ Researchers say that people skills are more important than either technical skills or knowledge for advancement in the business world.

♦ Gender plays a minor role in business relationships. Rank plays the major role.

♦ When in doubt about how to dress, take your cues from the people who are running your company.

♦ Before buying any piece of clothing, consider the position you hold and the specific business environment, as well as factors such as climate, geography, and occasion.

Introductions

In This Chapter

- ◆ How to make an introduction and how to respond to one
- ◆ What to do when you're not introduced
- ◆ What to do when you forget someone's name
- ◆ Tips on greeting people

Introductions are an area of business relationships in which too many people get off on one wrong foot and then trip over the other. Knowing the rules is critical because it will help you feel more relaxed and confident. Your confidence will come across when you are introducing people and will put them at ease.

The most important thing about an introduction is to just do it. If you don't, people around you end up feeling invisible. It's better to attempt and botch someone's difficult name than to ignore it. Another thing to remember is that Americans expect three things when they meet people: eye contact, a smile, and a handshake. Let's take a look.

Who's First?

When making an introduction, introduce the person who is being presented last. Also, keep in mind that social etiquette is based on chivalry, so in a social situation we defer to people based on gender and age by introducing women first and then those oldest. Business etiquette is different because it is based on hierarchy. Gender and age play no role, but rank and authority do.

The rule is that people of lesser authority are introduced to people of greater authority: "Mr./Ms. CEO, I would like to introduce Mr./Ms. Junior Executive."

Live and Learn
The forms we use when introducing people these days have been in use for so long that it is difficult to know when they first came into being. The earliest etiquette guides I am aware of advocate mentioning the name of the most important or highest-ranking person first.

One important exception to the "who's first" general rule is that no one, not even the CEO of your company, is more important than your client. A client is always more important that those in your company. The same goes for an elected official: "Mr. Muldoon, I would like to introduce Ms. Cooper, our chief executive officer. Mr. Muldoon is our client from Dublin." And, "State Representative Jones, I would like to introduce Ms. Cooper, our chief executive officer." Again, remember eye contact. Look at and speak to the greater authority first; look at and speak to the lesser authority second.

Background Info

As you make the introduction, include a brief bit of information about those being introduced: "Jim just joined our Newark regional office." When in doubt, be less personal rather than more personal. There's no reason, for instance, to add the fact that Jim is a real good guy.

Providing a bit of information gives the two people being introduced some basis to begin a conversation. Never underestimate the power of sincere flattery: "Without Jim, our softball team would never win a game." When the people you have just introduced begin to talk, you can excuse yourself, depending on the situation.

Introductions at Business Functions

The host at a business function should meet and greet the guests upon their arrival if at all possible. If not, he or she may appoint other guests to be greeters. The host's job is to make guests feel welcome.

In this case, the greeter introduces him- or herself and escorts the guest to the host. After making the introduction, the greeter should introduce the guest to others or show him or her to the buffet table or the bar. The idea is to leave the host free to greet other guests.

It is not necessary to introduce a new-comer at a business/social function to everyone else. A good tactic is to intro-duce the person to the closest group by saying his or her name first and then naming the others or having someone in the group name them.

Mind Your P's and Q's

When introducing anyone, par-ticularly a public official, to a member of the media, make sure you include the affiliation of the media person so that the other person knows he may be speaking "on the record."

Introducing Yourself

It is helpful to others and important for you to introduce yourself promptly and appropriately.

First, here's a bit of advice about actually entering a room. Most people make the hori-zontal approach to a room. That is, instead of walking to the center of the room, they freeze in the doorway and then head sideways to the bar or refreshments. Once there, they lock onto someone they know and remain joined at the hip for the rest of the occasion. This strategy is a big mistake because they never give themselves a chance to advance their own agenda, which is the reason they came in the first place.

If you are at a business social function or with just a few people and you are not intro-duced, you should introduce yourself just as promptly as is decently appropriate. If it looks as if the person who should introduce you isn't going to do so (he or she may have forgotten your name), you have to take over. Just smile, offer to shake hands with the nearest person, and say: "Hello. I'm Tom Engles. Jim and I are responsible for the Technec account."

In some situations, describing yourself in terms of what you do rather than by your title promotes conversation. However, don't interject endless details, such as how long you have been with the company or where you live.

Mind Your P's and Q's

Sometimes a title is all the infor-mation you need to give about a person, especially if the title is something like Senator.

Responding to Introductions

How you respond to being introduced by others is just as important as how you make an introduction.

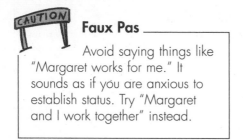

Faux Pas

Avoid saying things like "Margaret works for me." It sounds as if you are anxious to establish status. Try "Margaret and I work together" instead.

If it's an informal introduction, you can simply respond with "Hello," or you can add a bit of information, such as "I heard you speak at the seminar." In any case, keep your response brief and friendly.

"How do you do?" followed by the person's name is the best way to respond to a formal introduction. With this type of introduction, don't use the person's first name until he or she invites you to do so.

Greetings

Very definite rules apply to the various aspects of meeting and greeting people in the corporate culture. Your mother was right when she gave you that advice about first impressions.

Standing

If you don't rise to the occasion, you will sink in the estimation of others. Everyone should stand when being introduced. At one time women remained seated when new people arrived on the scene, but not nowadays. However, when newcomers arrive at a very large function, they are greeted only by those nearest them. If it is impossible for you to rise—if perhaps you are wedged behind the table—at least lean forward or rise slightly so as not to appear distant.

Mind Your P's and Q's

Think of the introduction as an equation. If you are formal with one person's name, don't be casual with the other. Don't say, "Mr. Jones, I would like you to meet Tommy."

When someone comes to visit at the office, stand and come out from behind your desk unless the visitor is a coworker or someone who comes into your office frequently in the course of the day. The frequency consideration comes into play even when a senior executive visits the office of a junior executive. If it's a common occurrence, there's no need to get up; however, you should certainly stop what you're doing and give your full attention to the senior executive whenever you're in his or her presence.

Shaking Hands

A handshake leaves a very definite and often lasting impression, and in the business world a handshake is the only truly appropriate physical contact for both men and women.

The proper shake …

- ◆ Involves eye contact.
- ◆ Is firm but painless.
- ◆ Lasts about three seconds.
- ◆ Takes only two or three pumps.
- ◆ Starts and stops crisply.
- ◆ Doesn't continue through the entire introduction.

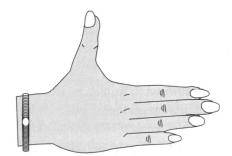

Begin with your fingers together and your thumb up.

Shake hands web to web, with a firm but not crushing grip.

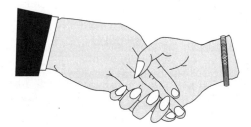

Never offer only your fingertips, causing a weak, limp handshake.

Keep your fingers together and your thumb up. Slide the web of your hand all the way to the web of the other person's hand. Otherwise, he or she ends up shaking hands with your fingers. Also, shaking web to web effectively prevents the other person, no matter how strong, from crunching your knuckles.

You shake when …

Mind Your P's and Q's

Keep your drink in your left hand to avoid giving someone a wet, cold handshake. Don't rock or sway. Handshaking is not a tango.

- ◆ Someone offers his/her hand to you.
- ◆ First meeting someone.
- ◆ Greeting guests.
- ◆ Greeting your host/hostess.
- ◆ Renewing an acquaintance.
- ◆ Saying good-bye.

Hugs and Kisses

In general, hugs and kisses are inappropriate in any business environment. In fact, touching others in the workplace, whether they are of the same gender or not, is impolite, even if you feel that the other person is your pal. This stricture includes patting someone on the back, putting your arm around someone, or putting your hand on his or her shoulder.

It is acceptable at a business/social function to kiss your spouse, if you happen to be getting along that day. Even then, keep it casual and cursory.

The Name Game

People wince inwardly when you mispronounce their names. It is a serious breach of business etiquette. If you don't know the correct pronunciation of someone's name, ask! If you are still in doubt, ask apologetically for the person to repeat it. Jokes or wisecracks about a person's name are not funny and are offensive.

If your own name is difficult to pronounce, help the person who is trying to pronounce it—and botching the job. You can smile and say: "It's a tough one, isn't it?" Pronounce it clearly without making a big deal about it. That just calls too much attention to the fact that the other person has made an error.

Say What? _____

If someone introducing you mispronounces your name or gives you the wrong title, wait until the introductions are over and say: "Jim is not the first person to have trouble pronouncing my name. It's …(give the correct pronunciation)."

And: "I'm afraid Jim has given me a promotion (or demotion). Actually, I'm now … (give title)."

In any case, don't make a big deal out of it.

Coming Up Blank

It happens to everybody. If you're the one making introductions and you forget the name of the person you're introducing, you can say something like "I remember our chat at the Cézanne reception. Please tell me your name again. I'm having a memory freeze."

Get the name and go right ahead with the introduction. Don't make a big deal out of it by apologizing more than once. Everybody has experienced mental vapor lock from time to time and will understand your predicament.

When you're introduced to someone, say the person's name and repeat it during the conversation to imprint it in your memory.

If you're the one being introduced and the introducer seems to have forgotten your name, jump right in, extend your hand, smile, and offer your name.

Titles

Because so much of the corporate culture is based on rank and status, titles are vitally important. You can't refer to a senior vice president as a vice president or to the chief operating officer as the chief executive officer.

In the company of others, especially with people outside your firm, show your boss respect by addressing him or her formally as Mr. or Ms. Smith.

Ms. is the appropriate address for a woman in business regardless of what she calls herself in her private life. Mrs. and Miss imply social, marital, and sexual distinctions that have no place in the business arena.

Faux Pas _____

Don't address someone verbally by a corporate title unless you happen to be speaking with the president of the United States, in which case you say, "Mr. President."

Of course, if a woman tells you directly that she wants to be addressed as Mrs. or Miss, it is best to comply. However, when using Mrs. in a business context, use the woman's first name rather than her husband's—for example, Mrs. Sally Kelly.

Career-conscious people entering the business world must be aware of more rules of behavior than they could expect to encounter in most social situations. You need to be aware of the sort of behavior that is expected in the world of work so that you can move within that world with confidence and ease.

The Least You Need to Know

- The most important thing about introductions is that you make them.

- When making introductions, mention the name of the most important person first.

- Customers/clients outrank even the CEO of your company, especially when they come to visit.

- If you don't know the correct pronunciation of someone's name, ask! If you forgot the person's name, politely ask for it and go right ahead with the introduction.

- A handshake is the one acceptable form of physical contact for men and women in the business world.

Chapter 16

The Arena: Etiquette in the Workplace

In This Chapter

- Relations with your staff, your colleagues, your boss
- The rules for interoffice visiting
- What about doors, elevators, smoking?
- Netiquette and nethics, the electronic world etiquette
- Home office etiquette

Nobody wants to spend eight hours a day with someone who just doesn't know how to behave.

Proper etiquette in the workplace means more than just displaying good manners. It generates efficiency, helps to eliminate distractions, and creates a pleasant environment in which people can work to their full potential. Because you spend so much time at work with so many others, you must learn to exercise good people skills—it is glaringly apparent if you don't.

Your Co-Workers

You must know how to establish cordial and respectful relationships with your support staff. Not only do you work closely with them every day, but they are also the foundation of your effectiveness. *Boss* and *bossy* are not synonymous.

Decide up front how secretaries or assistants will address you—as Tom or Mr. Smith, for example—and let them know your preference with courtesy. Always acknowledge their presence and keep greetings cordial. If you are introducing an assistant to a client or an associate, make the introduction according to the way those involved will later address one another. If you expect your assistant to address your client as Mr. Foster, introduce him that way and use your assistant's surname as well, even if you normally use your assistant's first name.

Say What?

A co-worker is a bully, stealing your ideas or just behaving in a heavy-handed or high-handed manner.

What do you say?

"You might not be aware of the fact that you are treating me unprofessionally, but I would appreciate it if you would be more respectful."

If you are sharing an assistant, consult with your associate about the workload to avoid overburdening him or her. Never ask someone else's assistant to do work for you without first clearing it with the assistant's supervisor. As a rule of thumb, never ask an assistant to perform a task you'd be unwilling to do yourself.

Watch those labels and nicknames. Never call anyone above the age of puberty a boy or a girl. The words *honey*, *dear*, and *hunk* have no place in the vocabulary of the workplace.

Your Superiors

Top management sets the tone of the workplace and the relationships therein, including such things as how people dress and how they address each other. This protocol probably won't be written anywhere. You will have to learn by observing those around you.

Address your superiors as Mr. or Ms., followed by a surname, not as sir or madam. Don't use first names unless and until you are specifically invited to do so.

And even then, be careful. Just because you have been invited to use the boss's first name or have had lunch or a golf game with her, don't assume that an intimate or even good pal relationship exists between you. Remember that relationships in the American business world are based on rank, and rank should always be observed and acknowledged.

Visitors

When you receive a visitor in your office, remember that you are the host and act accordingly. Greet your visitor cordially, which means that you or your assistant should go out to the reception area to meet the guest. Shake hands, make whatever introductions are necessary, and escort the visitor to the office.

If you stay in your office to receive the visitor, be sure to come out from behind your desk to greet him or her, or better still, meet the person at the door, usher him in, and show him where to sit.

Faux Pas

Never stay behind your desk when a visitor arrives—unless you're planning to fire him!

Visiting

Your role, when visiting someone else's office, is that of a guest, whether it is within your company or without. Don't walk in and settle down as if you were entering your own office. Here are some guidelines:

◆ Don't be late. If you are, apologize and explain.

◆ When you tell the receptionist your name and mission, also present your business card if you have one.

◆ Ask where you can hang your coat, if you have one.

◆ In the office, wait to be told where to sit. If there are a number of chairs, ask which one you should use.

◆ Don't remain standing if your host is seated.

◆ Don't lay papers or documents on the desk or the floor.

◆ Put your briefcase or handbag on the floor beside you.

◆ Don't fiddle with or touch anything on the desk.

◆ Leave promptly when your business is completed.

◆ Send a thank-you note for the meeting within 24 hours. E-mail if you must; just remember that few efforts make so positive an impression as a handwritten note. Try to make the thank-you note not look like a generic, one-size-fits-all product. Here's an example of a good note:

Dear Helen: Thank you for making time yesterday to help me out with the Anderson projections. Your insights are very much appreciated. Best regards, Tom

Doors

For such simple things, doors can cause a lot of confusion. Let's simplify matters:

◆ If you reach a door first, regardless of gender, you should open it, go through it, and hold it to ensure that it doesn't hit the person following. Men no longer hold doors for women just because they are women.

◆ If you are in the company of a senior executive, it is a good idea to allow him or her to reach the door and go through it first.

◆ If someone's arms are laden, hold the door regardless of the person's gender or status.

These rules are set aside when you are hosting others, in which case you open the door for your guests and motion for them to precede you. For a revolving door, you go first and wait for the others to come through after you.

In any case, always thank a person who holds a door for you.

Elevators

Yes, even an elevator calls for a certain amount of etiquette:

◆ Do not dodge or delay so that somebody can be the first to get on or off.

◆ If you are nearest the door, you get on the elevator first; then hold the door until everyone else has entered.

◆ If you are near the control panel, ask the others what floor they need and select those buttons for them. You can also hold the Open button to keep the doors open until everyone has had a chance to get on or off.

◆ If you are nearest the door, step out to let the people behind you get off; then, reboard.

◆ If you are among the first to enter and first to exit, stand to the side near the door rather than in the back. This way, you won't have to push through others to get off.

◆ Men should keep their hats on in a crowded elevator.

The only thing to say about escalators is that whoever arrives first gets on first and gets off first. Don't crowd the top of the stairs waiting for someone.

Smoking

It must seem to smokers as if the only place where it's not illegal or improper to smoke is the dark side of the moon. Smoking, once seen as a sign of sophistication, is now seen by many as offensive and even dangerous to nonsmokers and smokers alike. Although it's not polite to rebuke smokers in public, it's acceptable to ask them to stop smoking or to smoke elsewhere.

In general, if you don't see an ashtray, it's a safe bet that smoking is not permitted there—so don't do it. Don't say, "Do you mind if I smoke?" The other person may say he doesn't mind and still be secretly resentful. It is okay to smoke in your office if the company permits, but it will leave a smell that others may find disagreeable.

Even outside, check for designated smoking areas, as many office buildings have abolished smoking at the door. Even if permitted, smoking at the entrance of a building forces nonsmokers to walk through the cloud. That is rude.

If hosting a lunch, it's polite to ask for a table in the smoking section if your guest is a smoker, whether you smoke or not—provided you aren't allergic to smoke. If you smoke, never light up during the meal. Wait until after everyone has finished eating and coffee is served.

Electronic Etiquette

Although this area of etiquette is fairly new, electronic etiquette guidelines have never been more necessary.

Yes, e-mail is easy and fun to use, and we have a tendency to be casual in our approach to it. That attitude is a big mistake in the workplace. Remember that e-mail does not just go away when you hit the Delete button. It can be retrieved and traced. In addition, your company owns your computer and is free to examine any functions you perform and any material you download. A major national bank recently fired a score of employees for improper use of e-mail. In other words, if you wouldn't want it posted on the office bulletin board, don't put it into an e-mail. The same basic policies and considerations apply to Internet use.

E-mail Minefields

The cardinal rule in cyberspace is this: If you wouldn't say it in person, do not say it online.

In the business world, the rule is: Never say anything in an e-mail that you wouldn't say in a company memo, in a letter, or in front of a large audience.

By law, companies can be forced to produce all internal documents—including e-mail—that are related to a case. So that "hilarious" off-color joke that you send to your co-workers can be the nail in your corporate coffin if it's seen as sexual harassment. Ditto for any kind of sexual commentary, racist remarks, and general disparaging comments about others. And don't even think about using company computers to get into porn and gambling sites.

Be equally careful in discussing highly sensitive company issues or engaging in disparaging commentary about your company or its business practices and associates. These messages, too, have found their way to corporate headquarters and even government authorities.

It might sound extreme, but loose chat can cost companies millions of dollars in jury awards, massive settlements, and criminal fines.

To Send, or Not?

E-mail is a flawed medium because it never will provide you with the tone of voice or gestures that say so much. When in doubt, use the telephone or have a face-to-face meeting.

Furthermore, its speed and convenience are not licenses to be sloppy in your communications. Here is a checklist for sending e-mails that will work for you, not against you:

- ◆ Is e-mail the best vehicle to send this message in the first place? Are you sure you aren't using it to avoid talking to someone?

- ◆ Does the information in it deal only with your job responsibilities and your approved functions?

- ◆ Is there anything in this document that would be embarrassing to your company or yourself if it came to public attention?

- ◆ Is the language professional rather than emotional or reprimanding?

- ◆ Does this message require an immediate response? If not, consider all appropriate response options—a return e-mail, phone call, note, or face-to-face conversation.

Once you are satisfied with your answers to the checklist above, make sure that you send the e-mail only to the people who need to know the information. Copy all the appropriate people. Don't expect the person who originally receives it to distribute it to all concerned.

Time Is Money

Without being cold, make sure you get rid of all wordiness and tangents. Keep your sentences short and factual. Keep paragraphs short. Make sure you explain technical jargon if anyone who receives the e-mail won't understand it.

Presenting Your E-mail

Make sure you use a format that is not flowery and adapts easily to all computer systems. Use upper- and lowercase letters. All caps is the cyber-equivalent of screaming, while all lowercase is tedious to read and absorb. Consider the reader's point of view when you write. Make sure you are considerate, direct, and factual, using professional language. Make sure you double-check all facts and figures.

Proofread, Proofread, Proofread!

Your punctuation needs to be consistent and correct. Ditto your spelling. Spell-check is better than nothing—yet it's not infallible. Check for meanings of words, and be careful to check minor spelling variations that have major implications if used incorrectly. For example, don't announce your intention to "resign" (quit, retire) a vendor when you really intend to "re-sign" (sign up again) the company.

Spell out abbreviated words such as "w/" and "info."

Your sentences should be complete and grammatically correct.

 Faux Pas _____

It's a big mistake to ignore a salutation in an e-mail as well as a closing. Just because the medium is speedy, it should not be rude. Use "Dear Jim," or perhaps even simply, "Jim," but never "Hey, you!"

Subject lines that are out of date or inaccurate can wreak havoc when you are trying to retrieve them later on. When something does not need a reply, write "NRN" (no reply needed) and "F.Y.I." (for your information) in the subject line when the message is purely informative. Never leave the subject line blank.

Answer, Man

Reply to business e-mails within 24 hours, even if you don't have all the essential information. For example, it's helpful to know, "I am out of the office and will be able to get the information you need on Wednesday." Reply to personal e-mails as soon as you can, at least within 48 hours.

Telephone Etiquette

Everybody knows how to use the telephone, but very few people know how to use it to their best advantage.

When you speak to someone on the telephone, vocal quality counts for 70 percent of the initial impression you make, and the words spoken count for 30 percent. Listeners base their opinions of you not only on what you say but also how you say it and the tone of your voice.

Mind Your P's and Q's

Smile while you're speaking on the telephone because—believe it or not—your listener can hear your smile. Use the old mirror-by-the-telephone trick: Place a small mirror next to the telephone so that you will be aware of your expression as you speak. It works.

Speak unto others as you would have them speak unto you. It's up to you, the speaker, to make sure that the listener gets the message loud (but not too loud) and clear. The person on the other end shouldn't have to work hard to hear you and understand what you are saying.

When using the telephone, use your mouth for speaking only. Eschew chewing, eating, or drinking.

Answering

Answer the telephone no later than the second ring if you can. Identify yourself with both your name and company or department.

◆ "Hello" is better than "Hi."

◆ Say, "May I tell her who's calling?" not "Who's calling?"

It is up to you to determine how your telephone will be answered, not only by you but also by members of your staff. You have to let them know what you expect. You can try calling your own office to spot check.

Also, don't let a phone call preempt an in-person visit. For example, if it's 2:00 P.M., the person with the 2:00 P.M. appointment has priority over the person you are speaking with on the telephone.

Caller identification is now available on many business telephone systems. But even though you may know who's calling, you probably shouldn't answer the phone as though you do. It might make people think you're avoiding them if you don't answer the next time. Also, it might be one person using someone else's phone—and that can lead to embarrassment.

Placing Calls

Place your own calls whenever possible. If the person you are calling has to wait for you to come on the line, she is apt to think you consider your time more important than hers. This perception could cause the conversation to begin with a standoffish atmosphere.

Let people know right away who's calling. Every business telephone call should begin with the caller introducing him- or herself, identifying the company, and saying whom the call is intended for. This information enhances your chances of being put through promptly to the person you are trying to reach, and you will sound confident and in control.

> ### Live and Learn
>
> With the proliferation of cell phones and digital telephones, the majority of today's business is still conducted over the telephone. That figure is not likely to go down, even with the increased use of e-mail. People are now using telephones in circumstances in which they previously would not even have considered calling. And e-mail, although convenient and accessible to a growing percentage of the population, can never have the intimacy and, perhaps, the urgency of a telephone call. The human voice will always have a power that cannot be duplicated by any form of written communication.

Try to call when you know it's convenient for the other person. If you call a business just before closing time, you will be rushed and given halfhearted attention at best.

If you get another call while on the telephone, remember that the first caller has priority. Tell the second caller you will get back to him or her and resume your first conversation.

Trivial or long-winded calls are annoying intrusions in a busy workday. Make sure you have a good reason to make a call, and deal with your business in a prompt, organized way. Another consideration is that such calls convey the impression that your job is of so little importance that you have time to make chatty, unnecessary calls.

If your call somehow gets disconnected in the middle of a conversation, you should call back immediately—whatever the circumstances.

Closing a Call

People remember the way telephone conversations end. At the end of your call, thank the person for the call and do your best to try to end on a positive note. Never conclude by just saying, "See ya," "Bye-bye," or "Later." Say good-bye and let the other person hang up before replacing the receiver.

If you have a chatty caller who is droning on too long, say something like "I'll have to hang up now. My 2:00 appointment is here," or "Much as I'd like to chat, I'm on a deadline at the moment. Is there anything else I can help you with?"

After the call, do your homework. Everybody appreciates a follow-up and follow-through. Keep any agreements you make. If you have promised to provide information or data, get that material to the other person promptly.

Telephone Tag

Playing phone tag is annoying, frustrating, and irritating, but it seems to be inescapable. You might make a couple of dozen calls a day at your desk and connect with only about a fifth of them on the first try. But you can improve your chances of success.

Let's face it: Part of an assistant's job is to give the boss a chance to get some work done. However, the assistant who acts as gatekeeper can become your ally if treated with consideration and respect.

If you don't know the assistant's name, ask the receptionist when you first place the call. If you are calling for Mr. Jones and you reach his assistant without going through a receptionist, simply ask the assistant his or her name after you identify yourself and be sure to use the name during all conversations with the assistant. This approach scores a lot of points. Using the name on subsequent calls has the added benefit of displaying confidence and courtesy, and it gives the impression you and Mr. Jones know each other well. It also indicates that you remembered his or her name.

Having established a cordial relationship with the assistant over the telephone can be very helpful in getting information, such as when Mr. Jones is apt to be free, when the best time to call him is, and what time he returns from lunch.

When you get the "best time," make it clear to the assistant that you will be calling then: "Fine, I'll call back about 2 P.M. then to have a five-minute chat with Mr. Jones about the Frazier property in Oregon. I know he's been anxious to get some information about it."

If you are put on hold, be patient. If the assistant has been especially helpful, a thank-you note or e-mail probably would be in order.

If you are asking that Mr. Jones return your call, tell the assistant the best time to reach you. Be as specific as you can. If you are not available for the return call, you will have to begin the whole process again.

Cell Phones

Cell phones have been compared to pacifiers for adults. They make people think they are connected to a vital source of informational nourishment. It seems to me that the most insecure and/or boastful people are the ones who are most loud and ostentatious about using their cell phones.

Nevertheless, ownership of a cell phone does not include a license to be rude. Do not whip out your cell phone in a restaurant, at a party, on the train, or in any situation in which the call inflicts your half of the conversation on those around you.

If you are going into a business meeting and are not expecting a genuinely urgent call to come in, turn off the cell phone. When you must leave the phone on to allow an urgent call to come in, apologize in advance to the meeting's chairperson. Explain that you will excuse yourself when the call comes through and return with the phone turned off. If the chairperson objects, then you must remain outside the meeting until the call is handled or rely on the minutes of the meeting to catch up.

The same goes for the theater, a museum, and other places where the ringing of a phone would be unwelcome. Some restaurants now require patrons to leave their cell phones with the maître d' and will inform you if you get a call. If you need to take a call when you are in a restaurant, leave the room.

Most cell phones have a voicemail backup that will handle your calls when it's inappropriate to have a conversation. Use it!

Use two-way messaging to send and receive messages without speaking.

Always keep your conversations as quiet and brief as possible.

Honor the rules about cell phone use wherever you are. Some hospitals, airplanes, clubs, and restaurants prohibit cell phone use. Pay attention to the rules and follow them.

When you're driving:

- ◆ Pay full attention to the road.

- ◆ Check out the road conditions before you make or take a call.

- ◆ Let voicemail pick up when it's unsafe or inconvenient to take a call.

- ◆ Make sure your phone is in a position where you easily can see it and reach it.

- ◆ Invest in hands-free speakerphones or hands-free accessories for your car. In many states, it's now the only legal way to talk on a cell phone while driving.

Beepers

The same principle applies to beepers. Be prepared to be out of touch in certain situations or get a beeper that can be switched to vibrate when necessary.

Camera and Walkie-Talkie Phones

Just when we thought cell phones—and their users—couldn't get much ruder, they have.

Cell phones with cameras aren't toys. The technology is miraculous; yet fraught with problems. In short, you can get yourself into a lot of trouble, so be careful.

Legislation is emerging barring their use and meting out punishment for their inappropriate use. Some communities prohibit their use in public park–owned restrooms, locker rooms, and showers. Never mind what the law says. There always will be loopholes and arguments and appeals.

Instead, consider this: Never take a photo with your cell phone without getting permission from the person whose picture you are taking. That might take some of the "jokes" out of life; yet it's the one certain way not to offend. Sensitivity to the subjects of the pictures must come before the picture-taker's sense of fun.

The bottom line: Photograph others as you'd have them photograph you. If you wouldn't like some of your actions immortalized, don't immortalize those same actions of others.

Walkie-talkies might have been fun when you were playing G.I. Joe in preteen years, but they have very little place in civilized society, if any at all.

Push-to-talk phones, as they are called, allow the caller to press a button on their cell phone and immediately chat with someone else who has this service from the same carrier. Think of it as the difference between e-mail and instant messaging. The phones chirp each time one side of the conversation begins and the other side ends. When the user has the handset on speakerphone with the volume turned up, anyone standing remotely near you can hear the obnoxious chirps as well as the conversation.

There are situations where such immediacy and speed are advantages—in medical emergency services, for example. Even in such emergencies, some manners need apply:

- Don't start talking immediately when you beep someone. Wait for a response before talking. (Remember those good-guy/bad-guy movies when the police used their walkie-talkies for good ends? The conversation always went something like: "Jake, are you there?" Jake: "I'm here, sir." Not a bad model to emulate.)

- Turn the speaker volume down, as low as possible.

- Turn the speaker off whenever possible and hold the phone next to your ear.

- Turn the phone on vibrate mode whenever possible.

Voice-Mail

Leaving voice mail is another business fact of life that is here to stay. It's a very good and useful tool for conveying information within your company. However, clients or others calling in from outside are apt to find it annoying. And, depending on the message, it can be almost as bad as dealing with a real and really disagreeable person.

The message on this medium should give the caller some choices—leave a message, call another extension, or switch to the receptionist. However, few things are more annoying than messages with too many, mostly irrelevant options.

The message you leave should embody the journalist's five W's—who, what, when, where, and why: "This is Mary Mitchell on Thursday, June 1. I'll be traveling all day today and will not be able to return calls until after 7 P.M., Philadelphia time. Please leave your name, telephone number, and a brief message."

When you are the caller, be brief and to the point. For example, "This is Mary Mitchell, calling on Thursday, June 1, about the training seminar. I'm calling to confirm that 12 people are registered from your company."

Mind Your P's and Q's

When it comes to leaving messages (outgoing or incoming), vocal quality is crucial. Make sure you know what you're going to say. Practice saying it. Speak clearly without being either sharp or loud. The message within the message should convey confidence.

Before recording your voicemail message, do the following:

- Write out your specific words and make several practice tries.

- Smile when you speak so that you sound enthusiastic and approachable.

- Forget about sound effects or other gimmicks; cute is unprofessional.

When you get someone else's voicemail:

- Be sure to leave a message, even if you get a wrong number. Saying that you dialed incorrectly will allay security concerns.

- Mention the best time for you to be reached.

- Leave your complete telephone number, pausing between the area code and local number.

The Fax

Rule 1. Don't tie up the fax machine. The transmission should be expected, important, and specifically addressed.

Rule 2. Start off with a cover sheet saying whom it's from, the number of pages (the cover sheet is included in page count), and to whom it goes.

E-mail Documents

Many companies now honor e-mailed documents, even invoices. Before you send such documents, check with your contact within the company. Alert them that the document is coming. Ask if a hard copy should be sent through the mail.

Home Offices

The era of the home office has arrived. Major multinational corporations support the concept in very real ways—providing technical support, flexible schedules, and making it clear to the public that its team members maintain home offices. Fortunately, consumers no longer believe that a person's ability to provide a service depends on bricks and mortar.

Perceptions Are Reality

Just as you don't need to wear a business suit to the home office, you don't help your professionalism by donning jammies and bunny slippers during the workday. Why? You simply won't feel professional, that's why. Shower. Shave. Put on street clothes. How we dress directly affects our job performance. When we dress for work, we can consider ourselves at work and then deal effectively with the distractions and relationships that come with any job.

Making the Rules

Setting boundaries with family members can be a major challenge. A bigger challenge is actually maintaining those boundaries. We must train our families. Just because we have a home office doesn't mean that it is an endless supply of paper clips, scotch tape, and pens—or that anyone can come in at any time to stock up.

Here are some tips to further your professionalism and peace of mind:

♦ Eliminate a home telephone line from your office.

♦ Establish your office number and tell your family that, during established hours, it's best to call you at work. Otherwise, you won't hear the telephone.

♦ Keep reasonable "available" hours. For example, keep your telephone ringer turned off during certain hours—say, from 6 P.M. until 9 A.M. Have a reliable voice mail system so that you can retrieve messages. After all, if you were on-site in a remote company building, there would be a limit on when you could be reached, reasonably.

♦ Hire childcare during your office hours. If you don't take your work time seriously, no one else will. And otherwise you won't be doing your job—either as an employee or a parent. It's well worth the investment both in professional effectiveness and family harmony. When you have someone taking care of your kids, it puts you off-limits during work hours. This is a good signal to give your offspring. They will perceive you as a working professional.

♦ Sound of body, sound of mind. Working at home usually is less physical an endeavor than working outside the home. Compensate for that by scheduling exercise and physical activity. Otherwise, your body and brain will turn to flab.

Say What? _____

Part of the Family/Friends Training Process 101 is conflict resolution. It looks like this:

A family member wants you to run an errand. After all, you're "at home." Trouble is, it's the middle of your workday. How do you handle it?

First of all, acknowledge the need for the favor. "I know it's important for the cat to get her shots. Right now is the middle of my workday. Let's figure out a time that works for everybody, okay?"

Say this in the same unemotional tone that you would say, "It's raining outside." No defensiveness. No argument. No apology. No rebuke. If you break your own rules, nobody wins—not your family, not your clients, not your employer, and certainly not you.

It's equally important that you let potential houseguests know your work routine, lest they assume you are at home to be their playmate. Make sure you advise them well in advance of the visit.

Your Branch Office

Your car becomes your branch office. Remember that. Make sure it's clean and neat. What is on the outside is simply a reflection of what's inside—you. Whether you are conducting a meeting or driving to one, your car must reflect professional conduct and accomplishment.

It's likely that your colleagues will see your car before they see your office space. Make sure you tend to its appearance and maintenance as you do your own. Pay attention to schedules for oil changes and service. Invest in a car vacuum and use it. Don't collect junk and trash—either in the seats or the trunk.

When you are on the job—no matter where it is—you are on display. Familiarity can't be allowed to breed carelessness; in fact, the necessity of spending a great deal of time with your co-workers demands even more attention to the details of courtesy and kind behavior.

The Least You Need to Know

- ◆ Treat your staff with fairness, your colleagues with friendliness, and your boss with honor.

- ◆ Holding doors and showing deference to women in other ways have long since vanished from the business arena.

- ◆ Develop good telephone skills. Speak clearly. Be courteous. Leave complete but concise messages. Return calls promptly.

- ◆ When visiting someone's office, be polite, be friendly, be brief, and be gone.

- ◆ Don't e-mail anything you wouldn't want on the bulletin board.

- ◆ Your home office is just that, an office. Dress for work, keep your office hours, and don't allow distractions that might throw your work performance off.

Chapter 17

Meetings: The Boardroom

In This Chapter

- ◆ Boardroom etiquette
- ◆ The agenda
- ◆ The business card

Don't be misled about meetings. You've probably heard that corporate America spends too much time in meetings, that meetings hamper rather than promote productivity, and that the world of telecommunications is making face-to-face meetings passé, often replaced by conference calls and teleconferences.

You may believe all of that or some of it, but the fact remains that important things do happen at meetings, and perhaps the most important of these is that people learn about—and form judgments about—each other.

Strategies for a Successful Meeting

Many of us go into meetings without being fully prepared and make the wrong impression by what we don't say (rather than what we do say) and by gestures we make unknowingly. Think of meetings as opportunities to impress your colleagues and superiors and to meet others.

With that in mind, here are some tips about how best to take advantage of these opportunities:

- **Do your homework.** Make sure to read all the materials provided in advance, including the agenda, before going to the meeting. Find out who will be attending and the purpose of the meeting; then, focus your preparations. Prepare any comments in advance so that you are not rambling and repeating yourself.

Live and Learn

Speaking of homework, you might want to familiarize yourself with *Robert's Rules of Order,* which you can find at any library. Several websites also contain the full 1915 text, and include revisions that accommodate such modern meeting elements as online documents. This universally recognized guide to procedure will only come into play at the most formal of meetings. However, you never know when you'll be at a meeting and someone will say, "How should we proceed with this?" And you'll hear yourself saying, "Well, *Robert's Rules of Order* suggests ...."

- **Arrive on time or a little early.** Nobody takes a latecomer seriously. Lateness is an affront to those who took the trouble to arrive on time. And, no, it doesn't convey the message that you are very busy, only that you are disorganized.

- **Bring all necessary materials.** Make sure to take along the agenda, papers, pens, and a notebook. Have them at hand so that you don't have to fish around while others wait.

- **Store your baggage.** Keep briefcases and purses on the floor, not on spare chairs or, worse still, on the conference table.

- **Don't play.** Leave the paper clips alone. Don't stretch the rubber bands or doodle on your notepad.

Mind Your P's and Q's

Invest in a fine writing instrument. People really do remember those nuances. Think quality over extravagance.

- **Turn off cell phones and pagers.** Unless you are expecting a genuinely urgent call, turn off your cell phone and switch your beeper to vibrate mode before the meeting begins. If you do expect an urgent call, let the chairperson know when you enter the meeting and sit near the door so that you can leave and return with the least disruption.

◆ **Keep your feet on the floor.** If you must cross your legs, do so at the ankles. Otherwise, you look inattentive and altogether too casual. Make sure your shoes are polished and in good repair. Scuffed shoes imply a person who disregards details.

◆ **Keep ties on.** Unless the person calling the meeting strongly suggests otherwise and actually sheds his own tie, keep yours around your neck.

◆ **Don't cross your arms in front of you.** It communicates hostility. You want your body posture to suggest open-mindedness and approachability.

◆ **Keep your elbows off the table.** Don't lean on them, propping up your head in your hand. It looks unprofessional, sloppy, and like you might be having trouble staying awake.

◆ **Sit straight and don't slouch.** You will look alert and attentive.

◆ **Maintain a high-energy and involvement level.** No matter how much your mind wants to roam, remember that meetings are a place for team players and enthusiasm.

 **Faux Pas** _____

Don't ask for food or a drink at a meeting unless refreshments are being offered. If refreshments are served, get rid of your coffee cup, plate, and napkin as soon as it is convenient. Your place at the conference table should be clean.

◆ **Enter the meeting room decisively.** Unless you are certain about how the seating arrangements work, ask where you should sit. Shake hands with your colleagues, introducing yourself to those you don't know and calling by name those you do know. Do these preliminaries while you are still standing. If you are seated and a new introduction is made, stand up.

◆ **Avoid electronic toys.** Don't even think about using your PDA or laptop at a meeting for reasons other than the specifics of the meeting. It's rude beyond words and unfair to others at the meeting. You're being paid to participate in the meeting, not just to show up. Use them only to retrieve info or note future meetings and important dates. Otherwise, take discreet notes and transfer data later.

Speak Up

Think before you speak and keep what you say as brief and to the point as possible. Avoid confrontational language and public criticism. Establishing battle lines helps no one. Say, "I disagree because it seems to me that …" instead of "You're wrong. If you took time to read the report, you would know that …."

Mind Your P's and Q's

Meeting etiquette is like stage lighting. You notice it only when it's bad.

Don't interrupt someone who is speaking. No matter how much you disagree, wait for the speaker to make his or her point before interjecting your opinion.

In addition, remember that it's better to make recommendations and suggestions than to give orders or take inflexible positions.

Other points to bear in mind:

♦ **Use positive language.** Don't introduce your points apologetically. "This might be a bad idea, but ...."

♦ **Use the editorial "we."** When discussing the work and position of your department or company, don't take personal credit for things when they're going well if you are not willing to take personal responsibility for them when they're going poorly.

♦ **Use proper titles.** Use an honorific to refer to others in the meeting, even though you may be on a first name basis at other times. Say, "Mr. Daniels just made the point that ..."; don't say, "Tom here thinks ...."

Teleconferencing

You can inadvertently put on a display of bad manners unless you are clued in to the new rules for the electronic meeting place.

♦ **Be prepared.** Bring everything you might need to the meeting. You don't want people to be staring at a blank screen while you go to fetch something.

♦ **Dress down.** The camera can distort bright colors, and bright tones and patterns will come across more intensely. Pale blue shirts are better than white. The camera will compensate for the brightness of a white shirt, making your face look darker. Because the camera doesn't like white, you might want to take notes on blue paper.

♦ **Think details.** Take it easy on the makeup and jewelry. Men should minimize five-o'clock shadow.

♦ **Sit up straight.** Posture is more important than ever.

♦ **Don't look at the monitor.** Speak to the camera lens. Stay within the range of the camera. When you move out of camera range, people wonder what you're doing.

Teleconferencing has become so commonplace that a rehearsal or two is a good investment of time and money. Gather some colleagues and stage a meeting. The tape should provide some important tips and insights.

As the Chair

If you are chairing the meeting, pick a time that's convenient for everyone. If possible, avoid scheduling a meeting first thing Monday morning or late Friday afternoon. People are often occupied and/or distracted at these times. In addition, give plenty of notice. Two weeks is an ideal minimum.

Decide on the seating. Remember that the two seats on either side of the chairperson are considered the most significant seats.

Create an atmosphere in which frank, open discussion is not only safe, but encouraged. If things get heated, it's your job to keep order and mediate any conflicts. Keep the spirit of the meeting positive. Don't criticize or chastise. Avoid undermining authority by hotly disagreeing with someone who outranks you, particularly your boss.

Consider the schedules and jobs of the participants. Make sure all paperwork is distributed well in advance. Provide breaks so that people can make telephone calls and use the restrooms.

At the end of the meeting, give credit to those who deserve it. Also, write a précis of the meeting within 48 hours, distribute it to the participants, and set the date for the next meeting.

Details

In some cases the use of formal name cards is appropriate. They should be two-sided so people across the table can read them. Nametags should bear the first and last names, without Mr., Ms., or Mrs. Use Dr. if appropriate.

Put out plenty of pads, paper, pencils, sticky notes, paper clips, rubber bands, and tape. Also, find out in advance if you will need a lectern, a microphone, a blackboard or whiteboard, a flip chart, audiovisual aids, or a photocopier.

If you are serving snacks, avoid greasy items like chips and Danish pastries and too much caffeine and sugar. They can make people sluggish and/or on edge. Always provide a decaffeinated, low-fat, healthy alternative. Make sure water glasses, pitchers, or bottles of water are close by.

The Agenda

The agenda should include all items to be discussed along with the amount of time to be devoted to each. It should be written so that the most important items are handled first, in case the meeting runs short. Make sure that everyone has a copy of the agenda well in advance of the meeting.

Here is a sample agenda:

TO: Marketing and public relations staff

FROM: Chairman's name

PURPOSE: Meeting, Wednesday, February 28, 2–4 P.M.

(If the meeting is to take place at mealtime, such as 8–10 A.M., or during lunch or dinner, say something like "Sandwiches and beverages will be provided.")

PLACE: Conference room, 10th floor

AGENDA:

1. Review quarterly goals and action plan (30 minutes)

    ♦ Summary by public relations director on achievements

    ♦ Report by publicity assistant on upcoming media coverage

2. Discuss upcoming media opportunities (15 minutes)

3. Establish priorities for next six months (10 minutes)

4. Open discussion (20 minutes)

5. Conclusion, summary, and action plan assignments (20 minutes)

Business Cards

Because the kinds of meetings discussed in this chapter are often occasions for handing around business cards, this is a good place to discuss them.

Your business card is an important and personal part of your communications within the corporate culture, and you should know how and when to use it.

Business cards have three main uses:

- They provide vital information about you—your name, your company, your title, and how you can be reached.

- They can be clipped to a document, a photograph, a magazine, or anything you're sending to someone who might find the information useful, letting the recipient know that you're the sender and providing your contact information.

- They can be used as enclosures in gifts or with flowers.

How and when to present your card:

- Present your card with the type side up. When someone hands you a card, look at the person to connect card with face.

- Don't appear anxious to thrust your card on a senior executive. Wait until asked.

- Be selective. If you are with a large group of people, don't give your card to everyone. Doing so is pushy and creates the impression that you're trying to sell something.

- Some people give their business card to anyone they meet. Not a good idea. On the one hand, it's irritating. On the other, you may regret supplying a stranger with your name and business address.

- Be unobtrusive about giving someone your card at a social function. Think of this action as a private exchange between two individuals.

- If your cards are soiled, damaged, or out-of-date, get new cards. It's better to give no card than to give one that looks bad.

- You never know when someone is going to ask for your business card, so carry a few with you at social as well as business functions. If you don't have a card, apologize and write out the information on a piece of paper.

- Whether you are dining at Joe's Chili Joint or at a black tie dinner, business cards should not surface during a meal. If asked, pass one as discreetly as possible. In fact, if the event has been billed as a social rather than business-related affair, you should be discreet about talking business at all.

All business meetings—regardless of location (boardroom or teleconferencing center) and participants (your colleagues, your boss, or your employees)—require preparation, a healthy helping of respect for all present, and a knowledge of the basics of meeting etiquette.

The Least You Need to Know

◆ Do your homework before a meeting and show up with everything you will need.

◆ If you haven't been assigned a seat, ask where you should sit.

◆ Show up on time or early. Stick to the agenda.

◆ Think body language. A slouch says you don't care.

◆ Keep your jacket on during meetings. Anything else looks unprofessional.

◆ Keep your business cards in pristine condition and always be discreet when giving your card to someone. Keep your cards with you at all times—you never know when an opportunity will present itself.

Part 5

Saying the Right Thing

Human interaction often involves conflict, criticism, and even some awkwardness. We have to be ready to respond appropriately and with grace to any challenge. Part 5 covers techniques for handing conflict situations and for receiving and delivering criticism, and how to apologize. These situations can be approached in a way that will reduce the tension and defuse some of the potential fireworks.

Meeting and dealing with people from different cultures or with disabilities too often causes confusion, apprehension, and tension. This situation occurs even when people on both sides are doing their utmost to make the encounter pleasant and relaxed.

We also discuss happier encounters—those involving giving and receiving compliments and gifts.

Chapter 18

It's a Small World

In This Chapter

- ◆ Stereotypes
- ◆ Greetings
- ◆ Business dealings
- ◆ Strange foods
- ◆ Too close for comfort
- ◆ Gestures you should avoid

Today Americans are encountering persons from different cultural backgrounds more often and more intimately than ever before. In 1980 the number of foreign-born people living in, but not citizens of, the United States was 14 million. In 1990 it was 20 million. More than 31 million people speak English as their second language.

The ease and speed of overseas travel; the ability to communicate instantly through satellite and computer; and the interlocking and overlapping business interests in the Americas, Europe, Africa, and Asia mean that we are in touch with the world's diversity as never before.

It's exciting, fascinating, and full of opportunity. It's also full of snares and dangers.

This chapter discusses ways of avoiding some of the more common errors. Although this information will be helpful, the best practices to keep in mind are the basic foundation stones of etiquette—kindness and respect for others. These precepts suggest a willingness to set aside your ingrained ideas about correct behavior and to approach new situations with an open, inquiring mind.

Smashing Stereotypes

A good way to begin to learn about others is to get rid of what you think you already know about them. Here are some common generalizations that you need to jettison:

- All Latin cultures hold the siesta inviolate.

- Visitors from abroad are eager to be taken to a restaurant that serves what Americans consider to be the visitors' favorite foods.

- Signs and gestures and loud English will bridge language gaps. (Noise never helps, and gestures send various and not always appropriate messages, depending upon the background and traditions of the observer.)

- Asians are remote and "inscrutable."

- Germans are cold and superefficient.

- Japanese are basically shy.

If you are visiting another country or are hosting or otherwise spending time with people from other cultures, don't hesitate to confess your ignorance of other cultures and ask for help. Your candor will be appreciated and your errors more cheerfully tolerated.

You can also do some research on your own. There are numerous resources, both in print and online available. A few suggestions are Norine Dresser's *Multicultural Manners: New Rules of Etiquette for a Changing Society* (John Wiley & Sons, 1996) and *Multicultural Celebrations: Today's Rules of Etiquette for Life's Special Occasions* (Three Rivers Press, 1999), as well as Roget Axtell's "Do's and Taboos" series, especially *Do's and Taboos Around the World* (John Wiley & Sons, 1993). Online, the National Coalition Building Institute International's website (www.ncbi.org) provides a variety of information dedicated to better understanding and bridge building among cultures.

Gracious Greetings

When greeting someone, an American's first instinct is to stick out his or her hand, look directly at the other person, and smile. In some situations this habit can mean making three mistakes at once. And the moment of greeting is when crucial first impressions are made. Methods and styles of greeting vary greatly around the world, and you need to know which practices apply in different circumstances.

- When greeting Asians for the first time, do not initiate the handshake. You may be forcing a physical contact that the other person finds uncomfortable. Many Asians, particularly Japanese, have learned to accept the handshake when dealing with Westerners. Because the bow is the customary greeting in Japan, a slight bow of the head when responding to a proffered handshake is appropriate. Westerners generally are not expected to be familiar with the complex Japanese bowing protocols.

> **CAUTION** **Faux Pas**
> A handshake is not the universally approved greeting. Also, "Look 'em right in the eye" is not always the best advice.

- Most Latinos are more accustomed to physical contact. Even people who know each other only slightly may embrace when greeting.

- Middle Easterners, particularly Muslims, avoid body contact with the opposite sex, but persons of the same sex commonly hug when greeting each other. When shaking hands, men should be careful not to pull their hand away too quickly. Orthodox Jews also avoid all physical contact with those of the opposite sex who are not family members.

> **Live and Learn**
> Same-sex hand holding, seen by some as a signal of a homosexual relationship, is a common gesture of friendship in many countries, particularly Mediterranean and Middle Eastern countries.

- People from France, Spain, Italy, and Portugal greet friends by kissing on both cheeks.

- The smile is the near-universal gesture of friendliness, and in America its meaning is usually clear. The person smiling is happy, amused, and/or sending out a friendly signal. In other cultures the smile may be sending other signals. In some Latin cultures, for example, the smile may be used to say "Excuse me" or "Please."

- If a person from another culture does not return your greeting smile, it doesn't indicate hostility or bad manners. In some Asian cultures, smiling is a gesture to be reserved for informal occasions, and smiling while being formally introduced would be considered disrespectful.

◆ In many cultures, avoiding eye contact is a sign of respect, but such behavior can lead to misunderstandings. For example, some Korean shopkeepers have been accused of disrespecting their non-Korean customers because the shopkeepers avoided making eye contact. The same sort of misunderstanding has occurred between American teachers and Asian students who do not look at the teacher while he or she is speaking.

Let's Do Business

When asked their impressions of American business people, foreigners often begin by saying Americans are very open and friendly. They find, however, that this friendliness tends to be shallow and short-lived. Americans come on strong at the beginning, but do not live up to the implied promise of an ongoing friendship or, at least, personal relationship.

Many business people from other cultures say they are put off by the abruptness with which Americans seem to want to get things done. We say that time is money. We work hard and play hard and eat lunch standing up or at the desk. Some people, particularly Asians and Middle Easterners, don't consider getting right down to business as an admirable approach to getting things done.

Another problem is that Americans tend to jump into a first-name basis rather quickly, apparently laboring under the delusion that everybody enjoys being called by his first name by everybody else.

High Context vs. Low Context

An insight into how to avoid these and some other problems American business people encounter on the global scene can be gained by considering what anthropologist Edward T. Hall calls high-context and low-context cultures.

The United States, Germany, Switzerland, Canada, and the Scandinavian countries are low-context cultures, meaning that business people tend to send unambiguous messages with a lot of specificity and clear descriptions. For them, time is a straight-line commodity when it comes to getting things done. You start at point A and you go right to point B.

High-context countries include China, Japan, Korea, Spain, Greece, Turkey, the Arab world, and Latin America. High-context cultures place more emphasis on nonverbal communication, indirect verbal signals, and implicit meanings. Rituals are important. Time is not a straight-line concept. The road from point A to point B is highly textured. The road has curves and detours and scenery.

Low-context people tend to view high-context people as sneaky, secretive, or at best, mysterious, and high-context people tend to view low-context people as moving too fast on the one hand and being excessively talkative and redundant on the other.

So, when dealing with high-context business people, you need to be patient and to recognize that a lot of things are happening at once. Let's take the example of a savvy American business executive visiting the office of a Korean colleague:

> The appointment is at noon, and even though the visitor knows it is important to arrive on time, he expects to be kept waiting. The American waits quietly. Reading or doing something else while waiting is not a good idea: Doing so would indicate that the upcoming meeting is not the visitor's primary focus.
>
> The host comes out to greet the guest. They shake hands, and the American gives a slight bow. Other people are in the office where the meeting is to take place. The American greets them: more handshakes, slight bows. The guest sits, keeping both feet on the floor.
>
> If refreshments are offered, the guest accepts after a mild and insincere refusal. He uses his right hand to drink.
>
> All the while, the Korean host is being gracious and hospitable, and the American responds in the same spirit. They do not discuss business just yet. The host may hold several conversations at once, talk on the telephone, and otherwise digress. But he will always return to the important issues, and inevitably, things will get done, and all parties will part cordially.

This experience may strike the American as inefficient, but it works for a considerable segment of the world.

Mind Your P's and Q's

In some cultures, if you effusively admire a possession of another person, particularly of your host, he or she may feel obliged to offer it to you as a gift. You, however, need not accept. In fact, you should firmly, but politely, refuse.

Is It Time to Eat?

Many foreigners find the customs and terminology that accompany eating in America odd, disconcerting, or baffling. Why do some American executives like to conduct business at breakfast, whereas we often consider lunch as little more than an afterthought? We load our water glasses with ice. We drink denatured (decaffeinated) coffee. We eat strange things and at odd times. Consider the following:

◆ The main meal of the day in other countries is taken at midday. In America the main meal comes at the end of the workday. We call the evening meal "dinner," a word that signifies the midday meal in other English-speaking countries.

◆ The evening meal in America is served, generally, within an hour either way of 7 P.M. Elsewhere it is generally later and generally lighter. In Spain, supper commonly begins at 10 P.M.

◆ The English have tea in the afternoon, usually around 4 P.M. This meal consists of tea, small sandwiches, and pastries. High tea is not a more elaborate version of tea. It is, in fact, an informal replacement for supper, which is eaten later in the evening.

In addition, brunch is considered a curious American invention in places where it is known at all. A foreign visitor will probably find its timing disconcerting.

Unfamiliar Foods

Here are some commonplace American foods that foreigners find unusual or, in some cases, repulsive:

◆ Marshmallows

◆ Corn on the cob, which many Europeans consider fit only for animals

◆ Pumpkin pie (also pecan pie)

◆ Sweet potatoes

◆ Crawfish

◆ Grits

◆ Hot dogs

When traveling in other countries, some Americans may have the same reaction to foods like sea urchins in Korea, horse meat in Japan, toasted grasshoppers in Mexico, sea slugs in China, sheep's eyes in the Middle East, haggis (sheep's organs and entrails) in Scotland, or kidney pie in England.

Also, what many Americans think of as Mexican food and Chinese food would not be welcome—or even recognized!—in Mexico and China. (When Chinese Americans want to say someone is losing touch with his Chinese heritage, they may call him "a chop suey man." Chop suey is a dish that Americans think is Chinese and Chinese think is American.)

Here are some general rules of etiquette to follow when you are confronted with unfamiliar food in a foreign land:

♦ If you don't know what it is, you might be better off not asking. Taste it. If you don't like it and are asked for your opinion, say something like "It has a very distinctive flavor."

♦ If you know what it is and don't want to try it, politely refuse. Or you can say something like "I know this is quite a delicacy, but I've tried it before and found it doesn't sit well with me."

♦ If you sense that a refusal would offend your host or fellow diners, cut it up and move it around on your dish so that it looks as if you are eating.

> **Live and Learn**
>
> Many Americans would just as soon eat a rat's tail as a cooked snail. And some people who consider snails to be a delicacy are repelled by the very idea of eating those good old Yankee standbys of corn on the cob and pumpkin pie.

Some cautionary notes:

♦ It is particularly important to respect the dietary rules of Muslims. They do not eat the flesh of any animal that scavenges, including pigs, goats, some birds, and sea scavengers like lobster. Food may not be prepared using the products derived from these animals, such as oils. Muslims do not drink alcohol and avoid foods cooked with alcohol.

♦ Do not point with your chopsticks or suck on them. Do not stick chopsticks upright in your rice. This placement is thought to bring bad luck.

♦ In Europe you may expect salads to be served after, rather than before, the main dish.

♦ Orthodox Jews do not eat pork or shellfish. Meat and fowl must be kosher, which means they must be ritually prepared. Meat and dairy products may not be eaten together in a meal.

♦ In Europe and elsewhere, the main dish is served at the beginning of the meal, so don't think of it as an appetizer. Also be careful at formal Chinese banquets. These events consist of many more courses than Westerners expect. Don't fill up too early, or you'll be too full to eat some wonderful delicacies later in the meal.

> **Faux Pas**
>
> What Americans call diapers are napkins in England. This could lead to some hilarious and/or embarrassing misunderstandings. When speaking to someone from the British Isles, refer to the linens you put on the table as serviettes.

You're in My Space

Whereas Asians stand farther away during conversations than Americans are used to, many Mediterranean people and Latinos stand so close that Americans believe that their personal space is being violated. Inexperienced Americans usually react by taking a step back. This strategy doesn't work because the other person will simply take a step forward. If you keep backing up, you may find yourself backed into a corner. On the other hand, if an Asian steps back during a conversation with you, control your urge to pursue him.

When with Asians, remember that touching can be a touchy subject. For example, you don't put your arm about the shoulders of a Japanese or take hold of his arm during a conversation. Don't be offended if Asian shopkeepers avoid contact by placing your change on the counter instead of in your hand. They are just being polite.

Making Gestures

When traveling abroad, some innocent or even friendly gestures can get you into trouble. These include making a circle of the thumb and index finger, pointing the index finger, and giving the thumbs-up sign.

Here are some other cautions:

◆ Avoid using the crooked index finger in a beckoning gesture. In many cultures the beckoning gesture is done with the arm extended and the fingers making an inward sweeping motion.

◆ In some places you may see people clap their hands or snap their fingers to get the attention of waiters or servants. In general, however, it is wise for the visitor to avoid doing either.

◆ Propping up your foot so that the sole of your shoe is facing someone is considered grossly insulting in most Asian countries and in parts of the Middle East.

◆ In some cultures it is considered rude to engage in conversation with your arms folded over your chest or with your arms akimbo (hands on hips).

Avoiding etiquette errors when dealing with people from other cultures, either at home or abroad, is difficult—and may even be impossible. The world is a complex mosaic of customs and attitudes, and even the most well-traveled and well-read person can transgress unknowingly.

> **Live and Learn**
>
> In Colombia people tap their elbows with their fingertips to say somebody is stingy. Americans point to their chest to indicate "me"; the Chinese point to their noses. The V for victory sign, when the palm turned inward, sends the "horns on you" message in England. It has an unpleasant sexual connotation. In general, it's not a good idea to copy gestures being made by others while traveling abroad. They may have meanings you do not fully comprehend.

So, although you may not always be correct, you must always be courteous. A willingness to confess ignorance and to ask for help, the ability to apologize gracefully, and a friendly, open attitude will get you through most difficulties.

Don't let anxiety about making social blunders cause your relations with those from other cultures to be mannered or stiff. Approach learning about new places and people with a spirit of adventure and a desire to learn, and you will generally find that people are more than willing to forgive innocent breaches of etiquette.

The Least You Need to Know

- ◆ In the United States, when you meet someone, you look him or her right in the eye, smile, and stick out your hand for a shake. In some places that would be making three mistakes all at once.

- ◆ Latin Americans and Middle Easterners are accustomed to physical contact. Many Asians find it disconcerting and even offensive.

- ◆ Foreigners say Americans tend to plunge into the business at hand too abruptly, that they are superficially friendly, and that they move to a first name basis too quickly—both socially and in business.

- ◆ Many familiar American gestures are considered offensive elsewhere—for example, the okay gesture, which involves making a circle of the thumb and forefinger. When in doubt, the safest thing to do is not make the gesture.

19

Conflict, Compliments, and Criticism

In This Chapter

♦ Giving and receiving criticism

♦ Giving and receiving compliments

♦ Delivering bad news

♦ Tips on handling difficult situations

Into each life a little strain must fall. Handling disagreements, delivering and receiving criticism and compliments, and working through conflicts are all crucial skills. Because conflict is inevitable, it is wise to be armed with some ideas and techniques for minimizing the pain and keeping disagreements from scarring a relationship or escalating into nuclear warfare.

The "Critical I"

Julia is having lunch with her cousin Carla. Julia has the egg salad on whole wheat. Carla has the smoked salmon. Even with the iced tea and tip, Julia figures her bill will come in under $10. Carla says, "Let's see: $16.50 should cover your end."

Julia can respond in a number of ways:

>Wrong: "Carla, you're wrong. How on earth do you get $16.50?"

>Worse: "What are you trying to pull?"

>Better: "I'm getting a different total. Shall we check the math?"

By using the last example and starting out with the magical "I" word, Julia effectively takes over the ownership of the comments and the situation. This method employs the critical I. Now Carla is less likely to feel she is under attack and thus in need of throwing up a defense or launching a counteroffensive.

Mind Your P's and Q's

The most important factor in any communication is the receiver of the information, not the sender. Thus, what you hear is more important than what I say. "I'm not sure I was clear about that" is much better than "You don't understand."

But let's assume that, instead of the "I" approach, Julia says: "Carla, you're wrong. How on earth do you get $16.50?"

Carla takes it calmly. She knows that it's always a bad idea to try to laugh off criticism or become defensive. People usually become defensive only when they know they are wrong.

Carla's possible responses:

>Wrong: "Are you accusing me of trying to cheat you?"

>Better: "I don't understand what you mean." Or "Let's have a look at this."

Julia, it turns out, forgot about that glass of expensive Chardonnay she had ordered. They had a little laugh about it and parted friends.

This little scenario is typical of the situations in which you find you must challenge or criticize someone. When that happens, think first of the critical I. If you do, here are some responses you might come up with in response to a similar sticky situation:

>"I think you've been misinformed."

>"That doesn't sound quite right to me."

>"I'm having trouble understanding why you ...."

Softening the Blow

When delivering criticism, keep these points in mind:

- **Avoid the "but" bomb.** "I thought the points you made in your report were excellent, but …." The but bomb immediately sends up a flare and triggers a defensive reaction. The person hears *but* and begins constructing a reply instead of listening closely to your further comments. Try: "I thought your report was outstanding, and next time I suggest you include …." *Next time* does not invalidate the first part of the sentence as *but* does.

- **Keep it impersonal.** Never say that some act or person was dumb or wrong. Talk about behavior, not personality. For example, rather than reprimanding someone for answering another's phone with "It was stupid to answer her telephone," try "It's best only to answer our own telephones."

- **Keep it private.** If you criticize someone in the presence of others, the person is not thinking about your message, but about being humiliated.

- **Be specific.** Don't criticize in generalizations. Mention specific incidents or behaviors.

- **Soften the impact.** Try beginning with a compliment: "You are usually a very considerate person. That's why I was so surprised at your behavior at lunch today."

- **Try advice.** You can also deliver criticism in the form of advice. Instead of saying, "You'll never even reach the basket if you shoot the ball like that," say, "I've found that keeping my elbows in close gives the shot more "accuracy." Or, a more proactive example of advice: "Try putting the knife handle in the palm of your hand so it will give you better leverage to cut your food."

The Receiving End

Whether you deserve it or not, you will be the subject of criticism at one point or another in your life. Be ready. If the criticism is justified, accept it and treat it as a problem that needs to be resolved. Acknowledge that you have a challenge ahead of you and make it clear to the person who pointed out the shortcoming that you intend to address it.

If you believe that the criticism is unjustified or delivered harshly or publicly, you have every right to react in a different way. However, if you get angry and start shooting back, you will end up saying things you will regret and so will the person who offered the criticism in the first place. In this situation it is usually best to put off discussing the matter: "Let's talk about this when we're both a little calmer" or "We ought to get together and work this out. What's a good time for you?"

If someone says something critical about you in the presence of others, you can try "freezing" your critic by stopping whatever you are doing or saying and looking the person dead in the eye for a moment. Or you can say something like "Very little good comes of criticizing others in public. Please tell me your objections (or problems) in private."

If you're not sure that the criticism is justified or if you need time to think it over, you can say, "I'm glad you're letting me know what's on your mind. I'd like to think about it and get back to you."

If you know you've goofed, it's sometimes best to just say, "I apologize," and that's all. Depending on the situation, something more may be required: "I never intended to (embarrass, upset, offend) you, but I can see that I did, and I'm sorry." But don't whine, don't grovel, and don't make excuses or try to shift the blame.

When All Else Fails—The Insult

It is never good manners to insult another person. But if you are going to do it, please do so with grace and style. Tradition, gossip, and literature present us with some excellent examples that may help you in such circumstances. The following conversation is reputed to have taken place between Lady Astor and Winston Churchill:

> "If you were my husband, Winston, I should flavor your coffee with poison."

> "If you were my wife, I should drink it."

Or consider the story of a Louisiana legislator who, having been insulted by a colleague, rose to say:

> "I am reminded that the Emperor Caligula once sent his horse to represent him in the Roman Senate. Caligula was more fortunate than my learned colleague's constituents. At least he was represented by the whole horse."

Another incident involved Dorothy Parker. Someone stepped aside to allow her to pass, saying:

> "Age before beauty."

She swept past, saying:

> "Pearls before swine."

Andrew Lloyd Webber wondered aloud why people took an instant dislike to him. "It saves time," responded Alan Jay Lerner.

The Fine Art of the Compliment

Whatever their source—our svelte new figure, our rousing speech, or our fabulous meal—compliments lift us, honor us, and validate our choices and efforts. A compliment is a two-way gift that benefits the giver and recipient alike. Too often, people deprive themselves of the pleasure of giving a compliment when they hesitate and let the moment slip by.

Compliments are *always* socially proper, if sincerely extended and kept appropriate to the context. (More on this later.) If someone always looks great, tell him or her. If someone is always efficient, acknowledge that. Compliments can break the ice with a stranger, defuse stress, lift spirits, or tighten a bond. The right words at the right time can motivate, comfort, reward, validate, and inspire.

Compliments are not the same as flattery. Flattery is insincere and excessive. Superfluous compliments are annoying and make others feel as though the giver is angling for something—as if the giver "expected a receipt," lamented one writer. What makes a good compliment? These are the basics:

- **Be sincere.** Complimenting someone just because you think it's a good idea is a bad idea. A phony compliment is easy to spot and instantly destroys the credibility of the speaker. If the luncheon speaker was a total flop, don't compliment the speech. Talk about the effort the speaker made to attend the function and the person's past achievements, if any.

- **Be specific.** "That was a marvelous casserole" is better than "You're a terrific cook."

- **Be unqualified.** Don't make the mistake of damning with faint praise: "That was a good report, considering ..." or "This casserole is okay."

- **Don't compare.** You can diminish the compliment by comparing the accomplishment to some other achievement—unless you are comparing it to something heroic, and then the compliment sounds insincere.

Compliments should be consistent with the setting and the relationship between giver and recipient. So what about the boss's new haircut? If she or he is a longtime colleague and you're on very friendly terms, it's fine to say so. In most cases, however, it's best to stick to compliments on a colleague's work, rather than his or her appearance.

That goes double for remarks made to someone above or below you on the organizational chart. Because these relationships contain a power dynamic, personal remarks may unintentionally become highly loaded or easily misunderstood. So feel free to compliment your administrative assistant—but for his or her skills rather than appearance.

Say What? _____

An acquaintance has changed substantially in appearance since you last met. It could be a weight loss, a major makeover, or cosmetic surgery. You want to say something complimentary about the change, but you don't want to refer explicitly to the reason for the changed appearance.

What do you say?

"You look absolutely marvelous!" with an exclamation point in your voice.

The other person may respond by saying something like:

"Yes, my dieting really paid off this time" or "Everybody seems to agree that a little bit of cosmetic surgery makes a big difference."

Then you can engage in a conversation about the rigors of dieting or new laser techniques for removing wrinkles. If the other person merely thanks you, talk about something else.

Caring for Your Compliment

When receiving a compliment, just smile and say thank you. Never try to shrug off a compliment or disagree with the person who is trying to compliment you. If someone compliments you on your dress and you say, "Oh, this old thing?" you're actually saying that the other person's judgment is poor or that she doesn't know what's fashionable.

If someone compliments you on doing a good job at the office, don't say, "It was nothing," or "It should have been more complete (or finished earlier)." This response is insulting to the other person, implying that his standards are not very high. "Thanks, I worked really hard on it" is much better.

Here's another important tip: Never unilaterally upscale a compliment by infusing it with even more praise and enthusiasm than the giver meant to give. For example:

"The sales managers liked your presentation."

"Liked it? They loved it. I knocked their socks off."

Finally, if other people deserve a share of the credit, don't fail to mention them when you acknowledge the compliment.

Facing Cosmetic Surgery

Millions of people undergo cosmetic surgery each year. Their reactions will fall somewhere between silent confusion and a straightforward willingness to discuss their decision to change their appearance.

More people than ever are electing cosmetic surgery, but today's motivations often are far different from the erstwhile stereotype of the suburban matron with too much time and money on her hands. In today's down-sized, competitive job market, many people elect cosmetic surgery for reasons other than vanity. They do it because they are convinced it will further their career.

And with more and more people appearing publicly in various stages of presurgical and postsurgical conditions, the problem of what to say and what not to say arises for both the patient and the friends and acquaintances of the patient.

Although most people today are open about having cosmetic surgery, it can still be a touchy topic for conversation. To avoid hurt feelings, follow these suggestions:

◆ Never tell a person that he or she is crazy to have cosmetic surgery.

◆ Wait until the person opens the subject before you ask whether someone had cosmetic surgery.

◆ If you are curious, try saying, "You look wonderful today." If the reply is that the person had surgery, ask only: "Are you pleased with the results?"

◆ Even if pressed, never criticize the results. If you must, you can say: "I see what you mean but only when you point it out."

◆ Never volunteer the names of others who have had cosmetic surgery.

◆ Never gossip about the subject.

◆ Cosmetic or not, it's still surgery. Be solicitous about the person's health and well-being.

Say What?

If you have had cosmetic surgery and look markedly different, make it easier for those around you by opening the door for comments. That might sound like, "I've just had a hair weave. Hope you are as pleased with it as I am."

Dealing with Bad News

More often than we'd like to think, and often when we least expect it, people we know end up getting fired, going into bankruptcy, having accidents, getting indicted, and experiencing the death of a loved one.

If it happens to someone you know well, you need to recognize the difficulty and offer your sympathy and—if appropriate—your help. It is less than useless to act as if nothing has happened. Don't wait for the other person to find an appropriate time to tell you about the misfortune and don't let the subject become the proverbial elephant in the living room that you both try to ignore.

Instead, be direct. For instance, you might say, "I heard about the fire at your house last week. I'm so glad that you're all right," or say, "I was so sorry to hear about Jim's sentencing hearing. It must be difficult for you."

If you attend a funeral, express your condolences as directly and simply as possible. You could say, "I'm very sorry about your loss," or simply say, "I'm so sorry." On the other hand, you may want to remind the bereaved of some characteristic of the deceased by saying something like "Our office won't seem the same without Bridget's daily baseball team updates" or "I'll miss seeing all her crazy T-shirts."

When someone begins to tell you bad news, be quiet and listen. Your concern will be mirrored in your attentiveness. You can nod and say, "Uh, huh," until you feel it's appropriate to add something like "This must be draining for you. I'm so sorry."

Don't think for a moment that it is helpful or encouraging to compare what your friend is suffering to another situation you've heard about or experienced—or to recount an even worse challenge or injury as a way to tell your friend that "it could be worse." That kind of one-upmanship only makes people feel even more upset. And you can see why. Just imagine that you're complaining to someone about your severe headache and, instead of sympathizing, she replies, "You haven't had a headache until you've had one of my migraines."

Nor should you choose this time to express opinions about proper behavior or judgments about people's character. (For example, "Well, if your husband hadn't cheated on his taxes, he wouldn't be facing prison, would he?") And don't offer unsolicited advice.

Above all, don't use the opportunity to pry into the other person's life. At a time like this, you two may reach a level of intimacy unprecedented in your relationship. A casual acquaintance might for a few minutes become uncharacteristically open and candid with you—and might regret it later on. Try to stay within the boundaries that previously characterized your relationship while remaining sympathetic and attentive.

Firings, Layoffs, and Demotions

The work arena is fraught with difficult and disappointing situations. People get fired, laid off, passed over for promotion, transferred against their will, and chewed out unjustly by the boss. In these situations nothing you can say will fix the problem, so it is important to mirror the person's distress. Let him know that he isn't alone, that he is, in fact, in good company. Reinforce the person's good qualities.

Don't say, "Things will work out for the best," or even worse, "I told you something like this would happen." Don't say that what happened to somebody else is even worse than what happened to him.

Instead, try one of these phrases:

> "I'm so sorry you must go through this."

> "Is there anything I can do to help?"

> "This must be very, very tough for you."

Do not indicate in any way that the unfortunate turn of events was predictable or even partially the fault of the injured party. If a colleague was denied promotion for what you believe to be very good cause, don't launch into a lecture about the skills she needs to acquire or improve upon or tell her that somebody else was more qualified for the position. If the injured party says, "Don't you think that this was rotten luck?" and you know luck had nothing to do with it, just say, "You must be really disappointed," or some other phrase that lets her know you identify with her emotional state.

Coping with Conflict

Because conflicts are unavoidable and inevitable, here are some short tips on how to handle everything from sexual harassment to embarrassing situations. Conflicts usually occur without warning, so we are often not ready for them. Let these ideas allow you to be better prepared.

Breaking Up with Associates

Very few of us enjoy conflict, so breaking up (with your hairdresser, personal trainer, lawn-cutter, manicurist, and the like), as the song goes, is very hard to do. Here are some principles to help ease the pain:

Be clear in your own mind about what you want.

Emotionally firing off salvos to end the relationship because you happen to be in a bad mood one day won't help anybody in the long run. So before you make the decision to end a relationship, determine just how valuable and practical it's been and weigh that against the downsides. No relationship is perfect, because we are not perfect.

Don't broadside anyone.

You might be irritated beyond belief or dissatisfied beyond belief. Does the other person know that? Before you amputate, give the person the benefit of the doubt. Say something like, "Listen, I'm concerned that … just doesn't seem to be working. What can we do to solve this?"

Don't skirt the issue.

Once you make up your mind and have given the other person fair warning, be direct and unemotional. Be a grownup and deal with it. Practice saying, "It's raining outside" to lock in an unemotional, non-judging tone of voice. Don't make any gestures—fidgeting, twirling your hair, and so forth, only give mixed messages. (Upset and coy gestures can be confused with, "I'm sorry … maybe this isn't really the end after all.") Let the words carry the message—that way the other person won't feel betrayed once you are out the door for good.

Mind Your P's and Q's

If you are more comfortable with the written word, write a personal note to the person with whom you're ending a professional relationship. This is not the kind of message that belongs on e-mail.

Own your decision and don't blame.

That might sound like, "I really appreciate all you've done for me and what we've done for each other. Now I think it's time for me to go in a different direction."

Grow up and recognize that business is business and these things are part of the game. When the game is played fairly, everybody retains their dignity and respect.

Never speak badly of the other person.

When asked, be objective and say something like, "I didn't feel that he was listening when I told him how uncomfortable I am with free weights." In other words, own your statements, don't blame, and stick to observable facts and behavior. Saying, "He/she was just impossible and I couldn't handle it anymore," serves no one.

Move on.

This scenario is no more nor less than treating others the way we would like to be treated—fairly, with dignity and respect.

Breaking Up with Friends

Relationships ebb and flow and people change as life changes us. So it naturally follows that a friendship in one period of life may not be sustainable in another with the same enthusiasm and participation.

Friends get angry with each other and often differ. Seldom are these differences good reasons to break a friendship. So before acting in haste, examine your feelings.

If you are absolutely certain you want to end the friendship, there are a few ways to go about it.

Letting things drift is a possibility. When a friend asks you to do something together, you can say you have plans. You can decline to make future dates by saying you think you'll be busy and can't make time commitments.

Be ready for the possibility that she will want some explanation for why you're backing off. Then you owe her the truth, but without being accusatory. You can say something like, "It just feels like we're not clicking lately and it might be a good idea to go in different directions for a while." Or you might say, "I just don't see things the way you do lately."

Keep a lid on your opinions about her/his character flaws. Reciting a list of shortcomings (as you see them) will solve nothing. You will only hurt someone with that. Should you be tempted to tell others, remember that it will only make you—not the other person—look bad. Instead, wish her well in your heart and with your words.

Friends become part of ourselves because of all we share. Never disrespect that fact. We all change and grow. Our needs and interests change. And although it's sad to call a friendship quits, it's a fact of life.

What matters most is that we never cheat friends or ourselves of the dignity, respect, and kindness we deserve.

To Inquiring Minds: Butt Out of My Business

Curiosity, the need or desire to know something, is a condition that almost everyone is born with. Many people look first at the gossip column of a newspaper or magazine. Some of the largest publications in the world are devoted to printing the details and dramas of "other people's business." It is human nature to be curious.

With this in mind, avoiding or quieting prying questions is difficult. It seems that the more you don't tell someone, the more he or she wants to know. However, you can handle an overly curious person in a few ways. Here are some examples:

Say What? _____

When all else fails, you might have to resort to another approach to respond to rude, intrusive questions—the put-down:

"Thank you for your concern. But why would you ask me that?"

"If you will forgive me for not answering that question, I will forgive you for asking it."

"That's really a family matter, and we don't want to talk about it in public."

"It's a personal thing, so let's leave it alone."

"Please don't ask about that anymore because it hurts to talk about it."

"Talk like that might hurt some people, so please drop the subject."

Your request might be ignored. If you make your statement strongly, seriously, and without anger, however, it's likely that the person you're telling will listen and act accordingly.

Helping Others Avoid Embarrassing Situations

Handling a friend's bad personal habits is easier said than done. Those moments of truth between friends often are tense and sensitive. Humor helps—if you can avoid sarcasm.

Bad Table Manners

Your lunch looks delicious, and you're having a great conversation in a cheerful, crowded lunchroom. All of a sudden your dining partner whips out a handkerchief the size of a tablecloth and blows his nose loudly. So loudly, in fact, that the entire room becomes silent for 15 seconds. The offender is oblivious to his disturbance, crumbles the mess into a ball, and stuffs the wad back into his pocket. Sound familiar?

The next time the offending behavior occurs, look your friend in the eye and say something like, "You know, I really value our friendship, so I have to tell you how much that disturbs me and I think it can be embarrassing to you even if you don't know it." Although the initial reaction may be denial and anger, a true friend will see your point and change the habit.

Above all, proceed gently. Don't attack, as you might be tempted to do when you feel uncomfortable and anxious. Any distraction that affects our senses adversely during mealtimes is offensive and therefore bad manners. When we ignore these basic rules, we find ourselves dining alone most of the time. Some of the most common infractions are cracking gum, chewing food loudly with an open mouth, or not being well groomed. Unwashed hair, dirty clothes, or grimy fingernails don't exactly spark an appetite.

Remember the "it's raining outside" tone of voice, and take care not to sound condescending or arrogantly heavy-handed and self-righteous.

Be specific so the other person understands the nature of your criticism and also what behavior needs correcting. Blurting out, "You eat like a pig," will serve no one. For example, "You might not be aware that you chew with your mouth open and it gets noisy." Or, "I noticed that you hold your knife like a dagger and there's an easier way to do it."

Body Odors

Tread lightly here, as the offending odor could be the unfortunate result of a medical condition. If it is a short-term problem, you might risk more by saying something than by putting up with it. If someone has been ill, for example, there might not be anything he or she can do. In that case, nobody is more aware of the problem than the offender. When the problem is long-term, try to speak with someone you know who might be friendly with the person first and ask for advice.

If you feel close enough to this person, you might say something like, "It's uncomfortable for me to say this to you. Still I am your friend and want to make sure you don't sabotage yourself with others without even knowing it. Others have noticed that your body odor/breath is pretty strong. It's distracting and not doing you any good. Perhaps you can change the products you are using now. Once I used a deodorant for so long that it stopped being effective. That might be the case here. I've had success with Brand O and you might want to give it a try."

Other Embarrassing Situations

Your colleague's fly is open, your friend has a giant run in her stocking, your lunch mate has spinach stuck between his front teeth, or someone has feloniously bad breath. What do you do?

First of all, you have to be direct but discreet. Get the person out of earshot of other people and say, "Your fly is open," in the same tone of voice you would use to say, "It's raining outside." If you don't know the person, find somebody in the group who does to give the message.

You are in a more serious situation if you have a friend who has a particular and persistent bad habit or something like chronic bad breath. If he's a real friend, you have to tell him about it even if you know he won't like it. Use the "critical I" if you can.

Mind Your P's and Q's

When you forget a name, you can try to bluff your way through, hoping the other person will drop a hint. Or you can focus on the solution instead of the problem by simply asking, "Please tell me your name again. I seem to be in a dead zone at the moment."

"I've been told that I've had bad breath from time to time, but it seems to be a chronic problem with you. Maybe you have a dental problem you don't know about, or it might be just a matter of using mouthwash more often. That's what worked for me."

The story or analogy you convey doesn't necessarily have to be about the exact problem that your friend has. If you haven't had that exact problem before, choose a story that shows parallels to the other person's situation.

Other Uncomfortable Situations

Sometimes we have to do things that make us squirm internally, but that must be done—to maintain our own self-respect, and more importantly, because it's the right thing to do. The key is to avoid squirming externally. Here are some strategies to help navigate these situations.

Saying No

It's a good idea to practice the rules of non-engagement when you want to say no. They are, basically:

> When you refuse to play the game, all the rules change.

> Tell people what you can do; not what you can't do.

We all have "pushers" in our lives. The "well-intentioned" host who insists you have another piece of dessert. The acquaintance who just knows how much you would benefit from a scrapbook party.

Simply, you respond, "No, thank you. I don't feel like so much dessert tonight." Or, "Thanks, I have other plans for that night." Basically, you are not playing their game.

The trick is to respond with no emotion in your voice. That way, when you decline, you won't sound apologetic. The very minute you sound apologetic, they have their hooks in you, and you'll be stuck doing something you do not want to do.

When you do this, nobody can argue with you. It's your reality. So if you don't feel like having dessert, end of story—you do not owe anyone an explanation. Your "plan" can be to watch paint dry. So what? They are your plans.

Let's suppose your neighbor pleads with you to take the carpool to soccer practice for the next month. Rather than argue how overwhelmed you are with other commitments, you might try something like, "I'd be glad to do it the first week of the month. Taking on the entire month as a whole just won't work for me."

Usually this strategy wins. After all, most people would rather have some of something than all of nothing. And by not ruling something out completely, you are honoring the other person's priorities.

Asking for Favors

This is where e-mail and third person messages just don't cut it. Neither does being vague. Be direct and to the point—in person or on the telephone. Whichever method of communicating you choose, make sure the other person knows that he or she has your full attention.

Don't expect anyone to read your mind. How many times have we heard, "Well, I talked about … for 15 minutes but she never volunteered to help out."

Instead, say something like, "I must ask you for a favor. Would you mind …? It would help me out a lot and I'd be enormously grateful."

When the person does the favor, be sure to make a special effort to thank him or her—a thank-you note, a special telephone call, a small gift—depending on the size of the favor.

Should the other person decline to help out, for whatever reason, don't get into a snit. Accept it graciously, say "I understand," and move on.

Apologizing

When we were children, sometimes our parents exhorted us to "take that back …. Tell Johnny you didn't really mean it." Unfortunately, as grownups we still think that that is what an apology means—denying how you feel. Not so!

Basically, apologies have three components: First, apologize for what you said or did that hurt or offended someone. Second, acknowledge the offensive or hurtful effects of your behavior on the other person. Third, assure the person that it never will happen again. The person we have offended wants to know those three things.

The bottom line is that we respect the other person's priorities, feelings, and values. At the same time, a sincere and authentic apology in no way diminishes our own convictions.

We apologize for the effects our behavior and bad judgment have had on someone else. That might sound like, "It was thoughtless of me to joke about fur coats, knowing how dedicated you are to animal rights. I apologize for saying anything you might have found distasteful. It won't happen again, and I hope you know that I never would deliberately hurt you."

When our apology sticks to observable facts and behavior, we steer clear of character judgments.

Apologies should be written and also spoken. Apologize in person or on the telephone—not on a cell phone while you are driving or multi-tasking; focus is important here—and follow the conversation up with a written apology. Even if all your note says is something like, "I really behaved like a jerk. It won't happen again. I am so sorry for hurting you."

Depending on how serious our misdeed was, it sometimes makes sense to send a gift such as flowers or chocolates.

Stand by Me

Somebody verbally attacks your friend when your friend isn't present, and you know you will regret it if you don't speak up. Here are some ways to respond:

> Wrong: "Look who's talking. You're the jerk who …." or "That's a lie."

> Better: "I'm not sure that's exactly the way it happened. Even if it is, I'm sure that Tom had a good reason for reacting the way he did."

If the other person asks what kind of reason Tom could have, say,

> "I don't know. Why don't you ask him the next time you see him?"

Dirty Jokes

If that jerk Phil starts telling what is sure to be an obscene joke, you can say, "I don't think I want to hear this," and move away.

If you don't realize what kind of joke it is until it's too late, just look right at Phil without laughing and say, "I didn't think that was the least bit funny."

One theme that runs though all the issues and situations discussed in this chapter is human dignity—a sense of self-worth and a respect for others. This quality allows us to deal with conflict without being diminished by it. It allows us to accept criticism without rancor. It allows us to give compliments generously and to receive them gracefully.

The Least You Need to Know

◆ When delivering criticism, use the "critical I." For example: "I've noticed that when you turn in your time sheets late in the day, the administrator gets annoyed. What can we do to solve this?"

◆ When being criticized, don't become overly defensive. Remember that people are most defensive when they know they are wrong.

◆ The best compliments are sincere, spontaneous, specific, and unqualified.

◆ When someone tells you bad news, don't try to be helpful by telling the person that his or her news could be worse.

◆ Proceed gently and discreetly but be specific when informing a friend of an annoying or embarrassing personal habit.

Chapter 20

Speak Up

In This Chapter

- ◆ Ways to deliver an effective speech
- ◆ Handling stage fright
- ◆ How to make small talk
- ◆ Keeping your conversation going and how to get away

Everyone, sooner or later, has to speak before a group of people. You may be called upon to give a toast or publicly welcome the guest of honor. You may be asked to speak at a club meeting or address the school board about a problem in your neighborhood school. On a larger scale, you may have to make a presentation before your superiors and colleagues that could have a profound impact on your career, or you may find yourself giving a speech before hundreds of strangers. Or you might be talking one-on-one with your boss about a raise or that managerial position that just opened up.

Guess what? No matter what kind of speech you give and to whom, the ways you prepare and deliver a speech are all the same. This chapter offers some advice on preparation and speaking techniques to help you become a more comfortable and accomplished conversationalist.

The Terror of Talk: Stage Fright

Everybody gets it. Everybody can get over it.

Third-degree stage fright manifests itself as a revved-up heartbeat, elevated blood pressure, a flushed face, and trembling hands. When you have stage fright, you're experiencing a reaction shared by your cave-dwelling ancestors. Experts call it the flight-or-fight reaction. When a cave dweller saw a saber-toothed tiger, adrenaline pumped into his blood stream and his body prepared itself to scamper up a tree or, if necessary, to do battle.

Most people have the same kind of reaction the first time they face an audience. Here are some physical and mental tricks you can use to control this reaction:

◆ Keep in mind that the audience is not a tiger. Audience members are disposed to like you. They want to relax almost as much as you do. They want you to succeed because that means they will be entertained. In other words, the audience is on your side.

◆ Because your stage fright reaction is a right-brain function—instinctive and emotional—counter it with left-brain activity. Count or work a numbers problem in your head. Think about how your talk is organized and how you've marshaled the various points.

◆ Breathe. Fitness experts recommend inhaling deeply through the nose and exhaling through the mouth.

◆ Smile. Just the act of smiling causes chemical changes in the body that can help you relax and feel more confident.

Live and Learn

The human brain starts the moment you are born—and never stops until you stand up to speak in public.
—Sir George Jessel

We'd rather be in the box than give the eulogy.
—Jerry Seinfeld

Getting Ready

When preparing to give a talk or, for that matter, when preparing for an important one-on-one meeting, ask yourself four questions:

1. **Who am I?** Does this person (audience) know you? What is your relationship, if any? How do you want your audience to perceive you? What attire would be most appropriate to communicate your role?

2. **Where am I?** The physical space will determine how you should use your voice and gestures, and whether you will need a microphone. Find out what audio-visual equipment is available and who will be running it. Think about what you will do if the equipment fails to function as expected. (It so often does.)

3. **To whom am I speaking and what do they expect from me?** Why are they here, and what are their expectations? Do audience members share any characteristics? Do they have a specific point of view concerning you or your topic?

4. **What do I want to accomplish?** To welcome, to instruct, to motivate, to persuade? Do you want to ask for a raise, explain your situation, or praise another person?

> **Live and Learn**
>
> People form impressions of one another in the following ways: visually (how you look), 55 percent; vocally (how your voice sounds), 38 percent; verbally (what you say), 7 percent. First impressions are formed within the first four to seven seconds.

The Delivery

Here are some insider tips on public speaking from experienced speakers:

♦ Speak while standing whenever possible.

♦ Adjust your language to the audience. Don't talk down to anyone, but do tailor your language and your references to the audience (for example, are you speaking to engineers or to artists?). A young audience has a shorter attention span than an older audience does, so you will need to sprinkle more spice into your talk—gestures, vivid images, jokes. Male audiences respond more to visual images; women, to verbal images.

♦ People like people who are like them, so try to make a connection by mentioning early something that connects you to the audience. For instance, you could say, "Some people think that, because we are volunteers and are not being paid, that our work is somehow easier or less important. We all know just how wrong that is, don't we?"

♦ Remember that you are more important than the material. The people are in the audience because they want to hear what you have to say and how you present the information. Otherwise, they could stay home and read the report.

◆ Decide what points you want to make. Don't try for more than four major points in a 20-minute speech. The usual technique is to make a point, give a descriptive example, then remake the point.

◆ Speak with feeling. Try to communicate your enthusiasm for your topic to your audience. Keep your head up and speak clearly.

◆ Control voice volume. Inexperienced speakers have a tendency to shout or to get louder as they go along. Think in terms of projecting. You can project your normal tone of voice without shouting and without sounding like a sideshow barker.

◆ Take your time. Another common error of inexperienced speakers is a tendency to speak quickly, as if every second has to be filled with information.

◆ Avoid rambling and repeating.

◆ When you've finished, if there is no question-and-answer session, say "thank you" and sit down. Don't wave or otherwise acknowledge applause.

◆ If you are having a question-and-answer period, say so and raise your hand briefly to indicate the protocol for asking questions. Restate and, if necessary, rephrase questions. Don't say "good question." This gives the impression you are judging the questions.

◆ Don't refer to the questioner by name unless you are prepared to address everyone in the room by name.

Mind Your P's and Q's

Let's face it—some people just can't tell a joke, and shouldn't. If your attempts at humor are frequently met with quizzical looks or strained smiles, leave jokes out of your speeches even if you think the joke is hilariously funny and your delivery cunningly droll.

The Opening

This is the second most important part of your talk. First impressions are critical because the audience is sizing you up; people are deciding whether they like you or not, whether they can learn from you, whether they are going to be bored or excited. Have the first few words and the first few ideas firmly in your mind. You may want to introduce yourself to the audience, even if the previous speaker has already done so. Some speakers open by complimenting the audience, making some startling or provocative statement, telling a joke, or quoting a prominent person.

The Closing

The closing is the most important part of your talk—the last impression the audience will have of you and the most lasting impression. We can be forgiven for weakness or lapses in the body of the presentation, but never for the opening or the closing.

If the talk has been of a rather light nature, you may want to end with a very good joke or a humorous spin on the material you've just presented. More often, the closing takes the form of a call to action. Don't be afraid to employ some dramatic or emotional language here. You may want to quote a portion of a great speech or use some lines of stirring poetry. Some experienced speakers have a whole arsenal of fiery or sentimental quotes they can use to close a speech.

Introducing a Speaker

Introducing a speaker is usually an easy job. Your basic objective is to get the speaker to the podium without a lot of fuss or delay. Leave yourself out of it as much as possible. Don't launch into a long story about what good friends you are with the person you're introducing.

Get hold of a biography and pare it down. Hit the highlights and emphasize what is of particular interest to this group. Make the tone warm and welcoming. If the event is a family gathering, a retirement party, or something similar, you can be a little more sentimental than at a seminar, lecture, or business function. But, still, brevity is the best policy.

> **Live and Learn**
>
> The average attention span of an audience is eight seconds. People forget 25 percent of what they hear within 24 hours, 50 percent within 48 hours, and 80 percent within four days. Varying your visual, vocal, and verbal delivery will help you hold an audience's attention.

Eulogies

Eulogies are supposed to be about the person who has died—not the sorrow of the person giving the eulogy. That is the most common—and most unfair and irritating—shortcoming of the speaker.

If there ever were a situation that should be scripted, it is a eulogy. Too often the speaker gets lost on tangents that mean something to him or her, and leave the audience baffled.

Here are the key principles for giving an effective eulogy:

- **Keep it short.** Sometimes even a moment of silence can be the most eloquent. Short of that, make sure that your remarks are prepared on paper and that you have both gone over them with someone close to the deceased and also given a copy of your remarks to a back-up in the event that you can't make it through delivering it.

- **Recognize the audience.** The people who are assembled hearing the eulogy were a part of the deceased's life. Mention others when you can.

- **Focus on the good.** Talk about what the person did in life—hobbies, fun times, characteristic expressions he or she used. Keep it upbeat and positive. The idea is to leave the audience happy to have been a part of the life that has just passed.

- **Avoid the bad.** Never talk about anything that might be embarrassing or controversial to either the person who has died or his family or friends. For example, "We all know that Johnny enjoyed the fruit of the grape and that's why he was a good storyteller" can be hurtful.

With eulogies, less is more. Keep it factual. Keep it upbeat. Keep it kind.

Making Conversation

There is nothing small about small talk. Just ask those who dread situations in which they must employ it, mainly because they think of it as uncomfortable, unnecessary, and trivial. Just ask those who know how truly valuable it can be and have learned to use it to their advantage.

You can overcome an aversion to small talk and learn to use and even enjoy it. Anybody can. It's what the experts call "learned behavior," which means a silver-tongued genius will be better at it than most, but anybody can be good at it.

First Impressions

It takes only about four seconds for somebody to size you up and make a preliminary judgment. Research shows that Americans expect three things when they meet someone for the first time—a smile, eye contact, and a handshake. So look directly at the person you are meeting. Smile sincerely. Shake hands firmly, but don't crunch.

Opening a Conversation

First, introduce yourself, and listen carefully to the other person's name, repeating it early in the conversation to lock it into your memory. If the person attaches any other information to the name, it may give you a conversational path to follow: "I'm with the volunteers from Aston," or "This is my first meeting with …."

Mind Your P's and Q's

Some people feel uncomfortable looking directly into someone else's eyes. If you have this problem, try the third-eye trick: Focus on the space above the nose and between the eyes.

Don't worry about using clichés. You can find out a lot about a person with a topic as seemingly banal as the weather. For example, you can start by sharing something of yourself to learn something about the other person:

"I don't know about you, but I sure don't thrive in this heat. Some people do. Are you one of them? Did you grow up in a hot climate?"

"Not really. I'm not a heat lover. I grew up in Ohio."

"Oh. What was it like growing up in the Midwest?"

"It was pleasant. I felt really safe there. People were friendly, things were a little slower paced."

"What brought you to the East Coast?"

"I came to New York to be an actress."

"Are you an actress now?"

"No. I'm a corporate trainer."

Thus, simply by asking about the weather, you have learned that the other person:

◆ Hates heat

◆ Is from the Midwest

◆ Lives on the East Coast

◆ Wanted to be an actress

◆ Is a corporate career person

More important, from nonverbal cues such as tone of voice and gestures, you probably have an idea as to whether you will want to know this person better and/or do business with him or her.

Don't be afraid to say that you're shy: "Big parties like this intimidate me" or "I like meeting new people, once I get over being a little shy." Nothing encourages people to open up like a desire to get other people to open up.

Keeping It Going

Listen. When people say, "He's a good conversationalist," they usually mean that he is a good listener. Don't lie in wait for one of those natural conversation breaks so you can jump in with your next prepared statement or question. Interrupting is the most common and among the most irritating errors people make in conversation.

Let people know that you're listening through eye contact, but don't stare fixedly at them.

Also, ask open-ended questions such as "Why did you decide to volunteer?" or "How did you become involved with our group?" Questions that result in yes or no answers stop the flow of conversation.

People like to be asked their opinions and impressions concerning major news events: "I heard this morning that the mayor resigned. Makes you wonder what's behind that, doesn't it?"

Every topic has its own natural life span, and if someone is going on endlessly about one thing, it is a good idea to cut in as tactfully as possible. If, for example, the back and forth about the mayor is lively and quick, settle down and enjoy it. If it begins to sag under its own weight, try changing the topic. The easiest way is switching to a related subject. "Speaking of politicians (or speaking of retiring or public figures or our city) ...."

When you're engaged in a conversation, keep in mind the following don'ts:

- **Don't perform.** Performing happens when you are concentrating too hard on the impression you want to make on the other person.

- **Don't speed-talk.** Sometimes people who are anxious to make a point try to spit it all out quickly, as if they're afraid they won't be permitted to finish the thought.

- **Don't slow-talk.** A sure sign that you're dragging things out is when other people finish a sentence for you or nod to indicate they understand even before you have reached the point of your remarks.

- **Don't let your mind wander.** Try not to watch other people moving around in the room while someone is talking to you.

- ◆ **Don't hold a drink in your right hand.** Doing so leads to damp, cold hand-shakes. If your palm is sweaty, it's okay to give it a quick swipe on the side of your trousers or skirt before extending it for a handshake.

- ◆ **Don't broach touchy subjects.** Avoid discussions about your health, the cost of things these days, mean gossip, off-color jokes, or controversial issues—particularly when you don't know where the other person stands on the subject.

On the other hand, it is okay to disagree. Wait until the other person has spoken and then introduce your point of view without being judgmental. Don't say, "That's completely off base," or "You couldn't be more wrong about that." Instead, say something like "I disagree because …" or "Well, another way of looking at it is …."

Difficult Conversations: Social Karate

We've all had the uncomfortable, unsettling experiences of saying exactly the wrong thing at the wrong time; having to deflect personal questions; or fending off constant interruptions.

Some basic principles to avoid making embarrassing gaffes are as follows:

- ◆ **Don't assume.** For example, just because someone looks pregnant does not mean she is pregnant. Or, just because that delicious young thing you see with your boss/neighbor/colleague is half his or her age does not mean it's a parent/child relationship.

- ◆ **Think before you speak.** For example, before you launch into a political diatribe against a candidate or a party, ask yourself if the person you are talking to has a relationship with them. It's just not very smart to rail against Republicans to a large Republican contributor.

- ◆ **Make sure you know who's within earshot.** For example, your discussion of Demi Moore's breast augmentation surgeries could hurt and offend someone nearby who's recently undergone breast cancer surgery. In short, stick to small talk because it's not dangerous.

- ◆ **Don't be afraid to admit what you don't know.** There is strength in defense-lessness. And it's far more appealing than trying to appear knowledgeable about something and making a complete fool of oneself.

Inappropriate Questions

Are you two sleeping together?

How much money do you make?

How come you don't have any children?

If someone comes up with a nasty or particularly inappropriate question, you can ignore it or tell the person that you consider the question to be rude. My favorite tactic is to say: "Why do you ask?"

Interruptions

Go lightly. In fact, wrap your comments in a compliment such as, "One of the things I like best about you is your enthusiasm. You might not even realize that you interrupt me a lot. So I'm asking you to do your best to curb the habit and listen to what I say. Then I'd welcome your feedback and listen to you."

You might be able to work out a private signal between yourselves in the future to help break the habit. Above all, keep in mind that your goal is to be helpful, not hurtful.

Body Language

Don't fold your arms, and do keep your hands away from your mouth. Both send negative signals. Try holding a drink in one hand and putting the other hand in your pocket or, perhaps, on the strap of your handbag. The point is to look relaxed and receptive. Lean forward slightly when the other person speaks.

Getting Away

It is very important to close a conversation gracefully. As humans, we need two things when dealing with others—acknowledgment and closure.

We need people to acknowledge our presence. That's why you might not mind waiting when a clerk says, "I'll be right with you," or even just looks at you and nods briefly. The need to be acknowledged also explains why you are so annoyed when a receptionist says, "Please hold," and cuts you off before you can say anything.

By the same token, it is annoying when people just drift away after a conversation without some acknowledgment that a conversation has occurred. When you feel a conversation has run its course or you have to move along, wait for a break in the conversation and then say something like …

> "Well, I've got to say hello to our host (or George or my aunt, for example)."

> "That food looks delicious. Think I'll have some. Excuse me."

> "I'm going over to the bar for a refill." (Don't try this one while holding a full glass.)

Then say something like …

> "It was good talking with you. I enjoyed learning about Ireland."

If others at a party interrupt and you cannot end the conversation properly, make some sort of parting gesture, for example, brief eye contact and a wave.

Giving a talk and holding a conversation have a lot in common. Both work better if you are relaxed and natural. In a way, both put you "on stage."

The Least You Need to Know

- ◆ If you suffer from stage fright, remember that the audience wants to relax as much as you do.

- ◆ Before you speak, run over the four big questions: Who am I? Where am I? Who am I talking to? What do I want?

- ◆ The two most crucial parts of your speech are the closing and the opening.

- ◆ Keep eulogies brief, positive, and noncontroversial.

- ◆ When people say, "He's a good conversationalist," they really mean that he knows how to listen.

- ◆ The most important aspects of a conversation are acknowledgment and closure: Greet people (and find out something about them) and end the conversation gracefully.

Chapter 21

Giving and Receiving Gifts

In This Chapter

◆ The gift quiz

◆ Giving gifts in the workplace

◆ Children and gifts

◆ Gift ideas for special occasions and age groups

Even if you don't accept the precept that it is better to give than to receive, you must acknowledge that it is important to do both graciously. There are times when spending too much is taboo, and there are times when "a little something" is just not enough. But time given to the thoughtful selection of a gift, no matter who is receiving it, no matter what the occasion, is never wasted.

And receiving a gift with a graceful expression of gratitude will be appreciated in direct proportion to the time and thought given to the selection of the gift. This chapter explains the fine art of giving and receiving gifts.

The Gift Quiz

Here are 10 questions to ask yourself when giving a gift:

- ◆ Why am I giving it?
- ◆ Is it sincere?
- ◆ Am I giving it without strings attached?
- ◆ Does it reflect the receiver's taste—not mine?
- ◆ Is it too extravagant?
- ◆ Is it kind? (Beware of gag gifts.)
- ◆ Is it appropriate? (No candy for a dieter.)
- ◆ Can I present it in person?
- ◆ Is it presented beautifully?
- ◆ Do I feel good about giving it?

Let's expand a bit on the first point, which is really the most important consideration. The first question you should ask yourself is why you're giving the gift. We give gifts to say thanks to a business associate for an introduction, to someone who gave a lunch or dinner in our honor, to a couple for dinner at their home, to a person who gave us information that helped land business, or to someone who treated us to dinner.

You might also give a gift to congratulate someone on a promotion, an award, a marriage, a birth, an anniversary, or a birthday. And when choosing a gift, don't forget the reason you are giving it. Fortunately, there are lots of ways to find, choose, and send gifts for every occasion. Keep the following tips in mind when choosing gifts:

- ◆ If you're tempted to buy a youngster war toys, check first with the parents. Some people have very strong feelings on the subject.

- ◆ Never give children pets unless you have cleared it with the parents beforehand.

- ◆ The value of a gift is enhanced by the fact that it arrives on time and is nicely wrapped.

- ◆ Handwritten notes should accompany gifts. If you must include a greeting card, add a written note to whatever printed sentiment the card contains.

Faux Pas

Joke gifts may get a laugh at the moment of giving, but can leave a sour aftertaste.

◆ A gift of money can be most conveniently given in the form of a check or cashier's check. Cash is more appropriate for a child. When giving cash, include a note mentioning the amount in case some is lost or mislaid and to help the recipient when it comes time to send a thank-you letter. Your note can say something like "I hope these ten dollars will fund your victory pizza after the game."

◆ Generally, money is a gift given by older people to younger people. It's a good idea to try to learn if the recipient is saving for something special and to include a note saying the gift is to bring the person closer to that goal.

E-Commerce and Registries

Selecting, purchasing, and sending gifts electronically can be a wonderful convenience, but you must do some thinking first.

Before placing the order, decide whether to have the gift sent to you, which will allow you to wrap and personalize it, or directly to the recipient. If you choose the latter, here are some things to consider:

◆ Find a reputable, reliable e-tailer, one you've used previously or that friends have recommended.

◆ Have the item gift-wrapped. Most e-tailers provide this service.

◆ Send a card or note telling the recipient that something is on its way.

◆ If you are the recipient, call or e-mail right away to say "thank you" and to let the person know the gift has arrived. You must then follow up with a thank-you note.

The Ease of Registries

Establishing an electronic gift registry is a bit more complicated than simply setting up a registry at an upscale department store. When you set up an e-registry, you can indicate the sort of gifts you would like to receive. The registry will contact your circle of family and friends to get some ideas about their interests and preferences when it comes to gifts they would like to receive. Those contacted can also provide hints about what to buy for others on your list.

Selecting a registry:

◆ Make sure the registry includes a large number of retailers to give you and others a wide range of choices.

◆ Make sure the items purchased are shipped directly from the retailer, instead of through the registry or another entity. You don't want the gift going through too many hands before it arrives.

Going Once, Going Twice

Participating in online auctions may be just the way to purchase specialized, hard-to-find gifts, such as an item to add to or round out someone's collection. You may know about eBay or one or two other big sites, but more than 800 auction sites are operating out there in cyberspace. You can use a filter such as AuctionRover to narrow your search.

Gift Giving at Work

Some of the most difficult questions about gift giving concern the workplace. Exchanging gifts with business associates is an area of behavior in which careful thought and prudence are especially important.

Faux Pas

Never send alcohol to a person's office. Most companies prohibit alcohol consumption on the job, and the mere presence of alcohol in the office is not very professional.

Rule 1: Extravagance shows bad manners and represents poor strategy.

Rule 2: Modesty and quality are the key words.

The gift should be personal enough to tell the recipient that you gave some thought to it. You might have to talk to someone's spouse or assistant to learn what a person's hobbies are or what kind of music, books, or foods would make a special treat.

It's the Thought That Counts

After you have an idea for a gift, consider how much to spend. Usually, $25 is an appropriate ceiling for gifts to employees and subordinates. That's the limit the government puts on such deductions.

However, if the employee has been working for you for years and has become a personal friend or almost part of the family—as is the case with many executive assistants—you might want to spend up to $100, but no more. But watch out. What you give sets a precedent that you might feel obligated to match or exceed in the future. Although proper etiquette doesn't require you to up the value of your gifts, the recipient may hope that you do and could be hurt and confused if your next gift is little more than a token. It's best to keep a record of what you gave whom and when.

On the other hand, an employee is under no obligation to give a superior a gift. There is always the danger of being suspected of apple-polishing. The truth is that you may be better advised to wait for a spontaneous reason to give your boss a gift of flowers from your garden or a batch of home-baked cookies or brownies.

In all cases, the best way to present a gift is in person. Gifts must be wrapped with care to demonstrate that time and thought went into them. Carry a nicely wrapped gift in something appropriate—shoving it into a plastic shopping bag can ruin the entire effect. And receiving a splendidly wrapped gift with a personal enclosure note in its own envelope is one of life's nicest experiences—especially if the note shows a bit more thought than the usual platitudes.

Faux Pas

Never send a gift to the office of a reporter, editor, or other media person to thank him or her for favorable publicity. It could look as if you're paying them off.

Mind Your P's and Q's

Flowers are appropriate to send the morning of a party or the day after. If sending flowers to a home, make sure the recipient will be there to receive them. Women, remember that it is perfectly acceptable to send flowers to men.

Children and Gifts

If a child wants to give a teacher a gift at Christmas or Hanukkah, on a birthday, or at the end of the school year, the gift should not be extravagant. In fact, encourage your child to get the class to offer a gift together. If, however, it is from a single child, a small token—perhaps something handmade—is appropriate. The gift should be wrapped and accompanied by a card.

This is an issue that has received a lot of attention in the press and among parents, many of whom feel pressure to "one-up" each other with gifts. One young parent relayed her experience to me, and it's a strategy I endorse. She had been in the habit of giving a token gift to her child's teacher at Christmas. When her child moved to a new school, she consulted with and followed the practice of the president of the school's Parents Association: a gift certificate to a bookstore at the end of the school year— "after grades were in, so there wasn't any question of play for pay." Both are excellent options.

And, like adults, children should send a thank-you note if they aren't able to thank the giver in person. In fact, it's a nice idea (and teaches a small lesson about the importance of sending thank-you notes) to send a note to Uncle Danny, even if your son or daughter was able to thank him in person.

Parents should impress upon their children that, no matter how dumb or ugly they think a gift is, the giver must never know: "Uncle Danny likes you and respects you enough to go to the trouble and expense of getting you something he thinks you will like. Telling him it's dumb or ugly will hurt his feelings."

Ages and Occasions

Here are a few ideas for suitable gifts for special people and occasions.

Babies

Many adults save and treasure gifts they received when they were babies. When giving a baby gift, therefore, you might want to consider purchasing some trinket in silver or gold. Pins, mugs, rattles, or bracelets that have the recipient's name and birth date are good ideas. Consider a one-of-a-kind drawing created around the child's name and birth date.

Another idea is to give the parents a photograph album with pictures of the baby and space for other pictures they can add to through the years.

A gift that will be appreciated by the parents, and later on by the child, is a savings bond or a savings account with an opening balance, giving the family a suitable foundation upon which to build.

Other useful gifts are rattles, crib mobiles, a car seat, clothing, a baby blanket, or a music box. It's also welcome when groups combine resources to purchase larger items such as a stroller, changing table, bureau, and crib bedding: blanket, sheets, baby pillow, and pillowcase. Be sure to check with the parents if you are considering a piece of furniture as a baby gift.

Children

Books, toys, a telescope, magic tricks, simple and "parent-friendly" (not messy) craft kits, computer games, and kaleidoscopes are all great gifts.

For a confirmation or bar/bat mitzvah, consider a piece of jewelry with a religious theme. Other possibilities include a subscription to a magazine like *National Geographic*, binoculars, an electronic dictionary, a nylon windbreaker, perhaps with the name of a favorite team on the back, rollerblades, or a skateboard. Consider, too, technology gifts such as MP3 players and Walkmen.

Teenagers

Teenagers always appreciate a gift of cash. Tickets to movies or a pop music concert will also be greatly appreciated. Other ideas include gift certificates to music and video stores, a camera, tickets to a sports event, sports equipment, or a portable MP3 player.

> **Mind Your P's and Q's**
>
> The trouble with gifts from gift shops is that they look like gifts from gift shops. An exception is the museum gift shop, particularly in the larger museums, where something interesting and/or classy can often be found.

High School Graduation

Graduating from high school represents one of the great turning points in life, a step from school kid into adulthood.

Money, of course, and savings bonds or stock and gift certificates are always appropriate and appreciated. A watch, a leather checkbook carrier, or a weekend travel bag can signal recognition of the graduate's newly independent status.

If applicable, you can give things to take to college: luggage, clock radio, bed linens and towels, hair dryer, a hand-held electronic organizer, perhaps with a dictionary and thesaurus included.

You might also check to see if the college-bound student is registered with any department or specialty stores to equip his college life.

College Graduation

Knowing the graduate's plans can help with your selection. If they include graduate school, a gift certificate to the college bookstore will help. If an office job awaits, a monogrammed leather briefcase may be appropriate. Also consider buying beer or coffee mugs, luggage, engraved stationery, a Palm Pilot, or MP3 player.

Wedding Showers

Shower gifts are almost invariably things that can be used around the house, such as small appliances. Be practical. Don't use this opportunity to pick something "she wouldn't buy for herself." Asking the bride's friends what they are bringing will help you avoid duplication and gives you an idea of the price range. Bridal registries are also a possible source of gift information, although they're used mostly for wedding gifts. Showers may take different forms. Guests may be asked to bring a gift for a specific room in the house.

Gift subscriptions to a couple's favorite hobby magazines are welcome, as are gift certificates to movie theaters and restaurants. These are especially appropriate when the bridal shower is co-ed.

If you decline an invitation to a shower, you don't need to send a gift. In any case, shower gifts are not supposed to be elaborate and expensive.

Weddings

The bridal registry at local stores can save you lots of time and concern. You will be confident that you are purchasing something that the happy couple wants. Shopping early gives you a wider selection when you use the registry.

Couples are registering at all kinds of stores these days, including mega-hardware stores like The Home Depot or Lowe's, electronic stores, and record stores, as well as traditional home and department stores. This variety opens up a whole new world of possibilities.

If, however, you do not want to go the registry route, you must first set a budget figure. Then consider the following categories:

♦ Money, in the form of checks, bonds, stocks.

♦ Art objects such as paintings, sculptures, or antiques. This can be a dicey route, however, unless you know the tastes of the people well.

♦ Silver flatware, candlesticks, salt and pepper shakers, chafing dishes, frames for wedding pictures, a box engraved with a facsimile of the wedding invitation.

♦ Crystal stemware, candlesticks, vases.

♦ Furnishings, such as card tables, coffee tables, mirrors, table lamps. Here, too, an intimate knowledge of the couple's tastes or desires would be an appropriate prerequisite.

> **Live and Learn**
>
> An old superstition, largely discarded now, suggests that clocks are not appropriate wedding gifts because they remind us that time runs out. If you are not familiar with family traditions or history, and you have any doubt about the appropriateness of a gift, check with the family.

Weddings are also occasions when treasured family heirlooms are passed along to the younger generation.

Anniversaries

For the most part, you will be giving gifts only on special anniversaries, such as a silver or 25-year anniversary. Remember that the recipients are probably at a stage in their lives in which they are not interested in collecting possessions, particularly household items or knickknacks. A good strategy is to get together with a group of friends or relatives and jointly purchase a vacation trip or a big-screen television.

For very close friends or relatives, you may want to give anniversary gifts more often than every 25 years. If so, you might be interested in consulting the traditional and revised lists of gifts given for different years. A comprehensive list is available on the Chicago Public Library's website, www.chicpublib.org

Birthdays

The only firm rules that apply to birthdays are the usual ones regarding thoughtfulness and timeliness. Remember that a birthday is a magical time for a child; a little extravagance is permissible, and a lot of creativity is recommended. In the workplace, a card and/or an invitation to lunch is appropriate. So are gift certificates to coffee shops and movie theaters.

Birthday gifts involving birthstones are always welcome. The International Gemstone Association (ICA)—www.gemstone.org—has an amazingly comprehensive list that includes birthstones for every day of the year. Another good website for birthstones by month is www.aboutbirthstones.com.

Housewarming

Stationery with the new address, a welcome mat (the practical kind), a plant that can survive some inattention, a coffee-table book, and gift certificates to the local bookstore or wine merchant are all wonderful housewarming gifts. So are gift subscriptions to hobby-related magazines. Another welcome gift is barware—corkscrews, glasses, wine stoppers, and so forth.

Other useful items are a board to hang keys on; a bulletin board for messages in the kitchen; telephone book covers; message pads with the family name on them; a supply of pens and markers to accompany them; an assortment of flashlights, light bulbs, and various size batteries; or a stamp box filled with postage stamps.

Coming to Dinner

Don't bring things that need immediate attention from a person who may be frantically busy in the kitchen. Cut flowers, for example, require the host or hostess to stop what he or she is doing, find a vase, and add water. Instead, try wine or an easy-care plant.

Retirement

Some people approach retirement with cheerful enthusiasm. Some, particularly if circumstances have forced retirement upon them, do not want to celebrate the event.

Mind Your P's and Q's

If you are bringing wine or food to a dinner party, say something like "We thought you might enjoy this later." This message relieves the host of the pressure of having to deal with the gift immediately, and he knows that it was not necessarily intended to be part of the meal.

Check with the retiree's spouse or close friends before deciding on whether to give a gift.

Some ideas: a tool kit for the handyman, a home-brew starter kit for the beer lover, sporting equipment, a backyard hammock, piano lessons, a trial membership in a health club or spa. Gift certificates to movie theaters and restaurants are always welcome. Even gift certificates to coffee shops are welcome to the person who complained, "I never have time to sit down and enjoy a leisurely cup of coffee."

Returning Gifts

When the party's over and your grateful smile flickers and dims, it is time to consider returning gifts. It might be a book you have already read, clothes that don't fit, or something you just can't stand to have around. Remember, however, that you can't return things made especially for you or things that the giver might expect to find on your bookshelf or coffee table during a subsequent visit. You may be able to tell a very close friend that you will exchange a shirt for another size or color or a book for another title, but never ask the giver of a gift to exchange it for you unless you are physically unable to leave the house. Common sense in this area will bring you many happy returns.

The Least You Need to Know

- A gift should be accompanied by a handwritten note and wrapped as beautifully as possible.

- Gifts of money are most conveniently given in the form of a check.

- For teachers, the gift ideally should come from the entire class. Gifts from individuals should be inexpensive tokens.

- In general, $25 is an appropriate ceiling for gifts to employees unless there are special circumstances.

- For the boss, flowers from the garden or brownies as a spontaneous response to a particular occasion will avoid giving the impression of apple-polishing.

- Remember that gift giving is not your golden opportunity to impose your taste on another person. Think about what would please the recipient, not you.

Chapter 22

Dealing with the Disabled

In This Chapter

◆ Ten enabling tips

◆ Taboo terms

◆ Wheelchair and visual impairment etiquette

◆ Hearing loss and speech impairment etiquette

◆ Developmental disabilities

Roughly one fifth of the U.S. population has some form of disability, according to the U.S. Census Bureau, making people with disabilities the largest and most diverse minority in our society. You will meet them in all walks of life, and, with the passage of the Americans with Disabilities Act, they have become a familiar and increasingly integral presence in the workplace.

Many people feel uncomfortable in situations involving the disabled, partly because they remind us of our own vulnerability, but mainly because we are unsure about how to behave toward those with disabilities.

On the other hand, the disabled may also be suffering discomfort in the same situations because of restrictions imposed on them by physical structures and the uninformed or callous attitudes of the nondisabled.

Disabled persons are sensitive to the reactions of those around them and want to put you at ease every bit as much as you want to put them at ease. A few simple rules of etiquette and some common sense can go a long way toward making everyone more comfortable. First, remember the three R's—respect, relax, and reason.

Respect. Persons with disabilities deserve the same respect you would extend to anyone else.

Relax. Meeting, talking to, and dealing with a disabled person should never generate undue tension. Relax and behave naturally.

Reason. Reasonable common sense and common courtesy will allow you to avoid or resolve difficult situations involving the disabled.

Ten Enabling Tips

Here are 10 practical tips that will help you avoid feeling socially disabled when dealing with the disabled:

- If you offer assistance, wait until the offer is accepted. Listen for information about what form the assistance should take.

- Speak directly to the disabled person, not through a third party. This tip is particularly important when addressing a hearing-impaired person and someone else is "signing" for him.

- Always offer to shake hands.

- Identify yourself and others to a visually impaired person. Always let the person know when you are leaving the room.

- Treat adults like adults. Don't use a person's first name until someone asks you to. Don't pat. Don't patronize.

- Don't shout.

- Don't touch, lean on, or move a wheelchair without permission. Treat the chair as part of the person occupying it.

- Don't distract a working seeing-eye dog.

- When conversing with a person with a speech impediment, listen carefully and never pretend to understand. If in doubt, ask questions. Be patient. Don't interrupt or inject comments during pauses. Don't try to fill in a word for someone with a stutter. Don't raise your voice. Louder is not better.

Mind Your P's and Q's

Remember, everything is relative: Some disabled writers have referred to nondisabled persons in general as TABs, for "temporarily able-bodied."

◆ Don't fret about phrases. Speak as you would normally and don't worry about using terms such as *running around* (to someone in a wheelchair) or *listen to that* or *see you later.*

Live and Learn

One who is sincerely interested in human communication and cooperation, in being genuinely helpful, will pay only so much attention to the disability as is necessary to give the other the help he needs and wants, will not call undue attention to it by extravagant gestures of sympathy and elaborate offers of undesired help, will give such help as is asked for or indicated in a matter-of-course way, neither evading nor emphasizing the fact of the disability, and will in general keep his companionship with the other on a basis that will keep communication and companionship as nearly normal as possible.

—Eleanor Roosevelt

What Should We Talk About?

People who have disabilities have families, pets, jobs, hobbies, cultural interests, or sports that they participate in. Get to know about them and their interests the same way you would with anyone else, by making conversation. You may be surprised at the range of interests and activities. Focus on who the person is and not the disability.

However, the subject of the disability is not taboo. If it comes up naturally, talk about it:

> The meeting is at four o'clock. Do you need me to come by for you, or will you get there on your own?

> I'll meet you in the auditorium. There's an accessible entrance to the left of the main entrance.

However, when talking to someone with a disability, avoid the term *handicapped.* Use the word *disabled* and save *handicap* for golf outings.

In addition, say, "the person with the disability," rather than "the disabled person." Say, "the person who has epilepsy," rather than "the epileptic." By doing so, you avoid defining the person as the condition. This practice is not only more considerate, but also more accurate.

Taboo Words and Phrases

The National Easter Seal Society advises us to eliminate certain words and phrases from our vocabulary and to replace them with positive, nonjudgmental terms:

- **Eliminate.** *Victim, cripple, afflicted with* or *by,* and *invalid,* which connotes "not valid."

- **Replace with.** *The person with a disability* or, more specifically, *the person with …* or *the person who has ….*

- **Don't say.** *Unfortunate, pitiful, poor, dumb* (as in mute), *deformed, blind as a bat.* These terms are stereotypical, judgmental, and downright vulgar.

- **Say:** *Uses a wheelchair* instead of *wheelchair-bound* or *confined to a wheelchair. Employed in the home* is better than *homebound employment,* when referring to people who must work at home.

Live and Learn

The reason that some people object to the word *handicapped* is that it derives from the phrase *cap in hand,* a reference to begging. Terms such as these are particularly offensive to the disabled because they are evocative of an era in which the rights of the disabled were ignored, when they were treated like children or, worse, kept out of sight. The term *disabled* seems, over the years, to have acquired general acceptance.

Wheelchair Etiquette

Think of the wheelchair as an extension of the person who uses it. Here are some tips, many of which also apply to those who use crutches, canes, or walkers:

- In general, you should keep your hands off the wheelchair.

- Respect personal space. Particularly avoid patronizing pats. Consider what your own reaction would be to this sort of behavior.

- Try to place yourself at eye level when conversing for any length of time with a person in a wheelchair. It's impossible to deal with another as a peer if one of you is looking up and the other is looking down. Besides, it's easier on the neck for both parties and generally more comfortable.

- Don't move a wheelchair or crutches out of reach of the person who uses them unless you are asked to do so. And if you do move them, remember to place them within the sight of their owner to avoid possible uneasiness or even panic.

Live and Learn

Pity for another implies inferiority. Pity avoids contact. It explains the man who will not employ the blind man even if he is proven as fit as the next man for the job, but instead makes out a check to the nearest blind service institution— his form of magical gesture to exercise.

—Ludwig Jekels, *The Psychology of Sympathy*

♦ Don't just decide to help out. Ask first. Push a wheelchair only after asking the occupant if you may do so. A good time to offer help is when the person in the wheelchair is encountering steep inclines or ramps or thick carpets.

♦ If you're planning a party or other social function, consider whether the location has access for wheelchairs. Think about such things as steep hills and obstacles when giving directions to the location. Remember that a disabled person may need extra time to reach the destination.

Visual-Impairment Etiquette

In general, guide dogs are working animals, not pets. So don't pet them. In fact, don't call their names or distract them in any way. Allow the dogs to accompany their owners into all stores and buildings. These dogs are trained to pay no attention to strangers while working except as objects to be avoided. Attempting to pet them while they are in harness is like urging someone to abandon a good, carefully formed habit. If the dog's harness is off, it's okay to ask the owner whether you can pet the animal—but don't touch it without the owner's permission.

If you are in an environment familiar to a blind person, don't move things, or if you do, put them back exactly as you found them. Leave closed doors closed, and open doors open. Never leave doors ajar.

Go ahead and offer assistance if you think it might be helpful, but remember that sometimes a person who is blind prefers to get along unaided. If you see a blind person without a guide dog waiting at an intersection, offer to help him or her across. The fact that the person has stopped at the intersection may signify that he or she is waiting for help.

However, if the person says, "No, thank you," don't insist. If the person wants your help, offer your elbow. You will then be walking a step ahead, and the movements of your body will indicate when to change direction, when to stop and start. Hesitate but do not stop before stepping up or down. You can say, "curb," or "step down."

Mind Your P's and Q's

In aiding someone who is visually impaired at the dinner table, use an imaginary clock to describe the placement of the food on the dish: The mashed potatoes are at four o'clock, the chicken breast is at two o'clock, and so on.

Here are some other tips:

- Give directions with the person who is blind as the reference point, not yourself. Say: "You are facing Broad Street, and you will have to cross it and turn to your right to go east on Chestnut Street."

- When helping the person into a car or taxi, place her hand on the inside door handle, and let her go in alone.

- When entering an unfamiliar office or restaurant, offer your elbow, use specifics such as right or left, and then place his hand on the back of the chair so that he can be seated without further assistance.

- Don't let self-consciousness or a misplaced sense of protectiveness make you hesitate to tell a blind person that he has egg on his shirt or that his tie is in his soup. Do so in a matter-of-fact tone of voice and let him deal with the problem himself.

- Some people have a tendency to raise their voices when speaking to a blind person. If you catch yourself doing so, stop. It's annoying.

- When accompanying a person who is blind, do your best to describe the surroundings, especially terrain and spatial relationships.

Recently, I witnessed the following encounter in one of those large chain drug stores. A blind man entered and stopped inside the door. Another customer walked over to him.

"May I assist you?"

"I want to have a prescription filled."

"The pharmacy section is in the rear of the store. I'd be glad to take you there."

"Great. Thanks."

"Take my elbow. We're going about six feet straight ahead. Now we're turning right. The floor inclines up, and there are some displays of soda in the middle of the aisle. About four steps more. Okay, shall I get the pharmacist for you?"

"No, thanks. I'm fine now that I'm here."

"Would you like me to wait and escort you out?"

"No, thanks. I can do it now. Thanks a lot."

As you can see, the person who helped out in this situation was able to combine common sense with simple courtesy in offering help and in providing just the right amount of assistance.

Meeting a Blind Person for the First Time

If the person is alone when you enter the room, make your presence known right away by speaking. Identify yourself when greeting the person, and if others are with you, be sure to introduce them and to specify where they are: "On my left is Helen Carver, and on my right is Mary Thompson."

When offering a handshake, say something like "Allow me to shake your hand." If the other person extends a hand, shake it or explain why you can't. "I'd like to shake your hand, but I'm afraid I may drop all these files."

Remember to talk to a person without sight as you would to a person who can see. In a group use the people's names as a clue to whom you are speaking. Address those who can't see by name if they are expected to reply and speak to them directly in a normal tone of voice. Excuse yourself when you are leaving. Doing so is especially important when ending a conversation so the person isn't left talking to thin air.

When a person with visual impairment has to sign a document, provide a guiding device such as a ruler or a card. When handing money to a person who is blind, separate all the bills into denominations and specify whether they are ones, fives, and so on. The person with the impairment can identify coins by touch.

Hearing-Loss Etiquette

Hearing impairment is a less dramatic disability than blindness, but is much more common. Hearing loss can be slight or complete or anywhere in between. Your response may be keyed to the degree of hearing loss. In any case, here are some tips that you will find helpful:

◆ Be sure that you have the person's attention before you start speaking. If necessary, wave a hand, give a tap on the shoulder, or make some other signal. Do so gently.

◆ Some deaf people depend entirely on lip reading to discern what others are saying, and many with partial hearing loss depend on it to one degree or another. Accordingly, face the person you are addressing and make sure the light is on your face so that he or she can see your lips more clearly.

◆ Don't get frustrated if you have to repeat yourself. If necessary, write it down or get someone to sign for you.

Mind Your P's and Q's

Shouting into the ear of a hearing-impaired person doesn't help him or her hear and may even cause damage.

◆ Don't keep repeating the same phrases. Be flexible. Choose another word or rephrase the whole sentence. Keep in mind that some words "look" similar to a lip reader. If "I'll drive the car around front" doesn't seem to work, try "I'll bring the car to the front door." Keep your hands away from your face while speaking and don't eat, chew, or smoke. You should be aware that a mustache might hide your lips and prevent a lip reader from understanding you.

◆ Remember that the person with the hearing loss will rely to some degree on expressions, gestures, and body language.

◆ Never talk from another room. When people who are hearing impaired can't see you, they may not be aware that you are speaking.

◆ Turn off the television or radio and reduce other background noises so that you can be heard more clearly.

◆ Don't shout. Don't use exaggerated lip movements. Speak slowly and clearly.

◆ Face the other person, preferably on the same eye level. Do not turn away until you have finished speaking.

Live and Learn

As far back as the second century B.C., deaf people were treated as fools or classified as children. Systematic efforts to understand and help educate those with hearing loss were not undertaken until the sixteenth century. Even then, the tendency was to treat those with hearing loss, and the disabled in general, as intrinsically inferior persons.

◆ You can bend down to get a little closer to the ear of the listener but don't speak directly into the ear, don't touch, and don't shout.

◆ Remember that fatigue, stress, illness, or fright affect everyone. External factors such as jet lag or a common cold can increase difficulty in communicating: Adjust your behavior accordingly.

◆ When a hearing-impaired person is in a group and the others are laughing at something he hasn't heard, explain the joke to him or let him know that you will explain it later. Because of past cruelties, your friend may be oversensitive and may think that the others are laughing at him or her.

Speech Impairment

The most important thing to remember is to give your complete and unhurried attention to those who have difficulty speaking. Give them time to express themselves. Don't interrupt or complete their sentences for them, but give help when they indicate that they need it. The following tips will help:

- Don't correct their pronunciation.

- Ask questions that require short answers or that can be answered with a nod or a gesture.

- Don't pretend to understand when you don't. Repeat what you thought you understood. The person's reactions will guide you.

Developmental Disability

Dealing with people with developmental disabilities may present you with the most difficulties and require the most patience, particularly in the workplace.

The key is to treat people with developmental disabilities as normally as possible and to set the same standards for them as you would for others. If, for example, the person tries to become too affectionate, explain that such behavior is not appropriate. Make sure your tone is firm but not reprimanding. Here are some other tips:

- Be careful about touching the person. Touching may signal approval of such behavior, which a person with developmental disabilities may use to curry favor.

- Some people with developmental disabilities are very sensitive to body language and tone of voice. Make sure your silent messages are nonthreatening. Be firm but pleasant. Speak with a smile on your face and in your voice.

- Criticism and accusatory language have a demoralizing effect on everyone. Instead of saying, "You made a mistake," try "How about doing it like this?"

- Recognize that repetition is important in teaching the developmentally disabled and be prepared to be patient.

 **Faux Pas**

Don't be so quick to say, "You don't look disabled" to someone getting out of a vehicle with a wheelchair license plate. Many serious health conditions are not immediately apparent to strangers.

The Lately Disabled

You may need an extra supply of tact and generosity with a friend or acquaintance who has become disabled later in life, possibly because of Ménière's disease, lupus, or multiple sclerosis. Often, you may know of such disabilities only if the person actually tells you.

One of the most common reactions among the lately disabled is a feeling of extreme self-consciousness in the company of able-bodied persons. The lately disabled are acutely sensitive to pity from others.

The lately disabled may also suffer from a loss of self-esteem. They may have lost their jobs and are worried about money. Keep in mind that they are unable to do many of the things that once defined them in their own minds—things that were part of their sense of self-worth.

They may also be suffering from depression, grieving for the person they once were, and struggling toward a realization of the new person they now must be.

The lately disabled may also experience boredom and wish for structure. You can help by getting them involved in activities, particularly those activities that involve exercise. Provide structure by offering to make appointments or arrangements for certain definite times and sticking to the plan.

Therefore, be prepared for displays of bad temper and frustration. And don't take them personally.

Hospital Etiquette

When a friend is hospitalized, you want to show that you care, but you don't want to demonstrate your concern in ways that will make the experience even more burdensome for your friend. Follow these tips:

- Do not telephone. Calls can be burdensome or exhausting for a patient. They can also be annoying to other patients. Call the patient's family or office to find out how things are going and have your message of concern passed on.

- Check with the family to see whether flowers are appropriate. Remember that nurses don't have time to take care of flowers, and nothing is worse than a hospital room with dying flowers in it. If you want to send flowers, send them to the home on the day the patient returns home.

- Check with the doctor before bringing gifts of food or sweets.

- Send attractive and/or amusing greeting cards and include a written message, for example, "The office is a lot less cheerful and productive without you."

- Send some light reading and/or books and poetry on tape. If the patient doesn't have a tape player, supply one.

- Speak softly and carry a big smile.

People with disabilities are very much like people without disabilities except, perhaps, that their daily lives may require a bit more courage and character than the rest of us need. If you are uncomfortable in their presence, it is your fault, not theirs. This discomfort will disappear if, while acknowledging that they have a disability, you treat them with the same respect that you expect for yourself. They don't want your pity, and they deserve your admiration.

The Least You Need to Know

- Disabled persons are often as anxious to put you at ease as you are to put them at ease.

- Avoid terms such as *victim*, *crippled*, and *invalid*. Instead of *handicapped*, use the word *disabled*.

- Do not pet or otherwise interfere with a working guide dog.

- Face the person with a hearing loss when you speak so that he or she can see your face. Never shout. It doesn't help and may cause damage.

- A wheelchair is an extension of a person's body. Don't touch it, even to help out, without asking permission.

Chapter 23

Obesity Etiquette

In This Chapter

- ◆ Who loses in obesity discrimination
- ◆ Invitations to avoid
- ◆ Entertainment guidelines
- ◆ Offering support

Most civil and civilized countries protect disabled citizens by law. Laws also prohibit discrimination on the grounds of race, religion, sexual orientation, gender, and age.

People who are obese enjoy few, if any, of these protections. Employers are forced by law to educate employees not to discriminate on the legal issues of race and disability. However, dealing with fellow employees who are obese is rarely in the curriculum. Obese individuals are routinely passed over for positions at school and at work.

Compassion has gone out the window. Compassion? Simple common decency—the cornerstone of good manners—seems to have taken a holiday in this society when it comes to those who are overweight or obese.

Even among those charged with treating the medical problems associated with obesity, cruelty is increasingly the norm. "Size discrimination is the last bastion of bigotry in this country, and the medical profession isn't any more sensitive than anyone else," said Dr. Butch Rosser in a 2003 *New York Times* article. "The people whose job it is to care for people, a lot of them have the attitude, 'You deserve it.' Right now, people with substance abuse issues get more respect and better health care treatment. Morbidly obese people get substandard medicine."

Putting America on the Scales

It's not as if we're talking about an obscure minority that reaches our attention every decade at census time or the few hundred afflicted with a rare disease—and therefore may fly under society's radar screen. Quite the contrary. According to a recent report by the U.S. Department of Health and Human Services, about 129 million U.S. adults are overweight or obese, a number that has risen sharply in recent years. That comes to about one in every four people in America.

Live and Learn
Researchers generally define obesity by using the Body Mass Index (BMI), determined by dividing one's weight (in kilograms) by the square of one's height (in meters). A BMI of more than 25 is considered overweight; 30 is the "cut point" for obesity; 40 for severe obesity.
A 30 BMI, a recent RAND Corporation study explains, corresponds to a person 5 feet 4 inches tall and weighing 174 pounds, or 5 feet 10 inches tall and weighing 209 pounds or more. Someone with a BMI of 50, for example, would be about 150 pounds or more overweight. The typical man in that group weighs 373 pounds and is 5 feet 10 inches tall.

Studies show that the causes of obesity vary. Genetics, medical and psychological conditions, diet, and a societal trend toward overeating are factors.

The decency, respect, and kindness we show to people who are obese should not vary. These people are our teachers, our doctors, our lawyers, our secretaries, our grandparents, our artists, our poets, our neighbors.

Think about it. If we deny ourselves the friendship, wisdom, knowledge, creativity, and love of one in every four people we meet, who really is the loser?

But just as thoughtless generalizations about the character, habits, or circumstances of such a large and diverse segment of our communities are, indeed, illogical, so too would be off-the-top-of-the head generalizations about the best and most polite ways to relate to people who are obese in various situations. For the segments that follow,

I've consulted with, among many others, physicians who perform weight loss surgery (WLS) and a group of remarkable, thoughtful patients who courageously shared their often painful experiences with me.

Live and Learn

James K. Weber, M.D., directs the weight loss programs at the Swedish Medical Center in Seattle and at the Stevens Health Center in Edmonds, Washington. He is a board certified surgeon and performed the first six gastroplasties ever performed at the University of Washington and more than 2,000 of the weight loss surgeries since then. His care addresses both the physical and psychological aspects of obesity. Indeed, his patients undergo significant counseling before a decision is made about having the operation, which requires a permanent commitment to lifestyle changes dealing with exercise and diet.

Over the years, he has compiled this list of the everyday hurdles that people who are obese encounter in a less-than-understanding world.

Some of the ways in which obese people differ from others:

♦ They see disgust registering in the eyes of others and feel shame as a consequence.

♦ They are well aware when they are eating in public that others are wondering how much and how often they eat, why they are eating *that*, why they couldn't exert a little more willpower, and other less-than-charitable thoughts.

♦ They cannot go to the average clothing store to find items that will fit; they must go to the "Big and Tall" shops, where everything is marked up threefold.

♦ They cannot reach down and tie shoe laces.

♦ They cannot balance anything on their lap; indeed, most do not have laps.

♦ They live in constant fear of getting stuck in turnstiles, breaking chairs and toilets, and not being able to get up if they should fall.

♦ They can well imagine the unkind thoughts going through the heads of those passengers who are assigned seats next to them on the airplane.

♦ They are usually the last kids to be chosen in choose-up games at school and are often ridiculed by their classmates.

♦ They are too embarrassed to be seen in gym clothes or a bathing suit.

♦ They can quickly see the disapproval in the eyes of those who are interviewing them for job opportunities.

♦ They are aware that everyone out there just knows that they could lose all that weight if they just exerted a little willpower, if they weren't so lazy, and if they didn't eat so much junk and fast food.

♦ They are really average-sized folks; it's just that they have become trapped under layers of fat, and they can't seem to find the way out. Most have spent hours and countless dollars trying to do something about their excess weight.

Common Assumptions

The most difficult thing for obese people to overcome is what nonobese people *really* know vs. what they *think* they know:

> *If you're overweight, you can't control yourself and therefore are not a good person.*

> *Fat people are stupid and lazy, ugly and sloppy.*

An article by researchers Nancy S. Wellman and Barbara Friedberg sums it up:

> Emotional suffering may be among the most painful aspects of obesity. American society emphasizes physical appearance and often equates attractiveness with slimness, especially for women. Such messages may be devastating to overweight people.

> Many think that obese individuals are gluttonous, lazy, or both, even though this is not true. As a result, obese people often face prejudice or discrimination in the job market, at school, and in social situations. Feelings of rejection, shame, or depression are common.

But the lifelong experience of "B.," clinically obese before undergoing WLS, brings it home:

> I am a smart, nice, personable person with a great deal to offer, but some people just won't see past the fat to the person inside. Most people can see past the color of a person's skin. I wish they could see past the fat.

Common Hurtful Remarks

The remarks obese people endure on a regular basis run a sordid gamut. They range from the openly contemptuous (and borderline illegal):

> *"Yes, we would have accepted you into this or that position if you looked a little more professional."*

> *"Why bother working out, you'll never be able to look like us."*

To the totally clueless:

> *"When is your baby due?"*

> *"Do you know that you are really fat?"*

To the condescending:

> *"You would be so beautiful if you just lost weight."*
>
> *"Why can't you control your eating? You manage to control everything else so well."*
>
> *"Do you think that eating that cheeseburger is in your best interests?"*

To the well-intentioned, but utterly …

> *"I don't think of you as overweight."*
>
> *"Some people are just not meant to be normal size."*

Think before you speak. Outright cruelty, levity at another's expense, unsolicited and patronizing advice, and misplaced compassion have no place in any civil discourse. It's especially cruel here. In general, discussions of another's weight without the full permission and acceptance of the other party is rude and inappropriate.

Let's not forget about the power of facial expressions—staring and looks of disgust or pity can cut as sharply as an insult.

Entertaining

Many severely obese people do not venture out of their homes unless it's absolutely necessary. They often can't be accommodated in many vehicles and almost no public transportation. Should that close the door to their enjoying your hospitality and deprive you of their company? Not at all. It does, as with almost any entertaining situation, present some challenges and require some forethought and planning. Start with the basic premise that everyone has the best intentions. Deal with what's comfortable—or uncomfortable. A decision-making process should emerge.

Here are some things to think about.

Invitations to Avoid Extending

A consideration, and often a dilemma, for any host is whom to invite for a particular occasion. Foremost in our minds should be the interests, convenience, and, most of all, the comfort level of our guests. Asking your elderly parents to join you in the throng at a Brittany Spears concert is probably not the wisest decision, as it would also put them in the uncomfortable position of having to decline a request from their darling child. So, too, is some commonsense forethought warranted in extending an invitation to an obese friend or relative.

"Obese people are for the most part very sensitive to the issue of being overweight," explains "M," another formerly obese patient. "They are *very* aware of spaces where they potentially won't fit—small chairs, bathroom stalls, seat belts, certain cars, buses, airplanes, and the like.

"They are also *very* concerned about furniture that won't accommodate them. They will stand at gatherings if the chairs look like they won't support their weight, or are possibly too small for them to fit into. They also avoid going to places themselves for all of the above reasons."

Other things to think about before extending an invitation:

- Avoid things like swimming parties, barbeques where there are only folding chairs, social gatherings where space is limited—small theaters, church functions (folding chairs again).

- Restaurants where there are only booths and no chairs without arms.

- Spa visits—make sure the spa has robes that can accommodate and massage tables that will hold up under the weight.

- Theaters and concerts—unless there are special seats for large people. (You'd do the same thing for somebody in a walker or a wheelchair.)

- Be wary of activities that require a lot of walking or standing.

"Personal space issues are really the ones that affected me," says "A," once 275 pounds. "Squeezing into chairs with arms at work, on airplanes. Fear of not fitting on things such as roller coasters."

Making Comfortable Accommodations

Try to ensure the invitation is going to a diverse group of people and that accommodations are made for everyone—after all, a 7-foot person would have difficulty with low ceilings, for example.

Assess whether door jams will accommodate the person. Make sure you have chairs without arms. It is easier to get on and off of them. Picnic table benches usually are strong. So are window seats. Couches can be scary—most don't have support in the middle. Big, soft chairs and sofas don't provide enough support.

Consider mealtimes—people often analyze what the obese eat, how fast, how much. If you can, find out if the person has a problem with that.

Don't go overboard with accommodations. For example, renting a park bench just so someone can sit on it safely only draws attention and thus separates the obese person rather than includes him or her.

Finally, says A., "Just treat them with the same dignity and respect you would a non-obese person."

Offering Compassionate Help

You see an obese person drop something, or you see someone challenged by something that's difficult to do. What do you do?

"For me, it would be to treat me as everyone else; just be kind and pick the item up and leave it at that," says B. "The person who dropped the item should say thank you and the person who picked up the item should say 'you're welcome.' Just don't make a big deal out of it. I would hope that the person who picked up the item would treat an infirm person or a pregnant woman exactly the same way."

In general, try these entrees to helping an obese person:

◆ "Is there any way that I can help?" (in a matter-of-fact voice)

◆ "How can I best help you?"

◆ "Will you need some accommodations for you to be comfortable?" This would be helpful at restaurants (offering to add a chair to a booth or retrieve one with arms); stores; hotels; public transportation—perhaps offering to get an extension on a seat belt. Make no fuss—simply drop the seat belt extender in the person's lap.

Anticipate helping out: Walk through doors first, stop for rest yourself if you're walking with an obese person. It doesn't have to be obvious.

Don't be afraid to offer help where it's clearly needed, says A.: "I think most people want to cover their eyes or look away naturally. For me personally, I would rather have it acknowledged than ignored while I continue to struggle."

Advice for Obese People

Perhaps the most important thing obese people must realize is that most people have no idea of what their limitations are and what their life is like, over and above the personal space issues. Thus, they need to take responsibility for getting the help they need.

"Obese people should speak out if there is something that they know needs to be accommodated," says M. "I am not a shy person, so I am not bothered by speaking out and asking for what I need. Many obese people are."

Among the areas where assertiveness is especially important is in retail settings, at restaurants, and similar venues where many obese people often find an apathetic and even hostile staff. Speak up if you're not being served properly or experience rudeness. It may smooth the way for the next person.

It helps to have a clear perspective and a thick skin, says B. "Obese people need to take personal responsibility for their obesity and deal with it. This is a hard reality for us, but it is reality. When obese people accept responsibility for their actions, they will be less militant.

"They also need to accept that there are some mean people out there and learn to let these nasty comments from mean people go, ignore them no matter how difficult and hurtful it may be.

"Obese people are super-sensitive about their weight, but virtually everyone is super-sensitive about something. There are nasty people out there to be mean to everyone about their sensitive issue. People being mean to others is not unique to obese people."

"The goal," adds M, "is to find the fine line between accommodation and excuse."

The Least You Need to Know

- Uninformed assumptions and generalizations about obese people is the greatest obstacle that deprives much of society the camaraderie, creativity, insight, wisdom, humor, and love of obese people.

- Facial expressions—looks of disgust or pity—cut as sharply as insults and condescension.

- Some commonsense forethought will accommodate obese people in your entertainment plans.

- Try to ensure your invitation is going to a diverse group of people and that accommodations are made for everyone.

- Obese people must be assertive and take responsibility to ensure that their needs are accommodated, their rights protected, and their lives led as fully as they want them to be.

Part 6

Correspondence

Living in the era of e-mail does not exempt us from the rules and responsibilities that relate to correspondence—business or personal, formal or casual. The pen, even if it takes the form of a computer keyboard, is still mighty, and people will still make judgments about you based on the quality of your correspondence, electronic and otherwise.

Correspondence should be structured. Different people are addressed differently. Various rules and conventions affect letters and notes that offer thanks, express condolences, convey congratulations, and so on.

How your correspondence looks is sometimes as important as what it says. The stationery should fit the occasion. It, too, speaks for you.

Chapter 24

Letters and Notes

In This Chapter

- ◆ The power of the pen
- ◆ The structure of a letter
- ◆ Kinds of letters and how to write them
- ◆ Writing notes
- ◆ E-mail correspondence

Not one of the communications marvels that enrich and bedevil modern society can replace a personal letter. It is more than a communication. It is a gift. A letter can have special powers. It can be more intimate and touching than even a conversation. It can be more personal than any telephone call.

This chapter discusses the proper form and content of letters sent for specific business or social purposes. It also addresses the easiest ways to open and close a note. Whether you're writing a letter or a note, you'll learn how to conquer writer's block.

Personal Letters

Simplicity and clarity lend grace to what we call plain language. The thoughts and ideas that touch another person most profoundly should not be hidden by or entangled in convoluted phrases and unfamiliar words.

The best letters reflect the personality of the writer. In a way, the letter is a gift of that personality to the reader.

Open and Shut: The Letter Format

Some people have trouble starting a letter but, once started, can continue comfortably. It's a good idea to mentally go over the main things you want to say before starting. You can begin with a bit of good news: "You will be glad to hear that ...." You can describe what you have been doing that day or depict the room in which you are writing. You can also refer to the most recent correspondence or the last time you met the person to whom you are writing.

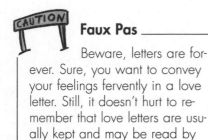

Faux Pas

Beware, letters are forever. Sure, you want to convey your feelings fervently in a love letter. Still, it doesn't hurt to remember that love letters are usually kept and may be read by others many years later.

Don't open a letter by apologizing for not writing sooner. You can say something like "You may have thought I'd forgotten all about you, but really, you have been in my thoughts often lately. It's just that there's been a lot going on. For instance ...."

Letters, by their nature, convey news. Therefore, in the body of the letter, talk about what has been happening to you and to those you both know. Talk about shared interests. Keep the tone conversational and let it flow.

Mind Your P's and Q's

Start your letters by addressing them to the person you're writing to. Indeed, *you* is a much better word than I for beginning a letter.

End formal letters with a *sincerely* and progress toward familiarity with *yours truly, regards, best wishes, affectionately, love,* and so on. The most informal and affectionate letters may end with *miss you* or *write soon* or *more later.*

Letter Do's and Don'ts

Over the years certain customs dealing with how the elements of a letter should be organized on the page have evolved and have been pretty much universally accepted. Knowing how the skeleton of a letter should look allows you to concentrate on the essential message you want to convey. Accordingly, here are some general rules for writing business or social letters:

◆ If your address is not printed at the top of the page, write it in the upper-right corner. (Don't bother if the person you're writing to knows perfectly well where you live.)

◆ The date goes under the address at the upper-right or at the bottom-left corner. Write out the month in more formal letters or if you think the letter might be preserved for posterity.

◆ The salutation goes flush left.

◆ Leave a space, indent, and begin the body of the letter.

Mind Your P's and Q's

Bag the ballpoint pens. Ballpoint does not suggest performance. Fountain pens make letters look so much better. Colored inks are okay for casual notes and letters to friends, but use black ink for a condolence letter or when replying to a formal invitation.

The complimentary close goes to the right, and it can take many forms:

◆ *Love* is a wonderful thing, and you can use it to close a letter if you're writing to a family member or close friend. You can also use *fondly* and *affectionately*.

◆ If you don't know the person very well, try closing with *as ever* or *as always* or *all best wishes*. A stalwart standby is *sincerely*, and you can soften it by putting *very* or *yours* in front.

◆ *Cordially* is considered to be out-of-date, but I like it and still use it because it is correct and, I think, warm.

◆ *Gratefully* is great for letters of thanks.

◆ *Respectfully* and *respectfully yours* are reserved for the clergy.

---

123 Margo St.
Hartford, CT 93433
Nov. 8, 2004

Dear Mr. Petersen:

Thank you so much for your letter of September 9. It certainly brought good news. We have had no difficulty organizing the workers according to your instructions, and I am certain you will be pleased with operations when you arrive for your inspection tour in January.

Sincerely,
Horace Grant

◆ Fold letter sheets vertically with the fold on the left, somewhat like a handwritten brochure. Start writing on page 1 and go to page 3 if the letter runs to a second page. Go with the usual sequence (1,2,3,4) if the letter requires all four pages. Number the pages as you write, at the top of the page in the middle.

The sequence of pages in a letter sheet.

Faux Pas

If you're not going to include a handwritten message, don't send printed Christmas cards at all. A handwritten message— even something as brief as "Holiday Greetings"—may go above or below the printed material.

◆ *Dear Madam* and *Dear Sirs* are outdated if you are writing to a store, for example. It is better to use *To whom it may concern* if you are writing to an unknown person.

◆ If you fold a letter twice, fold the bottom third first and then the top third. The letter should be inserted into the envelope so that when it is removed and unfolded, it is ready to be read— right side up and facing the reader. A letter that is folded only once doesn't require special treatment.

Insert a fold-over note into the envelope in this way.

Leave letters unsealed if they are to be hand-delivered unless they are of a highly personal nature.

Postcards are useful for sending out notices of meetings or confirming appointments. They can be used as thank-you notes for casual parties, but never for dinner, gifts, or for being a houseguest.

> **Mind Your P's and Q's**
>
> Handwrite letters, if possible. However, most formal letters, particularly business letters, may be typed. In addition, if your handwriting is truly cursed beyond redemption, typing is an alternative preferable to illegibility.

Sample Letters

Whether you're writing a thank-you letter or an apology letter (or even a Dear John letter), here are a few do's and don'ts, tips, and samples to help you along the way.

Thank-You Letters

These notes can be boring—boring to write, boring to read: "Thank you for the present. It was nice of you to think of me." To avoid this sort of letter, you can follow my foolproof, three-step formula:

1. Be sure to thank the person for the specific gift and mention the gift by name.

2. Acknowledge the effort and energy the giver put into selecting, purchasing, or making the gift.

3. Let the giver know how you have used or will use the gift.

When thanking someone for a gift of money, don't mention the amount in your letter of thanks. A reference to "your generous gift" will suffice.

When you refuse a gift, a letter, or at least a note, is required. It should say that you don't feel you can accept the gift (perhaps in the case of a woman receiving expensive jewelry from a male acquaintance) but that you appreciate the thought.

> ### Live and Learn
>
> If you thanked the giver at the time the gift was presented to you, it may not be necessary to write a thank-you note. For example, when your sister who lives a block away gives you a gift in person, you need not send a note (although it's nice to do so). When your Aunt Tillie, visiting from across the country, presents you with a hand-knitted sweater, you should acknowledge all her efforts with some extra effort of your own.

Dear Helen:

Tom and I and the two girls want to thank you very much for the handsome Deluxe Edition Monopoly game you gave the family. I happen to know that you can't get this beautifully produced version of the game at most stores, and you must have had to do some shopping around to find it. The four of us spent last night playing the game. (Tammy won.) Your gift has made this familiar game very special for us.

Fondly,
Margaret

Condolence Letters

A letter of condolence should do three things:

- Acknowledge what a terrible loss the death is for the bereaved and that you sympathize with his or her suffering

- Convey a sincere desire to help in some way during this time of grief

- Praise the accomplishments, character, and devotion of the deceased

Remember that many people may read this letter, and it may be saved as part of the family archives. Therefore, although it will be personal, the style should be at least somewhat formal.

In a condolence letter, avoid stressing how much you feel bereaved. The purpose of the letter is to comfort others, not to have them feel sorry for you.

Dear Mrs. Thompson:

Please accept my deepest sympathy on the terrible loss of your fine husband, George, even though I know no words of mine can ease your grief.

I met George on my first day of work at MicroTech, and I will never forget his kindness to me, a confused newcomer. He helped me to get settled and to understand how things worked there—all out of the goodness of his heart. George had that rare combination of kindness, good humor, and competence.

I think you know that we live just a few blocks away, and if there is anything my family or I can do to help during the days ahead, we would consider it a privilege if you would call upon us.

Yours,
Tom

Writing after you have heard some bad news about a friend or acquaintance is a different matter. In this letter, you want to convey not only support but also a bit of optimism.

Dear Margaret:

We just heard that Tom was among those laid off at MicroTech. I know it must be a shock for you and your family. Joe and I will be home all weekend in case you and Tom want to stop by for a drink or dinner or just to chat.

Warmly,
Helen

Congratulations Letters

The congratulations letter is one of the easiest and happiest of letters to write. It is also the sort of letter that a family may keep for years.

Dear Mark:

Congratulations on receiving the fellowship and study grant from Princeton. It is not only a tribute to your brilliance and hard work, but it will give you the opportunity to explore some of the avenues of investigation we have been talking about so wistfully. All of us here at the lab share the joy of this moment with you. We will miss you during the term of your studies and look forward to welcoming you back.

With best wishes,
Jerry

Apology Letters

If you've offended someone and are sorry about it, the best thing to do is apologize in person and follow up with a letter. In any case the letter must say clearly and humbly that you are sorry. If there is some way in which you can make amends, promise to do so.

Dear Mrs. Fitzhugh:

Please accept my sincere apology for having failed to attend your dinner party after assuring you that I would be there. I know how the unexpected absence of a guest can upset the plans of a hostess and am deeply sorry for any distress I may have caused.

My guilt is even greater because I do not have the excuse of a family emergency or other crisis. I simply got the date wrong, and forgot to check to make sure.

Once again, I most humbly apologize and hope that you will forgive my carelessness.

Sincerely,
Elizabeth

Dear John

The overriding objective in this case is to end a romantic relationship with as little pain to the other person as possible.

> **CAUTION**
> **Faux Pas**
>
> Printed thank-you notes from a gift shop are not acceptable as tokens of gratitude. Gratitude does not come prepackaged. And, no, a telephone call is not good enough. Telephone calls always are interruptions. We tend to call people when it's convenient for us—not for them.

- You have to start with a straightforward statement giving the reason for the letter.

- Apologize and offer an explanation that does not blame the other person, something—if possible—that is beyond the control of either of you.

- If there is blame involved, blame yourself.

- Don't lie.

- Don't leave the door open—not even by a crack.

Dear Robert:

After a lot of thought and soul searching, I have come to the realization that it is time to bring our relationship to an end.

Our personalities, interests, and backgrounds are so different that conflicts and unhappiness are inevitable for both of us. I am firmly convinced that I will never be the sort of woman who would fit into your world. I am sure that you will come to realize that as well. I recognize that the reason for this is a lack of flexibility on my part, but I can't seem to help it.

I think we should make a clean break and not try to contact each other again. I wish you nothing but success and happiness.

Sincerely,
Mary

Letters to Politicians and Other Power Brokers

Letters to people in power do have an effect. Ask any politician. These letters should be …

- **Concise.** Put the heart of your message at the very beginning of the letter.

- **Unemotional.** Don't carp or bluster. State your position and the reasons for it with as little emotion as possible.

- **Identifiable.** Say whom you represent. You may be speaking for a group or organization, or you may be writing as a father, businessman, or just a concerned citizen.

Dear Senator Fulton:

I am writing to oppose the proposal to drain the wetlands in the Westphalia section of your district. As you know, wetlands are a critical part of the ecosystem in that area. Draining would not only damage the environment there, but would bring in the sort of development that would put great strain on the area.

I am writing as a resident of Westphalia, as well as someone concerned about the dangerous erosion of the environment through overdevelopment.

I hope you will vote no on SB 188 when it comes before your committee.

Yours truly,
Elizabeth Gordon

You can be even more terse when writing to the White House. The president almost certainly will not see your letter. However, staff people keep a careful tab on how many people are writing with opinions on each issue, and these tabulations are passed along to the president.

Dear Mr. President:

I strongly oppose the idea of sending American troops to Bolivia. In fact, I oppose military intervention in the affairs of any nation in the Americas.

Sincerely,
Robert Anderson

Complaints

One situation in which a face-to-face conversation is preferable to a letter is when you have a complaint about the behavior of a neighbor or friend. Keep things as pleasant and nonconfrontational as possible.

However, a letter to a retailer, business, or government agency is sometimes necessary. Keep your letter as unemotional as possible and state the facts emphatically.

Keep a copy of the letter and follow up within a week with a telephone call.

To Whom It May Concern:

On May 1, 2004, I purchased a Populux 5000 dishwasher from your firm, and it was installed at my home a week later. I have had trouble with it ever since.

First, there was a leak under my sink. Your repairman came four days after I reported the leak and left without fixing it, saying he did not have a certain part with him. When he did not return within three days, I called to complain. Two days after that, he returned.

He worked for more than two hours in my kitchen. When he left, the leak was fixed, but the dishwasher did not work at all. I called again, and another repairman came three days after the call. He said the problem was with the wiring in my kitchen and that I should call an electrician. I did. The electrician said the wiring is fine and charged me $45.

I have now had this dishwasher for one month and have yet to wash a single dish in it. Because your people apparently are unable to repair this machine, you should replace it or refund my purchase price.

Please contact me as soon as possible concerning this matter.

Sincerely,
Paula Smith

Notes

Sometimes you have a great thought about a certain person or situation that you want to share. Of course, you can always place a phone call, but you know what usually happens. You have an idea of what you want to say, not the exact words, but an idea. You may hesitate. The other person says something. The mood shifts. The moment is gone.

On paper you can say exactly what you want to say, and you can take your time in finding the very words that you know will please the object of your thoughts, affection, or concern.

A note can work the magic. It doesn't have to be long (Wish I was there—with you.). It doesn't have to be poetic (I wish you chicken soup.). It doesn't have to be particularly clever (It was great to see you last week. Happily, you haven't changed a bit.).

While drafting your note, think about these points:

- **The recipient.** Is he or she an intimate friend, someone you feel affection for, a person you know and like and would like to know better, someone you know only slightly? A personal reference to that individual or to your relationship separates your note from the anonymous platitudes on printed greeting cards.

- **The occasion.** A birthday is not the same as a confirmation or bar mitzvah. Are you sharing someone's joy, offering condolences, helping to mark a milestone in life?

- **The root message.** When you know what you want to say, you can find pleasing or proper ways of delivering the message. Some root messages are …

  I love you.

  I miss you.

  Thank you.

  Sorry you're sick.

  Congratulations.

When writing a note on an informal note card, don't write anything on the front if it has a monogram in the center of the page. Short notes go inside under the fold. If the note is longer, lay the paper out flat, start the note at the top of the page, and continue onto the bottom half of the back page. Sometimes you cannot write on the back of the monogram or engraving because of the indentation.

Here is a formally engraved informal note in which a woman is using her husband's name—the classic "informal."

Mrs. Timothy Randolph Bennett

Start writing here, on to the bottom half of the back of this sheet.

Openings

You can always use these perennial openers:

- *What a ...* can be followed by *great trip*, *nifty surprise*, *grand occasion*, or *excellent gift*. Another similar beginning is *That was a ....*

- *I was thinking (or remembering) ....*

- *I can't tell you how much ....*

Mind Your P's and Q's

Two good sources of quotations are the *Oxford Dictionary of Quotations* and *Bartlett's Familiar Quotations*.

You can probably come up with a few perennials of your own. When you find a good one, write it down for future use. But remember that perennials wear easily and should be used sparingly.

Quotes

"No wise man ever wished to be younger."

—Jonathan Swift

Sometimes a quote sends just the right message. Every library has books of quotations. A paperback book of quotes for your library is a good investment even if it comes to your rescue only once.

You can even use a tired old saw such as "You inherit your family but you choose your friends." But you have to follow up with something like "With you in my family, I feel as if I am an heir to a fortune." Or "I am so glad you chose me to be a friend."

Closings

A closing to your note should reflect the nature of your relationship with the recipient. A flat *yours truly* will disappoint and perhaps offend a close friend. Leave the *L* word alone unless the recipient is a very close friend.

Here are some closings listed in a more or less declining order of intimacy.

All my love	Affectionately
Best love	Warmly
Much love	Best regards
Love	Regards
Fondly	Or just sign the thing

The following type of letter would receive *love* as a closing:

Dear Sandy:

You know me so well! I'm dashing through my living room in another headlong rush to another boring meeting, and I see your flowers and remember your admonition, "Take time to smell the flowers." So, I am taking time—time to write this note and time to smell the flowers. They smell wonderful. They smell like friendship.

Love,
Mary

E-mail and Netiquette

The ease of e-mail makes it ideal for casual correspondence, but it should be seen as a supplement to, and not a replacement for, other types of correspondence. Some situations demand a formal letter, a telephone call, or a handwritten note.

The rules of grammar and usage are not suspended for e-mail. Exotic punctuation, such as dashes, slashes, and dots, makes the copy hard to read and gives it a juvenile look, like signing a letter with X's and O's. If your system has a spell checker, use it, no matter how good a speller you think you are.

Picturing your correspondence printed out and tacked to a bulletin board will help control the temptation to use e-mail gimmicks. Always use the subject line to let the reader know what the message is about. Tabs and centered or justified text can be lost in transmission. Type single-spaced with a blank line between paragraphs. Using all lowercase makes the message look trivial. All uppercase is equivalent to shouting.

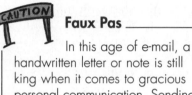

Faux Pas

In this age of e-mail, a handwritten letter or note is still king when it comes to gracious personal communication. Sending a note of thanks or condolence by e-mail has the virtue of being an immediate expression of gratitude or sympathy, but it is not a substitute for sending a handwritten letter.

If you want to forward a message, check first with the original author of the message. You also should get permission before passing around another person's e-mail address. In addition, tell people where you got their address when you are sending them e-mail for the first time.

When sending e-mail internationally, keep the language formal. Casual language, slang, or jokes can confuse and/or annoy someone from another culture.

The Least You Need to Know

- When writing a letter, remember that the address goes at the upper right of the page with the date under it. The salutation is flush left, and the closing and signature are to the right.

- Always write a draft. This practice also helps when you can't think of what to say.

- Don't type your letters unless your handwriting is truly atrocious.

- Make sure notes do their job. Focus. Brevity is the best policy, but don't be curt.

- Keep in mind that letters are a reflection of your personality, and some letters are saved and reread for years.

Chapter 25

Invitations and Addressing

In This Chapter

- ◆ Sending invitations
- ◆ Replying to invitations
- ◆ Formal/informal invitations
- ◆ Addressing people and envelopes
- ◆ Dr., Ms., and Mr. President

We're all sensitive about the way people address us verbally and in writing. And while many of us might be entrenched in the technological age, we still live in a multicultural, multigenerational global village. And many inhabitants of this "village" retain a reverence for the written word and a concern for addressing people correctly.

Even though we live in an age of e-mail and faxes, some formal occasions will always require formal correspondence and invitations that must be addressed properly. The correct way to prepare invitations is the subject of this chapter.

Invitations

People are almost always pleased to receive an invitation, and they are especially pleased to receive one that is properly composed and presented.

Replying

We provide examples of formal invitations later in this chapter. First, let's have a look at some suggestions that apply to the entire invitation scene.

My mother would rather a rattlesnake bite her than include a reply card in an invitation, but that's another generation. These days, the RSVP card is a fixture in most social situations. It evolved because so many people stopped replying formally and in writing to invitations without them.

The practical host must decide whether or not to use the reply cards, and either decision is acceptable. However, experience shows that it is far less stressful to use them than to mount a telephone campaign before the event to find out how many people are coming.

Reply cards follow the same style as the invitation and are made of the same stock. If you do not enclose a reply card with your invitation and you need to know who's coming, be sure to mark the invitation RSVP and provide an address or a telephone number.

Mind Your P's and Q's

Print directions in a similar stock as the invitation and also in its style. If you enclose a map, keep it as uncluttered and clear as possible. Sometimes, including too much information only causes confusion.

When responding to a formal invitation that does not contain a reply card, follow the same general form as the invitation. Write by hand and in the third person. Use conservative stationery or engraved personal stationery. You can use a personal letter sheet, a half sheet, or an informal note sheet. Couples responding should use a Mr. and Mrs. informal. (See Chapter 26 for a rundown of these and other types of personal stationery.)

Faux Pas

Leave the "Jrs." behind. When responding to an invitation from a couple whose name is followed by Jr., II, or III, leave out these designations if you leave out the host's given name. For example, Mr. and Mrs. Paul Gallagher III becomes Mr. and Mrs. Gallagher.

Regrets

When you decline an invitation, briefly state the reason for the refusal in your reply. Two standard reasons to refuse an invitation are a previous engagement and absence from town. Don't give illness as the reason because that is a signal to the host to inquire about your health. If you know the host, call to explain your regrets more fully. Otherwise, a detailed explanation is unnecessary and "regrets she is unable to accept" will suffice.

Informal Invitations

Written on personal notepaper or on an informal or correspondence card, informal invitations are nonetheless written in the third person but are less structured in form than truly formal invitations.

Informal invitations come in various forms. For instance, you can send a fill-in invitation that you buy in a card shop. You can write on informal notepaper or on a folded note with a monogram. On a note with a monogram, start writing on the front if the monogram is placed to one side; start inside, under the fold if the monogram is in the middle.

You can reply by phone if the invitation includes a telephone number. Otherwise, respond on your own stationery—either plain, informals, or correspondence cards.

If the invitation says "Regrets Only," you need not respond if you can attend. However, it's still a good idea to let the host know you're planning to attend.

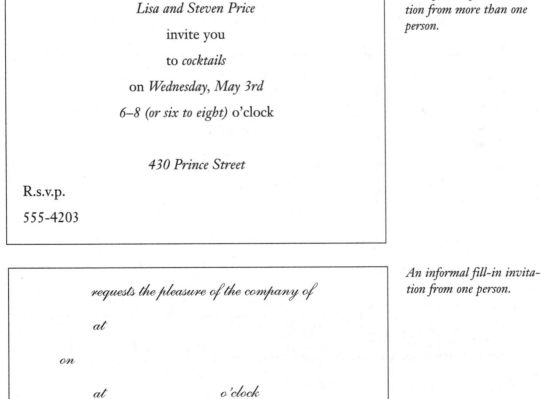

Lisa and Steven Price

invite you

to *cocktails*

on *Wednesday, May 3rd*

6–8 (or six to eight) o'clock

430 Prince Street

R.s.v.p.

555-4203

An informal fill-in invitation from more than one person.

requests the pleasure of the company of

at

on

at   *o'clock*

An informal fill-in invitation from one person.

Formal Invitations

The following examples of formal invitations apply to both handwritten and engraved invitations.

A dinner invitation.

> Mr. and Mrs. Harold Smith
>
> request the pleasure of your company
>
> at dinner
>
> on Wednesday the third of May at 8 p.m.
>
> 1234 Beverly Drive, Toledo, Ohio.
>
> RSVP   Black Tie

If the dinner intends to honor a specific person, the phrase to use is "at 8 P.M. to meet Harold Stasson." Some dinner invitations specify "dinner and dancing."

A formal dance invitation.

> Mr. and Mrs. Harold Smith
>
> request the pleasure of
>
> Mr. and Mrs. Jones' company
>
> at a small dance
>
> on Saturday, the first of May at ten o'clock
>
> at the Ashmead Beach Club
>
> RSVP   Black Tie
>
> 1234 Beverly Drive
>
> Toledo, Ohio 54321

If a single person may bring an escort, add "and guest."

An official luncheon invitation.

> Mr. and Mrs. Harold Smith
>
> request the pleasure of your company
>
> at a luncheon in honor of
>
> the Honourable Edward Rendell,
>
> the Mayor of the City of Philadelphia,
>
> Saturday, May 2, at 1 o'clock
>
> at the Four Seasons Hotel
>
> Logan Square, Philadelphia
>
> RSVP
>
> Office of the City Representative
>
> City Hall
>
> Philadelphia, Pennsylvania

RSVP invitations require an immediate reply.

Accepting a formal invitation.

> Mr. and Mrs. Peter Haas
>
> accept with pleasure
>
> the kind invitation of
>
> Mr. and Mrs. Harold Smith
>
> to dinner
>
> on Saturday, the tenth of June
>
> at eight o'clock.

These days a telephone reply is acceptable. However, meeting your host on the street or at the office and saying you will attend does not constitute a formal acceptance. You must still write or call.

If one half of a couple is accepting, write this type of response.

> *Peter Haas*
>
> *accepts with pleasure*
>
> *the kind invitation of*
>
> *Mr. and Mrs. Harold Smith*
>
> *for Saturday, the tenth of June*
>
> *at eight o'clock.*
>
> *Mrs. Peter Haas regrets*
>
> *that she will be unable to accept*
>
> *because of absence from the city.*

Sending regrets.

> *Mr. Paul Gallagher*
>
> *sincerely regrets*
>
> *that because of a previous engagement*
>
> *he will be unable to accept*
>
> *Mr. and Mrs. Smith's*
>
> *kind invitation for the tenth of June.*

Addressing People

Before dealing with addressing envelopes, let's talk about addressing people. The name game can be confusing—who's a Ms., how to hyphenate, Misses, Messrs., and so forth.

Remember that information about forms of address and titles is merely what has been the custom and what most people have accepted. These titles and forms of address, however, are no more correct than any you may decide upon for yourself.

You can use this information as a starting point, but you will ultimately make up your own mind about what titles and forms of address are most appropriate for you and for those with whom you're corresponding.

Women

Ms. is the correct form of address in the business arena, and it is widely accepted in the social arena as well. Its use, however, is sometimes confused. A divorced woman who goes by her married name would use Ms. because Miss is reserved for a woman who has never married. Thus, when Mary Mitchell marries Dan Fleischmann, she becomes Ms. Mary Mitchell (which is also fine if she is single) or Mrs. Daniel Fleischmann. She does not use Mrs. Mary Fleischmann.

Other rules for addressing women are as follows:

♦ **Married.** A married woman who keeps her maiden name may be known professionally as, for example, Mary Mitchell and socially as Mrs. Daniel Fleischmann. When a married woman hyphenates her name, a practice that appears to be waning in popularity, the maiden name comes before the hyphen and the married name after.

♦ **Widows.** A woman using her husband's name does not change her name when her husband dies.

♦ **Divorced.** When a woman does not drop her married name entirely, she uses her given name in place of her former husband's given name. If she is known professionally by her former husband's name, she can continue to use it even if she remarries. When a woman resumes her maiden name, she becomes Ms. Mary Mitchell, dropping her former Mrs. and never using Miss, which denotes a woman who has never been married.

♦ **Separated.** A woman who is legally separated continues to use her husband's name—given and surname—until she is divorced. A separated woman may use her given name if she chooses.

♦ **Single mothers.** Using Ms. makes more sense than using Miss (although it is technically correct) or Mrs., which designates someone who is legally married. Ms. can refer to either married or single women.

Men

A man is Jr. if his name is identical to his father's. If you spell out the junior, as I have in this sentence, use a small j. If a woman marries a junior, her married name includes the Jr. If a junior gives his son the same name, the son becomes III or 3d. A comma is used between the name and the Jr. or Sr. but not between the name and a Roman numeral.

When a junior's father dies, the son drops the junior. If the surviving son and his mother live in the same city, she may add Sr. to her name to avoid confusion with her daughter-in-law.

A man named after a family member other than his father—say, an uncle or grandfather—uses II or 2d, which is dropped when the family member dies. Men with III or IV usually keep it until death.

Signatures

A married woman should sign legal documents and checks with her given name plus her married name—Mary Fleischmann. If she has a common name such as Jane Smith, she might want to distinguish her signature by using her maiden name as well. A single Jane Smith might want to use a middle initial.

When writing to a person you know very well, sign using your first name only. Never give yourself a title when signing your name. Thus, if writing to someone not on a first-name basis, *Mrs. Daniel Fleischmann* goes in parentheses under the *Mary Fleischmann* signature. If *Mrs. Daniel Fleischmann* is printed at the top of the stationery, simply sign *Mary Fleischmann* at the bottom.

A single woman may write in parentheses (Miss) or (Ms.) to the left of her name. A professional woman who uses her husband's name socially and professionally wants to make it clear that she is married. She signs business letters with (Mrs. John) Alana Kelty. In social correspondence, she proceeds as described in the previous paragraph.

Ambiguous Names

If your name can be either male or female, help the recipient to know your gender. You may include a title on your printed or engraved stationery, even though the rules dictate otherwise. Help the reader by including Ms., Miss, Mrs., or Mr. to the left of your signature. You can also write your full name, including title and address, at the top right of the notepaper or on the upper-left corner of the envelope.

Joint Signatures

Only one person can write a letter, so only one person can sign it. If one half of a couple is writing to a mutual friend, relative, or acquaintance, he can say at the end: "Helen joins me in wishing you the best in your new job."

It is perfectly fine, however, for one half of a couple to sign both names on a postcard, greeting card, and so forth.

Addressing Envelopes

Here are some do's and don'ts on addressing envelopes:

◆ Type or write by hand all social envelopes. It's okay to address an envelope by hand when the letter is typed. Neatness counts, however.

◆ Keep the lines aligned on the left or indent each line slightly more than the previous one. City, state, and ZIP code are on a single line.

◆ It is no longer necessary to write out the names of states in full. And the practice of writing out numbers in full in the most formal situations has virtually disappeared. People use numerals rather than risk trying the patience of the Postal Service.

Mind Your P's and Q's

When writing, Mr., Ms., and Dr. are the only titles that are abbreviated. All others are spelled out.

◆ Middle names are not always written out on formal envelopes. For example, if Michael Jack Schmidt uses Michael J. Schmidt, follow his lead.

◆ The return addresses may appear on the envelope flap, but it is more convenient all around, particularly for the Postal Service, if the return address is on the front of the envelope.

Here's how to address an envelope to a married couple when the wife uses her maiden name:

Ms. Margaret Ferguson

and Mr. Horace Fitzhugh

Yes, the woman's name goes first. Writing out the *and* indicates that the recipients are married. However, if the husband has a professional title, his name goes first:

> The Reverend Horace Fitzhugh
>
> and Ms. Margaret Ferguson

If Margaret uses her maiden name professionally but not socially, the correct address is Mr. and Mrs. Horace Fitzhugh or The Reverend and Mrs. Horace Fitzhugh.

If Horace is deceased, do not address the envelope to Mrs. Margaret Fitzhugh because that would indicate she is divorced. Widows keep their husband's first and last names. If Margaret's son is a Jr., she may add Sr. to her name to avoid confusion.

If Margaret is divorced, address it to Mrs. Margaret Fitzhugh unless she has resumed her maiden name. Then it's Ms. (not Miss) Margaret Ferguson. A separated woman may continue to use her husband's name until she is divorced.

Doctors

When both halves of a couple are medical doctors, the envelope can be addressed as follows:

> The Doctors Peterson

or

> Doctor (or Dr.) Judith Peterson
>
> and Doctor (or Dr.) Michael Peterson

or

> Doctors Judith and Michael Peterson

If Judith goes by her maiden name, the correct form is

> Dr. Judith Holmes and Dr. Michael Peterson

If only the husband is a doctor:

> Dr. and Mrs. Michael Peterson

or

> Dr. Michael Peterson and Ms. Judith Holmes

The name with the title goes first. So, if Judith is the doctor:

Dr. Judith Holmes and Mr. Michael Peterson

Unmarried Couples

Address the envelope to a couple living together but not married with each name on a separate line, flush left, alphabetically, with no *and* between the names.

Children and Teens

Girls are *Miss* from birth until 21, when they may wish to become *Ms.* However, girls' envelopes are generally addressed by name only until they become teenagers, when Miss is used more often.

Boys are correctly (but not necessarily) addressed as *Master* until age eight, when that term is dropped in favor of the given name and no title. He becomes *Mr.* at age 18.

Messrs.

Abbreviated from the French for Misters (Messieurs), *Messrs.* applies only to brothers, not to other male family members like uncles or fathers. If the envelope is going to all of the brothers in the family, it is addressed to The Messrs. Smith. If it is going to two of the three brothers in the family, for example, it is addressed to The Messrs. Lawrence and David Smith. The same rule applies to Misses.

Esquire

Originally, *Esquire* was the title applied to a knight's eldest son or to the younger male members of a noble house whose hereditary title was borne only by the eldest male heir.

The title is seldom used today and only if the person being addressed is a lawyer, male or female. It follows the person's name and is usually abbreviated as Esq. It can also be written out in full in the address. Do not use a prefix (Mr., Mrs., and so forth) when Esq. is being used after the name. When writing to a lawyer and spouse, drop the Esq. and address the letter to Mr. and Mrs. John Smith.

Addressing Officials

The proper forms for addressing various officials follow. The honorifics, Mrs. or Ms., may be substituted for Mr. where appropriate. If the official is a woman, give her husband's full name: Elizabeth Smith and Mr. Harold Smith. If the wife of the official uses her maiden name, use that instead of Mrs. Smith.

Person	Official Address	Social Address
The President of the United States	The President The White House 1600 Pennsylvania Ave. Washington, D.C. 20500	The President and Mrs. Smith The White House 1600 Pennsylvania Ave. Washington, D.C. 20500
Former President of the United States	The Honorable Gilbert Scott Office address	The Honorable Gilbert Scott and Mrs. Scott Home address
Vice President of the United States	The Vice President Executive Office Building Washington, D.C. 20501	The Vice President and Mrs. Smith The Vice President's House Washington, D.C. 20501
The Chief Justice of the Supreme Court	The Chief Justice The Supreme Court One First Street, N.E. Washington, D.C. 20543	The Chief Justice and Mrs. Smith Home Address
Associate Justice	Mr. Justice Smith The Supreme Court One First Street, N.E. Washington, D.C. 20543	Mr. Justice Smith and Mrs. Smith Home Address
Cabinet Member	The Honorable Joseph Smith Secretary of the Interior Department of the Interior Washington, D.C. 20240	The Honorable Secretary of the Interior and Mrs. Smith Home Address
U.S. Senator	The Honorable Mary Smith U.S. Senate Senate Office Building Washington, D.C. 20510	The Honorable Mary Smith and Mr. Harold Smith Home Address
U.S. Representative	The Honorable Harold Smith House of Representatives Washington, D.C. 20515	The Honorable Harold Smith and Mrs. Smith Home Address
American Ambassador*	The Honorable Harold Smith The American Ambassador American Embassy 2 Avenue Gabriel 75382 Paris, France	The Honorable and Mrs. Smith The Ambassador of the United States of America 2 Avenue Gabriel 75382 Paris, France

Person	Official Address	Social Address
Foreign Ambassador	His Excellency Ricardo Smith The Ambassador of Brazil Embassy of Brazil 3006 Massachusetts Avenue Washington, D.C. 20008	His Excellency The Ambassador of Brazil and Mrs. Smith Home Address
Governor	The Honorable Harold Smith Governor of Connecticut State Capitol Hartford, CT 06115	The Governor and Mrs. Smith Home Address
Mayor	The Honorable John Street Mayor of Philadelphia City Hall Philadelphia, PA 19101	The Honorable John Street and Mrs. Street Home address

* When addressing or referring to the American ambassador to a Latin American country, call him or her the Ambassador of the United States of America. Latinos consider South and Central America to be "America," too.

Judges are addressed as *The Honorable*.

The pope of the Roman Catholic Church is addressed as *His Holiness, the Pope*, or as *His Holiness, Pope John Paul II, Vatican City, 00187 Rome, Italy*.

A cardinal is addressed as *His Eminence, Cardinal Justin Francis Rigali, Archbishop of Philadelphia*.

A bishop or archbishop is addressed as *The Most Reverend Thomas Jones, Bishop of Dallas*.

A monsignor is addressed as *The Right Reverend*. A priest is addressed as *The Reverend Father*, a nun as *Sister Mary Catharine*, and a brother as *Brother Thomas Mann*.

A member of the Protestant clergy is addressed as *The Reverend Thomas Jones*, with the letters *D.D.* after the name if the person has a doctor of divinity degree.

An Episcopal bishop is addressed as *The Right Reverend*. The words *The Venerable* precede the name of an archdeacon.

A Jewish rabbi is addressed as *Rabbi Thomas Wise*, with degree initials following the name. A cantor is addressed as *Cantor Thomas Wise*.

The patriarch of the Eastern Orthodox religion is addressed as *His Holiness, the Ecumenical Patriarch of Constantinople, Istanbul, Turkey*. In this religion an archbishop is *The Most Reverend*, a bishop is *The Right Reverend*, and a priest is *The Very Reverend*.

The rules and customs for addressing people and for extending and acknowledging invitations are not new. They have evolved over many generations and have come into existence for very good reasons. All of us care about how we are addressed, and part of having good manners is caring enough to address others properly.

The Least You Need to Know

♦ If you do not enclose a reply card with your invitation and you need to know who's coming, be sure to mark the invitation RSVP and provide an address or a telephone number.

♦ Reply to invitations promptly. If you are sending regrets, briefly state the reason, but do not cite illness. The host would then feel obligated to inquire about your condition, taking up her or his valuable time before the function.

♦ A reply should have the same form and structure as the invitation.

♦ If a title is in the address, it should also be in the salutation, as in Dear Dr. Smith. Never give yourself a title, such as Miss Abigail Dunwoody, when signing correspondence.

Chapter 26

Stationery

In This Chapter

- ◆ Paper quality
- ◆ Your personal stationery
- ◆ Stationery styles
- ◆ Engraving and monograms

Just as we judge others more by what we see than by the words they speak, we also make judgments based on the appearance of the correspondence we receive. A single-sentence letter can speak volumes about the person sending it, which can be an advantage or a disadvantage.

People are far less restricted and rigid about their correspondence these days than in the past, especially when it comes to correspondence mediums. Computer programs for word processing and graphics provide more resources for expressing personal style and creativity than anyone ever dreamed of in the past. Hence the strict formulas for correspondence have been stretched to reflect the times.

It is still valuable to know and to understand the process for taking pen to paper and what's what when it comes to stationery. Your personal choice of fuchsia paper with hot-pink type might be great for a missive to your former roommate. It would be the kiss of death, however, if used to apply for a job with a conservative law firm.

As with any issue involving personal presence, grooming is more important than a fashion statement. If the engraved letterhead isn't even close to your sense of self or concept of reality, then clean paper, crisply folded with its written components done perfectly, will speak better in your favor than costly stationery, carelessly used.

Paper

People judge paper by its texture and weight, both reflections of the material from which it is made. The best stationery is made from new unlaundered and undyed cotton rags. Cheaper papers are made from vegetable fibers, sometimes combined with wood pulp. The higher the rag content, the better the paper. Rag content is usually noted on the package.

Watermarks reveal the quality of stationery. A watermark is the manufacturer's identification, which can be seen when the paper is held up to the light. A genuine watermark looks slightly blurred. There are imitation watermarks, but they look artificial in their sharpness.

Printing

The kind of printing you use is another important factor in the overall quality of your stationery. Engraving is the highest quality printing.

Raised lettering, or thermography, imitates the look of engraving, but cannot approach the quality. It is the pretender to engraving, and personally, I think you should decide either to engrave or not. Stationery, like people, ought not to pretend to be something that it isn't.

Most printing involves a process known as offset lithography. It is the least expensive method but, with good design, can achieve a high-quality image.

Personal Stationery

Your personal stationery is as important and as noticed as any clothing accessory—for example, a wristwatch. Most people should own three kinds of personal stationery: formal writing paper (which can be engraved or plain), personal business stationery, and personal notepaper. Household informal stationery is an additional option.

You use formal writing paper for writing condolence letters and responding to formal invitations. Do not substitute informal writing paper when formal writing paper is called for.

Personal business stationery is used for matters relating to your career or home life, such as applying for a job or letting the store know that your drapes have not arrived.

Use personal notepaper for writing informal invitations and replies, friendly correspondence, thank-you letters—basically for all informal social correspondence. Stationery stores call this kind of item informals. They are generally folded and about 5 by 7 inches in size. The most widely used colors for notepaper are white and off-white. Folded notes, which are available in pale pink and other pastel colors, are slightly less formal than informals.

If you print household informal stationery, you might choose to include your telephone number for convenience. This fairly impersonal type of stationery is used for notes to vendors, the post office, electric company, and so on.

You don't need to use custom-printed or engraved stationery. Any good stationery store, department store, or jeweler who provides engraving services will also carry plain stationery. Personalizing it is a nice and useful luxury, however.

Make sure your stationery meets U.S. postal regulations—that is, envelopes must be at least 3½ by 5 inches. The Postal Service still allows envelopes with the return address printed on the back, which is a formal social custom. As a general rule, however, printing the return address on the front of the envelope is much more practical if the letter has to be returned to the sender. It is good manners to heed the Postal Service request to put the return address on the front of the envelope for everything but the most formal invitations.

Women and Stationery

There was a time when every well-bred woman used only fold-over notes, rather than flat stationery. Today, women are free to select stationery that complements their handwriting, style, and taste. For example, I know several women who choose large letter-size paper for casual notes because it accommodates their large-script flair. However, unless you have a wardrobe of personal stationery, it's a good idea to avoid wild ink colors in favor of more conservative colors such as black or gray, which are appropriate in all situations.

With personalized stationery a woman has the option of using her social title. Thus a married woman might use Mrs. Daniel Fleischmann or the more contemporary Ms. Mary Fleischmann. It is unnecessary and perhaps a bit pretentious for single women to give themselves the title of Miss, although it is not incorrect. The name itself does just fine.

Faux Pas

Engraved stationery for a young person is pretentious; wait until he or she is 18 or in college.

Printing notepaper with your address only is probably more practical if you use different names or titles, for example, your maiden name in business and your married name socially.

Men and Stationery

For men's stationery the name appears without a title unless he happens to be a medical doctor, in which case it is fine to use Dr. before the name. Use M.D. only professionally. A man would also use a title if he is a clergyman or member of the military so that others will know how to address him correctly.

Children and Stationery

Children are often "bribed" into writing thank-you notes with the prize of personal stationery. A wealth of children's stationery is available in designs ranging from colorful sports motifs to delicate dolls and animals. You'd be wise to purchase lined paper for young children.

Monograms

Monograms continue to be popular. They should appear either centered at the top of the page, centered on the front of the folded note, or in the upper-left corner.

A single-initialed piece of stationery leaves too many questions in the readers' minds. Stationery stores sell preprinted notes with single initials, but these seem to me to be useless and silly.

If you choose to monogram your stationery, it is best to use three initials, unless they happen to spell something graceless. Alice Stanton Smith, for example, would be better off using just two initials.

Mind Your P's and Q's

Any good stationer—Tiffany & Co. or J. E. Caldwell & Co., for example—can guide you through deciding what kind of stationery you need and how to use it. Most major cities have respected stationers who cater to established families. When in doubt, shop in these places. The advice is usually free.

The most common styles for monograms are either three initials set in consecutive order or the initial of the last name in a larger size in the middle of the other two. A single woman or a married woman who retains her maiden name uses the initials of her first, middle, and last names. A married woman who uses her husband's name uses the initials of her first name, her maiden name, and her husband's last name.

Always write out the names of your city and state in full with no abbreviations. Numerals for street numbers are fine. Spelling out numbers greater than 10 is generally unwieldy and pretentious.

Engraved monogram styles.

Stationery Styles

Here are some descriptions of traditional stationery styles. All listed measurements are approximate.

Letter Sheet

Size: 5¼ by 7¼ inches high.

The letter sheet is a formal stationery style. It can be used for extending and replying to informal invitations or for replying to formal invitations. (You may not want to use a letter sheet that is engraved informally with the address only to extend an invitation.)

This stationery should be of white or off-white stock. The sheet comes folded vertically with the crease on the left. You can engrave it with a crest, monogram, name only, or address only—although it doesn't have to be engraved at all.

Informals

Size: 5 by 3½ inches wide.

In spite of its name, the informal is a pretty formal piece of stationery. Men use informals only when they are engraved with a couple's name on the front. Informals can also be engraved with a woman's full name. They are appropriate for writing notes, gift enclosures, extending and replying to informal invitations, and replying to formal invitations.

Message Cards

Size: 5 by 3½ inches high.

A message card is a single white card with a very smooth (satin) finish. It can have a woman's full name or a couple's name engraved at the top center of the card. The street address can be in the upper-right corner. You can use these for thank-you notes or other kinds of notes and for extending or replying to an informal invitation.

Correspondence Cards

Size: 6½ by 4¼ inches high.

The correspondence card is a most useful investment for both men and women, especially in the corporate arena. The single card can be colored and sometimes has a colored border. The card can also be plain or engraved with a monogram, the name alone, or the name with address. The correspondence card is used for any kind of short note, sending or replying to invitations, thank-yous, and so on. Men find these particularly useful and often have only this one stationery item for personal use.

The correspondence card is probably the single most used item of stationery in a businessperson's arsenal.

A woman's and a man's correspondence cards.

Half Sheets

Size: 5¾ by 7¾ inches high to 6¼ by 8½ inches high.

A half sheet is a single sheet in any color. Use it for writing letters. If you are engraving it, the monogram or crest, or name and address, is centered at the top. You will need plain second sheets if you write long letters. The second sheets can be used interchangeably with the letter sheets for most correspondence, although the letter sheet is more formal and traditional. Pale colors are fine, although you should not use anything other than white or off-white to send a condolence letter or to extend or reply to a formal invitation.

WILLIAM WARREN REDFIELD

A half sheet.

Folded Notes

Size: 5¼ by 3½ inches high.

Folded notes look just like informals but may be in pastel colors. The front page is blank or engraved with a centered monogram or with the monogram in the upper-left corner. Folded notes are great for general correspondence, especially thank-you notes.

Monarch Sheets

Size: 7¼ by 10½ inches high.

Both men and women use monarch sheets for general correspondence and informal business letters.

Sample man's monarch sheet.

KENNETH BRADLEY HAZARD

Sample business monarch sheet, engraved.

Uncommon Courtesies®

215-574-1666

facsimile 215-574-1667

Post Office Box 40008

Philadelphia

Pennsylvania 19106

The
MITCHELL
Organization

As you consider which style, color, and types of stationery to invest in, remember the factors that transcend these details. The stationery you choose is part of the message you will be sending and should reflect your personality.

The Least You Need to Know

♦ Paper quality is judged by the weight of the paper. The better quality paper has a higher rag content.

♦ Most people need three kinds of stationery: formal, personal business stationery, and personal notepaper.

♦ Informal writing paper is generally white or off-white.

♦ Engraving is the finest and most expensive type of printing.

Part 7

Travel

Travel etiquette involves not only getting from here to there with style, but also maintaining safety and comfort while on the road. This section examines tipping, luggage and packing, personal space issues, proper attire, and other crucial matters.

Security has taken center stage among travel concerns, with delays, searches, long lines, and cancellations a new fact of life. But it's important to remember amid the frustration that these precautions are designed to serve us and are for our own good.

Having said all this, travel should be fun and our attitude about it often can make the difference between a good trip and a miserable one.

Chapter 27

On the Road

In This Chapter

- ◆ The importance of being prepared
- ◆ Services you can expect from hotels, motels, and bed & breakfasts
- ◆ Tips on tipping the concierge, porters, maids, and more
- ◆ Wise advice for women traveling alone

Travel can bring out the best and the worst in people. And no wonder. Travelers are forced to deal with lots of people, most of them total strangers, in sometimes difficult and stressful situations—situations you probably have no control over. The people around you may be tired, edgy, anxious, excited, or gabby. You may be any or all of the above.

Yet pleasant travelers seem to be welcome everywhere. They get the best service and end up meeting the most intriguing people—and deservedly so. The pleasant traveler begins each journey armed with a positive attitude and a willingness to deal with new situations and meet new people. Each journey also should begin with a sure knowledge of the "rules of the road."

Are You Ready to Travel?

Rule number one is to be prepared. People get into unnecessary travel trouble because they haven't prepared properly, and the pleasant traveler is the well-prepared traveler.

Take Pride in Your Appearance

Most people you will meet on your journey will be strangers, and their only way of judging you—at least at first—is by your appearance. The fact that you may be squished into cramped seats for long periods and may have to spend a lot of time in the same clothes does not mean that your attire should be sloppy or grungy. The way you dress represents what kind of person you are. If the way you dress sends out the signal that you are careless or unkempt, you don't have a prayer of successful, convivial travel. People will tend to shy away from you if you give the impression that you are poorly groomed. Close quarters demand scrupulous cleanliness.

Calculate Your Finances

In calculating how much money you'll need for a trip, be realistic about meals, tips, admission charges, recreation, and other activities. Remember that if your plans include a stay in a luxury hotel, tips can add another 25 percent to the final tab. More people are waiting on you there than at Motel 6, and anyone who "leaves the light on for you" wants to be compensated for it.

If you're traveling to a foreign country, know its exchange rate and, if possible, carry a small exchange chart with you. Confusion over exchange rates and fumbling through different kinds of currency can be annoying to you and those around you. Make sure you have a small amount of local currency on hand when you arrive to take care of things like taxis and tips. If not, the currency exchange window should be one of your first stops at the airport. Hotels will exchange money, but they don't give the best rates. Banks are your best bet. The airport exchange window is often more expensive than the windows at banks and hotels.

Check to see whether you can use your ATM card to get cash in local currency while you are away.

Mind Your P's and Q's

Pack metal items in a separate bag so that you can get through security metal detectors with a minimum of hassle. All luggage should have identification tags on the inside as well as the outside. Exterior labels sometimes come off during a trip.

Pack Well

In general, less is better, and that's especially true when it comes to packing. You don't need to be prepared for every possible emergency. Some people pack as if every necessity of life will have to come from their suitcases. An overabundance of luggage looks ostentatious and can make your trip unnecessarily complicated and burdensome. Remember, you will find stores at almost every destination.

Proper Documentation

Check to see whether your passport is up-to-date well in advance of any international trips. You will need about six weeks to obtain one. If you apply by mail or during the peak travel season, allow even more time.

To get a passport, you need proof of citizenship—an old passport or birth or baptismal certificate will do. You also need two identical passport photos. If you're traveling with your family, every member of your family will need a passport. Most major cities have a passport office. Otherwise, your county courthouse or local post office can help.

Check at least six weeks in advance to see whether you need a visa to travel to your destination. You can find out from a travel agent or an airline ticket agent.

If possible, obtain an international driver's license. Your local auto club can help you. Whether you get an international license or not, carry your regular license with you, as well as other identification.

If you're attending any official functions during your trip, bring some documentation of that fact with you. For example, I arrived in London expecting to attend an international banking reception that evening. My luggage was lost, and the airline could not guarantee that I would have it in time for the event. As a result, once I showed them my ticket for the reception and my luggage claim check, the airline gave me a voucher and sent me off to Harrod's to purchase a dress suitable for the occasion.

Make sure you have copies of your eyeglass prescription and any medical prescriptions with you at all times when you travel. Keep them with your passport. Also, have records to prove that your inoculations are up-to-date. Your travel agent or board of health can give you the necessary information.

Some inoculations are mandatory, and some are merely recommended. Don't be so quick to disregard the "recommendations." I was not required to get typhoid shots before going to Egypt. So I didn't. You better believe I regretted my decision once I caught typhoid.

> ### Live and Learn
>
> Always read the fine print on the back of your airplane ticket. You will find out how much liability the carrier accepts for things like lost possessions. You also can learn about circumstances under which the carrier will cease to honor your seat reservation. (You might arrive five minutes before your flight and find your seat has been given to a standby.)

Don't Leave Home Without It

If you do not have a printed itinerary from a travel agent, draw up one of your own. Take one copy with you and leave a copy at home (include emergency telephone numbers in case someone needs to reach you).

Also, make a list of items in your luggage. Take the list with you (but not in your luggage) and leave a copy at home.

Travel Agents

Working with a travel agent can save you time and money. Agents' compensation comes from commissions they earn from companies like airlines, hotels, and cruise lines. However, it is appropriate for a travel agent to charge you for out-of-pocket expenses incurred on your behalf, including unusual long-distance telephone charges or messenger services.

Some travel agencies specialize and primarily handle particular types of travel, such as cruises, hiking, or other special-interest trips. Some agents are more knowledgeable than others about places and topics that are of special interest to you. The best way to shop for a travel agent is to ask friends who have interests similar to your own.

> ### Live and Learn
>
> Here are some points to keep in mind about travel insurance:
> - Your credit card may automatically provide travel and life insurance.
> - Many people believe in trip-cancellation insurance. It reimburses you if you must cancel a trip because of a medical emergency or a death in the family.
> - Check to see whether your homeowner's policy covers loss of luggage and personal items while traveling.

If you're consulting a travel agent who can't provide the information you need or if you sense that the agent isn't giving you adequate attention, feel free to say something like "I'll get back to you" and try someone else.

Travel agents can arrange car rentals, chauffeur services, tour guides, theater tickets, and even meal reservations. They know about guided tours and group trips and can handle details as small as a one-shot AMTRAK ticket.

However, you need to be clear about your preferences and about your budgetary limitations. And be reasonable. You can't accommodate Ritz Carlton tastes on an EconoLodge budget.

Hotels

Hotels can be so much more than places to sleep while traveling. They can be among the most interesting and memorable aspects of a trip. However, because hotels range from elegant luxury establishments to country inns to chain hostelries off the interstate, they can be a bit confusing unless you know what to expect from them and what they may expect from you.

Luxury Hotels

It's usually a good idea to book rooms in luxury hotels well in advance. These hotels provide many extra amenities and services. You probably can count on having bathrobes, hair dryers, and a minibar in your room. (Beware of minibars: You can be in for a very expensive and sobering surprise when you pay your bill.)

When you arrive, a doorman greets you, and a porter takes your bags. Tip the porter at least $2 per bag. If the doorman hails a cab for you, tip him at least $2. If he has to stand out in the rain, tip more.

Proceed to the registration desk and give the clerk your confirmation number. Married couples should sign in under both of their names. If a woman uses her maiden name in business, she should include that in registering so that telephone calls can be fielded accurately. Unmarried couples should both sign in as well. These details may seem unnecessary, but they are important for security purposes and, practically speaking, for things like telephone calls.

The porter takes the bags to your room. Sometimes the desk clerk will direct you to the room, and the porter will follow with the bags. The porter or bellman will open the room, turn on the lights, adjust the air-conditioning, put your luggage on stands, draw the curtains, show you the minibar, and explain how the television works. If you don't like the room, ask the porter to call the front desk about a replacement.

Remember that the porter is not authorized to change your room and must clear your request through the front desk.

> ### Mind Your P's and Q's _____
>
> The Citizens Emergency Center at the State Department in Washington, D.C., can give you up-to-date information on health precautions for virtually any place you plan to visit. Call 202-647-4000. The State Department's Bureau of Consular Affairs website (travel.state.gov/travel_warnings.html) also provides security advisories and other useful information for any country you can visit. In addition, you can find a variety of helpful tips on new security regulations, baggage restrictions, prohibited items, and preparation strategy on the U.S. Transportation Security Administration's website (www.tsa.gov/public/).

The next thing you should do, no matter what sort of hotel, motel, or inn you are staying at, is to find the emergency and fire exits. Check to see whether you need more towels, pillows, blankets, hangers, or an iron. If you do, call housekeeping right away. Calling late at night when there is a reduced staff can create difficulties and delays.

Luxury hotels have a concierge, in the European tradition. The concierge desk is generally located near the registration desk. Here you can obtain theater, concert, and sports tickets; look at local restaurant menus and make dining reservations; and find out about car rentals, sightseeing tours, baby-sitters, and even traffic and weather conditions. A good concierge is a miracle worker who seems to know everything about everything.

Commercial Hotels

These hotels, typified by those in the Marriott and Hyatt chains, are designed for the business traveler. They are clean, comfortable, and efficient. They also are cheaper and offer fewer frills than the luxury hotels. Available for business travelers are conference rooms, computers, facsimile machines, copiers, secretarial services, and fitness facilities.

Pack a travel iron and hair dryer. You might be able to borrow these things from the hotel, but you might not be able to borrow them exactly when you need them. You can't afford to be held up for an appointment because you are stranded waiting for an iron.

Business people suggest you avoid doing business in your hotel room. And if you are on a business trip, never share a room with a member of the opposite sex—colleague or not. This behavior damages your credibility, as well as that of your company.

Room Service

Especially if you are traveling on business, put in your breakfast order the night before and allow yourself plenty of time to receive and eat it before leaving for your business appointment. It's fine to greet the room service waiter in your robe. The waiter will set up the meal in your room. When you're finished, call room service to come for the tray or cart, instead of leaving it in the hall. A service charge is added to the bill. If a tip is not included on the bill, the usual amount to leave is 20 percent.

Security

Hotel guests, even guests in the most prestigious hotels, must be aware that they always have at least some responsibility for their security. Here are some basic rules to remember:

◆ Never keep cash or valuables in your room. Use the hotel safe.

◆ Never open the door when someone knocks unless you know who it is—especially at night. If the knocker claims to be a hotel employee and you have any doubts, call the front desk to ask whether this person has been sent to your room. If not, call hotel security, give your room number, and state that someone is at your door.

◆ Always double-lock your door. You may want to leave the television on when you're not in the room to dissuade burglars.

◆ If the desk clerk announces your room number in a loud voice and this practice bothers you, as it should, quietly ask for another room and explain that you are being cautious in case someone overheard.

◆ Don't flash a wad of bills in the hotel bar.

 Faux Pas _____

Bathrobes, ashtrays, wineglasses, and the like are not souvenirs. Neither are towels. If you like, you can arrange to purchase these things at the front desk. This approach is far superior to finding the items listed on your hotel bill because you have been caught in the act.

Checking Out

Confirm your departure the day before and verify the checkout time. Usually, you can arrange a late departure if the hotel isn't full. Call the porter to collect your bags. Tip about $2 a bag. If you need to check your bags at the hotel for the day, the porter will take care of it and give you tickets to redeem them.

Motels

Motels come in many shapes and sizes. Some offer little more than a bed, bathroom, and television, whereas others resemble small resorts with pools, restaurants, and gyms.

The variety of possibilities is one of the advantages of motel travel. They are usually clustered at the convergence of major highways so that motorists have a wide range of options within the distance of a mile or so.

You can easily make your own reservations, since most major chains have toll-free reservation numbers and websites for reservations. Most offer discounts for members of auto clubs, holders of certain credit cards, and senior citizens. In some cases "seniors" can be as young as 50.

When you check in, the clerk may want government-issued photo identification, your driver's license number, and a credit card, even if you are paying in cash.

You will carry your own bags. Ice, snacks, and some personal items like toothbrushes probably will be available at a vending center, usually located one to a floor. Dress is casual, of course, but wear a cover-up at the pool, and avoid dripping all over the lobby. Don't leave children alone in the pool or Jacuzzi.

If you arrive late at night or leave early in the morning, be considerate of those still sleeping. If there is a disturbance late at night, don't elect to straighten it out yourself. Call the front desk, and do not open your door. Tip the maid $2 or $3 for each night you stay. Leave your tip on the pillow or sink each day as you leave the room. That way, the person who cleans your room will be sure to get the tip.

The Bed and Breakfast

Antiques. A canopied bed. Tea or sherry in the afternoon. A convivial host. These are among the charms of the bed and breakfast.

Often for the price of a good hotel, you can spend the night in a charming Victorian or colonial-era house, usually an interesting place with interesting owners who have an agreeably old-fashioned idea of comfort and hospitality.

And then there's breakfast. Some hosts offer a simple continental breakfast of juice, coffee, and a roll. Others offer such a variety and quantity of food that you'll feel dazzled—and quite sated after eating! The best ways to find out about B&Bs are from friends or from the many guidebooks that are available in bookstores and public libraries. Always call for reservations. Some establishments require a stay of at least two days.

When you arrive, the host will probably be on hand to greet you personally. He or she will take your bags, help you get settled, and show you the dining room and other spaces devoted to the guests. It is very bad form to stray into the host family's living quarters.

A good rule of thumb is to behave much like a houseguest at a friend's home. Avoid loud conversations or television late at night. You may borrow books from the library to read in your room but be sure to return them. Don't use the owner's private telephone without asking first.

Many such places have shared bathrooms, so don't luxuriate in the tub while someone may be waiting. And be sure to leave the tub and the rest of the room as clean as you can reasonably make it.

At breakfast, which is included in the price, introduce yourself and say, "Good morning," all around. If you don't feel chatty in the morning, just smile and give minimal answers, and people will get the message. Be alert for such signals yourself.

Leave your room reasonably neat and say good-bye to the host before leaving. No tipping is required.

Houseguests: How to Be a Good One

Most times we are houseguests first with our families—visiting cousins, grandparents, aunts, and uncles. Those experiences teach us lots for later years, and as the poet says, "Good fences make good neighbors." In other words, it's important to know how to behave so you get a return invitation, and keeping the house rules is essential. Here are some tips that will serve you well, both with family and others.

Whether you are host or guest, it's important to know …

- ◆ Only go/invite when you *really* like the people and know you can spend extended time with them. Being a houseguest or houseguest's host is a lot different from a single dinner, lunch, or afternoon outing.

- ◆ Communicate! Arrival and departure times should be clear to both host and guest. Host should clue guest in about the activities planned and if any special clothing/equipment will be needed. For example, "Be sure to bring your tennis racquet and you'll need a jacket for dinner on Saturday."

- ◆ Make sure there is "down time." Whether you are host or guest, or if the visit has a business context, both are "on" the entire time. Exhausting! The host should let the guest know that there will be some free time: "Saturday you're on your own from lunch until dinner. There are lots of shops to explore and, of course, the beach, if you like. Or you can just take a nap and curl up with a good book."

◆ Positive attitudes mean a lot. After all, everybody loves a lover, so to speak. So if everyone is determined to play volleyball, don't be a wet blanket. Similarly, hosts need to be positive about their guests' quirks and roll with the punches. Sulking ruins the visit for everyone.

◆ Break something of the host's? Replace it or repair it at once. And apologize profusely—probably by sending flowers once you return home.

◆ Don't bring your pets!

◆ When the host says, "Make yourself at home," he/she doesn't *really* mean it. Hosts want you to sleep well, have a good time, and to be well fed. They do not want you to leave bathrooms littered with your shaving paraphernalia or cosmetics. They do not really want you to search for hidden treasure. (Once I awakened to discover my guest rummaging through my drawers and cabinets!)

◆ Cell phones are to be seen very infrequently and not heard. If you're tethered to your cell phone, why visit in the first place? Of course, if you have children to keep tabs on, it makes sense to bring your phone along. Keep the ringer off. If you have calls to make, schedule them during your "down time." It's amazing how the world goes on even when we're unplugged for a little while.

◆ Come bearing gifts! Or you can send something in advance of the visit; and flowers after you leave are always welcome (although they do not replace the hostess gift). If you plan to bring food to be consumed during the weekend (not my favorite idea—it can throw the host's plans way off) be sure to ask the host well in advance. They might not want your grandma's famous lasagna. If you bring nice wine—a few bottles, please!—say to your host, "This is something for you two to put aside for a quiet evening sometime with each other." "Rainy day" gifts are a good idea—games, coffeetable books, and the like. Be generous.

◆ It's gracious for the guest to take the hosts to dinner one night—just be sure to let the host know that you plan to do so.

◆ A thank-you letter—handwritten—is an absolute must. Detail the special parts of the visit, compliment the atmosphere and your host's graciousness, food, and planning. Let the host know that you appreciate all the work that went into the visit. E-mails only are acceptable when followed by a handwritten letter: "We just got back and although my letter will be on its way very soon, I just want to tell you what a super time we had this weekend—it was difficult to re-enter the 'real world.'"

Travel Tipping

Tipping is so solidly ground into the fabric of the economy and culture, it is unavoidable. If you plan to travel, you must plan to tip.

Cruise Control

Cruise lines can provide a list of recommended tips. In general, tips on your cruise will amount to 15 to 20 percent of your cabin fare.

The porter who takes your bags at the pier gets $2 to $5 a bag, more if you have trunks. On board, you might get better service if you give your cabin steward and your dining room steward $20 or $30 at the beginning of the cruise. These stewards usually are tipped a total of $3 to $5 a day, more if you are in a suite. Bar and lounge stewards are tipped 20 percent of the bill. Wine stewards get 15 to 18 percent of the wine bill, just as they do at a fine restaurant. For personal services—hairdressers, manicurists, and so on—tip as you would on land.

Don't tip officers or the cruise director. A thank-you note will do.

On the last day of the cruise, put tips in envelopes with a note for each recipient. Hand them out personally or, if necessary, have the purser distribute them. It is worth the effort to write a note because the staff will appreciate your personal thanks.

Mind Your P's and Q's

When traveling by plane, a buck a bag is the correct tip for a skycap. No other tipping is required. Tip a private driver, limousine or taxi, 18 to 20 percent of the total bill.

Trains

In first class, the ticket covers the costs of meals and service. However, you may tip $10 or $20 at the end of a long trip if service was good. If meals are not included in the ticket price, tip as you would in a restaurant.

For overnight trips, tip the porter about $10 a day if he makes up your berth, wakes you, brings coffee and a newspaper, or performs similar services.

Redcaps, or baggage porters, get $1 or $2 per bag whether you are traveling first class or coach.

Buses

Someone will be designated to collect tips at the end of a bus tour. The usual rate is $3 to $5 a day for the tour guide and $2 to $4 a day for the driver. If you want to contribute individually, put your tips in a sealed envelope with a note.

Hotels

The following are general tipping recommendations at an upscale, urban hotel. Tip slightly less at less expensive hotels.

Doorman: from $2 to $10, depending on how much baggage he takes from your car or cab. Figure $2 per bag, and include odd items that might not be suitcases. After that, he gets a dollar or two, having supervised installing your bags from the car or cab.

Bellmen who bring luggage to your room: at least $5 and up to $10.

Room service: Check first to see that your gratuity is on the bill. Give the server an additional $5 in cash, since frequently they do not share equally in their tips.

Valet: $5 to $10, depending on how much he assists you with dry cleaning, etc.

Engineering and technical support: If someone comes to fix your heating or air-conditioning, or to help with your Internet connection, tip $5 to $10.

Concierge: $20 if the concierge obtained dinner reservations or theater tickets for you, arranged for plane reservations, and so on, depending on the time and skill required.

Housekeeper: $3 to $5 left on your pillow each morning.

Valet parking attendants: $2 to $5 when they fetch your car.

Taxi drivers should receive 15 percent to 20 percent. I usually give a minimum of $5.00.

Note: Some luxury hotels and spas include tips with the room charge. Even so, you might want to tip the maître d' in the dining room $20 or $30 at the start of your visit, as a sort of insurance policy for good seating and service.

Wise Words for Women Traveling Alone

Women traveling alone have some special considerations with regard to safety and companionship. Fortunately, traveling alone in the United States poses no real difficulties culturally. Before going to another culture, however, do some homework. For example, I spent a long stretch of time in a Cairo hotel during which my husband was away frequently. Unfortunately, I felt forced to dine alone in my room because a woman dining by herself is thought of as less than morally upstanding. Not very pleasant.

Even in the United States, certain social difficulties confront a woman traveling alone. In general, a good guide when talking to strangers, especially men, is to pay your own way, even though you may be invited for drinks or a meal. Always make sure you are on equal footing.

Don't be afraid to talk to strangers. They might become the most interesting part of your trip. Just be wary of putting yourself in jeopardy because you are unaware of personalities and customs. An invitation to dinner may mean that the host expects you to be dessert.

You can communicate the fact that you are not interested in getting to know someone better by giving one-word answers, nodding, or saying that you need to take a nap.

Women dining alone are still at a disadvantage these days, but less so when the dinner hour is early, say, 6 or 6:30 P.M. Traditionally, women are thought to eat less, drink less, and tip less than men. Do yourself a favor, and call first for a reservation. Tip the maître d'. If you act like you know what you are doing, you will get better service. Don't be afraid to challenge a manager about discriminatory practices if you think it's warranted. Do so quietly and with no emotion in your voice.

Here are some other tips:

◆ If you agree to have dinner with a man you don't know, dine in the hotel dining room. Be sure to charge your meal to your room, thus averting any miscommunication about the nature of the date.

◆ If you have a drink in the bar alone, make sure you have a briefcase, files, or something diverting with you so that you don't look as if you're waiting to be picked up. Sit at a table rather than at the bar.

◆ If you are traveling on business and staying at a hotel (hotels are a better idea than motels for single women travelers), you may want to let the reception desk know that you are alone. Some women do; some don't. Better still, ask your travel agent to investigate which hotels are known for safe procedures when it comes to single women guests. Double locks on doors and windows, for example, are necessary, not optional.

◆ When you check in, make sure the clerk does not call out your room number to the bellman. If that happens, tell the clerk discreetly to give you another room and to be quiet about it.

◆ Make sure the bellman checks all the spaces in your room when he lets you in to be sure you are the only person there. Be alert when you approach your room for persons lurking in the hall nearby. Check your window locks, and make sure there are no other accesses to your room from outside.

♦ Never go into your room if you think something has been tampered with. Notify security immediately if you think an unauthorized person has been in your room.

♦ Never admit anyone to your room whom you haven't invited or requested through the hotel (such as housekeeping or a repairman) without calling the front desk first.

People in the travel industry use the term *good traveler* to describe someone who doesn't expect things to be as they are at home, knows that things can go wrong, and doesn't panic when they do. Good travelers have good manners, particularly when it comes to dealing with the people whose very job it is to serve them, provide for their safety, and get them from one place to another.

The Least You Need to Know

♦ Casual travel attire does not mean sloppy or grungy.

♦ If you're not absolutely certain that you will need it, don't pack it. If you do need something you haven't packed, you can probably purchase it at your destination.

♦ Have some local money ready for tips, taxis, and so on, on arrival. The best place to exchange your money is at a bank.

♦ Apply for a passport and visa well in advance.

♦ Be sure to factor travel tipping into your financial calculations. If you stay in a luxury hotel, for example, you can expect to spend up to 25 percent of your bill in tips.

♦ Women traveling alone often must be especially careful about meeting and dealing with strangers and handling security matters.

Chapter 28

Getting There: Planes, Trains, Ships, and More

In This Chapter

- ◆ Airplane etiquette
- ◆ Ship etiquette
- ◆ Auto etiquette

Different modes of travel present us with different adventures, different problems, and different questions when it comes to behavior and the standards of etiquette that are required. Stress, proximity, and the occasional need to hurry lend a certain urgency to knowing what to expect and how to react in various travel situations. Also, you should know about and be prepared to observe certain traditions, particularly aboard ship.

But as always, when in unfamiliar circumstances, respect and concern for others will get you through most difficult situations. Let's begin with keeping your feet on the ground when you fly.

Airplanes

You can choose from three classes when you fly: first class, business class, and economy.

First class flyers on regular flights get more space, more service, and more to eat and drink than others on the plane. Drinks—alcoholic and otherwise—are free, as are meals and snacks. Seats are larger and more comfortable in first class. Video equipment and telephones are available, as are sleeper seats. Each airline is different, so it's a good idea to check which services are provided. In general, first class tickets do not carry any penalties for exchanging flights and have no minimum or maximum stay requirements.

Business class is available on most international and domestic flights. It is considerably more expensive than economy class. Seats are roomier than economy and more comfortable. Refreshments are more lavish, and service is upgraded. Most businesses no longer approve first class travel at their expense, but some find that, for long flights, business class is often worth the investment.

Economy class is the least expensive form of air travel. Seats are small, and space is limited, but the cost is so much lower that it compensates for such minor inconveniences. You might get a meal if you fly during mealtime, but usually only sparse snacks are available.

At the Airport

Here are some things to be aware of (and to beware of) when you arrive at the airport:

◆ Avoid the "bag lady" syndrome. Don't show up with both arms encumbered by plastic bags overflowing with newspapers, knickknacks, and snacks.

◆ Make sure your luggage ID tags are secure. Air travel is very hard on luggage. Most domestic flights have no weight restrictions on luggage and permit a carry-on suitcase or garment bag, plus a personal bag, one placed overhead and the other under the seat.

◆ Remember that you may have to carry your own bags. If a skycap is not available, look for a cart. Tip the skycap $1 to $2 per bag. Don't expect skycaps to supply you with luggage ID tags.

◆ To take advantage of curbside check-in, you must have your ticket in your hand.

◆ Know where the metal objects in your luggage are when you go through the security checkpoint. Other travelers won't appreciate waiting for you to go through an entire suitcase for a small silver mirror when it could have gone in a handbag.

◆ Alert security personnel if you have unusual items in your luggage. For example, I often travel with a formal place setting of silver when I'm on the road teaching dining etiquette. I save time and avoid being searched by letting security people know what I'm carrying. Your ticket will list items not permitted on the airplane such as lighter fluid, pocket knives, explosives, and poisons. A full list of prohibited carry-on items, as well as the latest travel security-related information is available on the Transportation Security Administration (TSA) website: www.tsa.gov.

◆ Keep an eye on your luggage and don't agree to watch someone else's luggage. You never know what could be inside, possibly a bomb or illegal substances. You may also need to move from your spot before the owner of the luggage returns.

On Board

Welcome aboard. Here are ideas to take with you as you board the plane:

◆ Be ready when your row is called. Remove your overcoat or other outer garments before boarding so that you won't block the aisle. People should get out of the aisle as soon as they can in the boarding process.

◆ If you intend to sleep during the flight, try to get a window seat so that others won't be inconvenienced by climbing over you and you won't be awakened by them doing so. Also, no matter how experienced a traveler you are, wait until you have heard the emergency instructions before putting earplugs and/or blindfolds in place for sleeping.

Say What? _____

Your neighbor on a plane, train, or bus wants to chat, and you want to be left alone.

What do you say?

"I wish I had the luxury to talk, but I really have to catch up on my work" (or sleep, or reading).

You want to chat, but don't know whether your neighbor does.

What do you say?

"Is this a business or pleasure trip for you?" Take your cue from the tone of the answer.

♦ Reserve an aisle seat if you have long legs or if you expect to be up and down a lot.

♦ Bring cash—in small denominations—for in-flight purchases, such as beverages that are not complimentary and headphones for movies.

♦ Flight attendants are there primarily for emergencies, not to chat and not to provide maid-valet service. Don't push the call button unless you have a very good reason. A very good reason might be that you need a drink of water, and you don't want to crawl over a row of sleeping passengers.

♦ Leave bathrooms clean. Be efficient with your time while in there. The lavatory is no place to perform a full make-up overhaul. Men should shave before boarding the plane, rather than trying to do so on the plane.

♦ Look behind you before you put your seat back in the reclining position, especially just before or after a meal. Moving the seat could spill a drink or dump a dessert into a lap.

♦ If working, keep your papers within the framework of your seat. It is polite to ask your neighbor if he or she minds your working on a laptop. Keep telephoning to an absolute minimum. Many passengers, including yours truly, find these things irritating at best.

♦ If a delay means you have to dash to make a connection, tell the flight attendants before landing. They can assist you in deplaning quickly.

♦ When leaving the plane, stop and let people who are ready to enter the aisle to do so in front of you. Don't get into the aisle until you are ready to proceed toward the door.

♦ It is imperative to respect the carry-on luggage requirements and restrictions. Exceeding them will only slow down your travel

♦ Backpacks are a blessing and a curse. As convenient as it is to have your arms free, it's also painful and irritating to get whacked by one when its owner is turning around or trying to pass. Be careful and considerate.

Delays

No airline ever created a blizzard, hurricane, thunderstorm, or tornado. No airline ever deliberately lost someone's luggage, especially yours.

Airlines do, however, overbook. They do it to protect themselves from some travelers, certainly not you, who make more than one reservation for a trip and then fail to cancel the ones they don't use. These merry travelers are called, among other things, no-shows.

Sometimes people with reservations, particularly those who arrive late, get bumped. The airline generally tries to make up for this situation by upgrading your ticket, getting you onto the next possible flight, and giving you vouchers for meals and a hotel room if necessary.

When delays or overbookings occur, remember that getting angry will not get you a seat. In fact, the person who explains the problem quietly and politely could have a better shot at getting that last seat—if one becomes open—than the person doing all the yelling and threatening.

Luggage

Luggage does get lost. Most often, it is retrieved. Airlines lose luggage with ID tags as easily as they lose untagged luggage, but they return the bags with the tags sooner.

As soon as you are certain that your luggage is missing, report the problem to the airline office, which is usually situated near the luggage carousels. Your itemized list now becomes invaluable. It helps you identify your property. It also helps provide validity for any claim you might have for loss. Airlines carry very limited loss liability, so if you must carry anything of unusual worth in your luggage, let your ticket agent know when you check your luggage so that it can be noted.

Here, too, is where forethought in packing pays off. Always pack medicines, toiletries, pajamas, cash, jewelry, and a change of clothes (if possible) in your carry-on bags. This stash will get you through the night and to your meeting in the morning.

Shipping Out

More people travel by water today than ever before. Cruising to all parts of the world has become a primary mode of pleasure travel, and it's easy to understand why. Your cruise ship is a little self-contained city designed for your comfort and pleasure. It's a city with constantly changing dramatic vistas and a place in which the most challenging decision facing you is what to eat. Decisions about where to eat, where to stay, where to go, and how to get there have all been made for you.

The lure of the cruise experience involves the adventure of being on the high seas and visiting strange and, perhaps, exotic ports and the security of knowing that, once on board, everything you need for a pleasant journey is being taken care of. Your journey will be even more pleasant if you have a good knowledge of shipboard etiquette. But first, take a look at some shipping details.

Extra Charges

The price of the cruise usually includes accommodations, meals, on-board entertainment, and the use of all shipboard sports facilities. Extra charges apply to wine and liquor, port taxes, and personal services such as the beauty salon, barbershop, dry cleaning, massages, and sometimes premium dining. Another consideration is tipping, which can be costly and should be factored into your budget.

Mind Your P's and Q's

If the captain gives a reception, it will probably be dressy. Ask the purser.

Getting Ready

Life is a breeze once on the ship, but preparation can be complicated. So it's a good idea to use the services of a travel agent, many of whom specialize in cruise travel. An agent will know which cruises are available and when, details about the style of the ship and the atmosphere created there, all costs, payment schedules for cruising, and other logistical intricacies. The agent can even make beauty salon appointments in advance, which you can confirm later when on board. Your agent will explain the ship's dress code, which can vary widely from ship to ship, see to your deck-chair assignment, and arrange for your seating in the dining room.

The following is a list of tips to follow when preparing for a cruise:

◆ Get a diagram of the ship in advance so you will know where you are staying. The most expensive accommodations are the larger rooms, higher up and on the outside.

◆ Don't even think about having a bon voyage party on board. They are no longer permitted for security reasons. In fact, your friends can't come aboard at all unless they are passengers. You can have a party in your cabin for fellow passengers. The ship's purser is the person to arrange it.

◆ Pack light. Space is limited on the ship.

◆ If you are prone to motion sickness, see your doctor about medication before leaving. Also, herbal remedies are said to be effective, so you might want to check with a health food store. (If you become ill on board, of course, the ship's doctor will assist you.)

◆ Be sure your bags are tagged and that the porter you give them to is wearing identification.

◆ Once you have made your plans and paid for the cruise, your travel agent will give you a packet of information. This packet, produced by the cruise line, will contain your ticket; boarding information; luggage tags; your personal ID tag; dining room reservation cards; general information about the ship; and a complete itinerary with mailing addresses, information about ports of call, currency exchange, local customs, and so on.

Shipboard Etiquette

Treat every crewmember respectfully. They work hard and deserve it. And you do get more flies with honey than vinegar. Address the captain as Captain, and the other officers as Mr., Mrs., or Ms.

If the captain has a reception, do not monopolize him in conversation. He is very busy and must do his best to meet everyone on board, in addition to performing other duties. If you are invited to dine at the captain's table, consider it a high honor. Be on time. Introduce yourself to your dining partners and wait for the captain to arrive before you order. Dinner at the captain's table is usually formal.

Most ships have two dinner seatings. The early seating is usually for families. The second is considered more fashionable. You may be assigned to a table with strangers. You don't have to wait for everyone to be seated to order. If you are unhappy with your table, you may be able to ask the steward to assign you to another one. Do not request seating at an officer's table. Sitting with the officers is considered a bestowed honor.

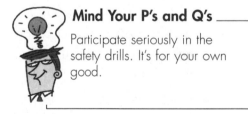

Mind Your P's and Q's

Participate seriously in the safety drills. It's for your own good.

Ship Wear

Traditionally, formal dinner dress is required only for the captain's dinner. Most other nights, jackets and ties for men and cocktail dresses for women are appropriate. Generally, short-term cruising is more casual than transatlantic travel or, say, a gala cruise around the world.

If you are traveling first class, dress will be somewhat more formal in the evenings than in, say, tourist class, where dressing for dinner or for special evenings is up to you. Even in first class, dressing is less formal than it used to be.

Because every cruise ship has its own flavor and most are becoming less formal, it is wise to ask your travel agent and people you know who have sailed on that ship about appropriate attire.

Daytime dress is casual. Dress as though you were at a fine resort hotel. Shorts, slacks, and sweatsuits are fine for breakfast and lunch. Never wear a swimsuit without a good-looking cover-up. Men should bring at least one good business suit and a dinner jacket (tuxedo). Women will find a shawl or jacket very useful on chilly nights.

On the world's most luxurious ocean liners, your cabin might determine where you dine. People who purchase the most expensive cabins dine in small dining rooms where formal dress is expected every night. Women should pack dressy cocktail dresses or suits.

Be sure to wear shoes that can handle slippery decks.

Auto Etiquette

A considerate driver is a safer, as well as a more appreciated, driver. Cars are so much a part of our everyday lives that we take them for granted and usually forget that driving manners cannot be separated from safety.

Here are general tips that should be helpful for drivers and passengers:

◆ If it's your car and you are in the driver's seat, you are the boss. It's up to you to make sure your car is in good condition and is sufficiently fueled. You have every right to ask your passengers to wear their seat belts and to insist that very young children have child safety seats. Pets, too, should be contained properly when you are driving.

◆ Taking chances is not only unsafe, it is disconcerting to your passengers. Speeding, passing, dashing through yellow lights—all create tension.

Say What?

A back seat driver is really getting on your nerves. What do you say?

"You know, your comments are really interfering with my concentration. Can you hold off until the car is stopped?"

◆ Never smoke in another person's car. The tobacco odor is nearly impossible to get rid of. Don't even ask if you can smoke unless the driver is smoking.

◆ Don't use a cellular phone unless it is absolutely necessary, particularly in challenging traffic. Driving requires complete focus. If you must drive and use a telephone on a regular basis, invest in a hands-free system so yours will be free to handle the steering wheel.

◆ Your trunk should be equipped with a first aid kit, flashlight, flares, blanket, ice scraper, and shovel.

◆ An investment in an emergency road service association such as AAA will pay off in peace of mind even if you never have to use its services.

When You're in Trouble

Lots of things can happen on the road. Here are some examples and some suggestions on how to react:

◆ If you are stopped by the police for a driving violation or for any other reason, don't try to schmooze the officer. It will only annoy him or her. Be straightforward and polite, never argumentative.

◆ If you're involved in an accident, stay cool. Don't trade accusations with the other driver. Exchange identification. Be sure to get insurance data and write down the license number on the car.

◆ If you scrape a car fender and the owner is not in sight, don't just take off. You would not want to be treated this way, and besides, somebody is apt to get your license number. Then you'll be hit with a charge of leaving the scene of an accident. Good manners and self-interest coincide in this situation. Leave your name and telephone number under a windshield wiper blade.

◆ If you are really frightened by the way somebody is driving, just tell the driver to stop and let you out of the car. If the driver says, "Maybe you would like to drive," take up the offer.

Seating Etiquette

It is up to the driver to suggest where people sit. The seat of honor is the front passenger seat. It is polite to defer to older persons and give them that seat. In a business situation, the client or the highest-ranking person gets that seat. If a couple has a single person in the car, it is best to offer the front seat to that person rather than to isolate him or her in the back.

(Note: Accommodating a passenger with long legs may have to take precedence over the above considerations.)

Faux Pas

The polite driver does not park in a handicapped zone, discard litter, use the horn unnecessarily, or take up two parking spaces.

Chit Chat

For some reason, people seem to feel chattier in a small car. Large sedans often feel studied and formal. Generally, it is safest to hold a conversation with the person you are sitting next to, rather than to try to turn around or talk over a seat.

Driving is an activity that requires focus and good reflexes, so no one should feel uncomfortable about remaining quiet during a ride.

A driver can signal "no conversation" by turning on the radio.

The Limousine

The seat of honor in a limousine is the curbside back seat. The guest of honor or senior executive is seated here. Junior executives take the jump seats or sit in the middle. A junior executive may also sit up front with the driver. Although the junior executive won't be able to schmooze with the boss, the driver is often a good source of information about the locale, information that might impress the boss later. When in doubt, ask the senior executive or host where you should sit.

It is polite to have the driver lower the seat divider when a member of the party is sitting in the front seat.

The Rented Car

Try to speak with the actual office where you are renting rather than the national reservation center. National centers are sometimes unaware of local or seasonal differences that may affect the rental. Specify exact times and, if you find you're running late, call the office to make sure that the agency doesn't give your car to someone else. Write down the confirmation number and the name of the person to whom you spoke. Make sure you're comfortable with the car and everything in it before you leave the lot. The rental company expects you to return the car clean and in good condition, so make sure it is clean and in good condition when you accept it. Return the car with about the same amount of gas as when you rented it.

Some companies won't rent to persons under 25, and all require some sort of deposit. The easiest deposit is a credit card. You can pay in cash when you return the car to avoid charges on your card. On the subject of credit cards, many customers have a false impression that their credit card company will provide all the insurance coverage they need. It's best to contact the card company and specify ahead of time what sort of car you intend to rent and what you intend to do with it. Most card companies provide only secondary coverage to your personal insurance. Some do not cover you at all if a third party is picking up the expense of the rental. Also, some credit card companies have limits on the number of days you can rent a car and the value of the cars you can rent.

Trains

AMTRAK offers three levels of service: first class, business class, and coach.

Some trains are designated "business class" trains, all reserved seating, and they have first class accommodations. Others are either reserved or non-reserved and you can upgrade to business class from coach.

Aboard, business class offers more room, better seats, good service, and meals. Overnight trips in business class include dining-car meals. The dining etiquette here is the same as it is in an elegant restaurant. Dress is rather casual but certainly not careless. The tip in the dining car is generally 20 percent of your check, easily determined by looking at the prices on the menu.

Overnight accommodations do not always include a private bathroom. If you do not have a private bath, it is all right to wear a robe in the aisles. Use the bathroom facilities efficiently and leave the room clean and orderly for the next person. Ask the sleeping car attendant to make up your bed at a reasonably early time—no later than 10 P.M. Tip the attendant about $3 per person—more if you receive excellent service or extra help.

Good manners are even more important in coach, where seats are not reserved and conditions can be crowded. Food is available for sale in coach, the café car, or the dining car.

The same basic rules of courtesy apply to both airplane and train travel.

- ◆ Don't ask the conductors for favors.
- ◆ Pack blindfolds and earplugs for sleeping.
- ◆ If you want to close or open the shade, ask the person next to you if he or she minds.
- ◆ Keep the reading light off if you are not reading.
- ◆ Remember to dispose of litter in trash receptacles and not in the pouch in front of your seat.
- ◆ Smoke only in the designated areas, which are scarce.
- ◆ Keep quiet. Listen to the radio only with headphones and use the cell phones minimally.

- Keep your children from running up and down the aisles.

- If you bring food on the train, keep it simple. Feel free to use your fingers for foods such as pizza or sandwiches. Keep the area around you clean and tidy. Use plenty of napkins or, even better, those dampened, packaged wipes. Stack the plastic mustard and ketchup wrappers. Put bones and scraps on the side of your plate, not on the tray.

Commuter Trains

Commuter trains have a culture unto themselves. Generally, passengers are not sociable, so don't expect them to be. As a matter of fact, commuters view train time as work time, and most of them want to use it productively. It seems the only time they talk to one another is when they have a mutual gripe about the train service.

Here are some important things to remember while traveling on commuter trains:

- Don't hog a seat with your briefcase, gym bag, or coat. If others do, it's perfectly okay to ask them to remove their things. But don't make a big deal out of it.

- Don't leave trash on the seat or the floor. Use the receptacle. Newspapers are an exception. You can fold your used paper neatly and leave it on the seat for someone else to read.

- Keep the volume down when using headsets or cellular phones.

- If you are able-bodied, giving up your seat to an elderly or disabled person is still the civil and decent thing to do. If other seats are at hand, you should move to allow people traveling together to remain together.

- If someone needs help heaving a bag onto an overhead rack, lend a hand if you are able.

- Have your ticket ready for the conductor, smile, and say "Thank you."

Busing It

Things that are annoying on buses include, but are not limited to …

- People hanging over your seat to talk or resting their arms on the back of your seat

- Loud radios or conversations

- Smelly food

Because bus travel is inexpensive, most travel agents don't deal with it. The commissions, if any, do not warrant their efforts. You're on your own as far as making reservations and gathering information. Here are some tips for more satisfying bus travel:

◆ Although bus seats are not reserved, people tend to keep the same seat for the entire trip. Some passengers can get testy about this expression of the territorial imperative.

◆ The baggage limit is usually two per passenger, plus two carry-ons. This number may vary, however, so check with the bus company in advance.

◆ Dress is casual, of course, but you should strive to avoid even the appearance of grunge. Layering is advised in all weather because of drafts and uneven delivery of air-conditioning.

◆ People with disabilities should notify the bus company in advance so that arrangements can be made.

◆ Take a book or a headset to turn off chatty neighbors.

◆ Do not talk to the driver while the bus is in motion. You don't tip drivers on commercial bus lines, such as Greyhound. (On bus tours drivers get a tip, usually in the form of a collection taken among the passengers.)

Security

It is great to try new things, have adventures, and meet new people while on the road, but considerations of security supercede these benefits. If you feel threatened, it is not discourteous to refuse to converse with someone, move to another location, or tell a crewmember or security guard that you are worried about a certain situation.

Getting Searched

Okay, so you're one of the lucky ones to get searched. Don't take it personally, and don't resist. Simply cooperate and it all will go faster. Travel-savvy people are quite unfazed by this anymore—and don't regard every searched passenger as a suspicious character. Very often these searches are conducted at random, most often dictated by boarding passes issued at the last minute.

When packing, though, keep in mind that you might be searched, so it's a good idea not to have embarrassing intimate items at the top of your suitcase.

The more cooperative you are, the more smoothly everything will go. Take it seriously when told to show up two hours before the flight. Learn and follow airline rules for baggage check-in and carry-ons. If you haven't followed procedures, you don't have the right to argue with security personnel if you're delayed.

All that said, *bon voyage!*

The Least You Need to Know

- If you intend to sleep, get a window seat and pack earplugs and a blindfold.

- If something in your luggage could possibly cause a problem, alert security in advance.

- Tag your luggage. You'll be glad you did if a suitcase gets lost.

- Don't plan a bon voyage party for nonpassengers aboard ship.

- Toiletries, a change of clothes, and other essentials should be in carry-on bags because luggage does get lost.

Part 8

Wedding Bells

Traditional weddings go in and out of fashion. Still, young girls dream of being a beautiful bride on "the most important day of her life." Parents often begin talking of her wedding when a daughter is born.

Traditional weddings again seem to be on the rise after years of variations—the weddings on the beach, in a hot-air balloon, in a field of flowers. Yet couples are getting married at a later age, when they often are more self-confident of their beliefs. Thus, a couple might be planning a "traditional" wedding, complete with white dress, veil, and so forth—and yet decide it makes more sense for the best man to, in fact, be a "best maid," a woman. Or that a religious ceremony makes less sense to them than a spiritual ceremony, officiated by a nondenominational minister.

Whatever kind of wedding they choose, it's up to the couple getting married to get a grip, to practice a large measure of diplomacy in the interest of family harmony, and to hang on to their sense of humor. It's also up to the couple's families to accept that it's the couple's wedding and defer to their values and preferences.

Chapter 29

Preparing for a Wedding

In This Chapter

- Getting engaged
- Prenuptial agreements
- Showers
- The ring
- Who pays for what
- Announcements and invitations

Ah, love. It has been said that weddings have nothing to do with marriage. Weddings are celebrations of life and love, grand parties, and times when family and friends become closer. Weddings have also been called ordeals and costume parties.

But as long as there is love, there will be weddings. They can be as elaborate as a coronation or as simple and as solemn as a promise. But whatever form your wedding takes, it is important to know the basic, practical rules of wedding etiquette. Here, in broad brushstrokes, are the guidelines you need.

You're Engaged!

Before people get married, they become engaged. Engagement marks the interval between the day the couple agree to get married and the actual wedding ceremony. What happens during this period depends on the people involved, but some basic rules apply.

Oh, Grow Up

First, tell your parents the good news!

Whatever your circumstances, regardless of age, whether you think they will approve or their heads will explode, your parents have to know what's happening, and they have to hear about it from you.

It doesn't matter if they're divorced or if your relationship with them is strained at best. They must know, and you should tell them personally. It is better for all concerned, especially the happy couple, for the two of you to be together when you break the news.

Practice your speech beforehand.

Even if your parents greet the announcement with great joy and hearty approval, expect an eventual "but …" or two, or more. Usually, the first and most serious concern involves financial security. Most parents know the effect of financial difficulties on wedded bliss.

Have your arguments and explanations ready to go. Don't make light of any issues or try to laugh them off. Don't become defensive. Act like an adult. Acknowledge your parents' concerns and talk about your plans for dealing with problems, however conceptual those plans may be.

Once informed, parents are expected to perform certain ceremonies. Traditionally, the groom's mother writes to the bride's mother to express her happiness about the betrothal and invites the bride's parents to visit. However, many parents are unaware that such traditions exist, so no one should be offended if the groom's mother overlooks this formality. Even if the groom's mother does not plan to invite the bride's parents for a visit, writing a note is a good idea. It should say something like this:

Dear Matilda:

Robert just told us his good news, and I don't want to waste a minute before telling you how pleased we are. We've heard so much about you already, and are grateful for all the kindness you have shown our son. We feel pleased and privileged to welcome Paula to our family. Both of us are eager to meet you in person when we can toast the happy occasion together.

Fondly,
Helen Thomas

The single most important thing here is for the parents to communicate, whether by mail or by phone. The idea is to share the good news, and to share it personally. E-mail is just too casual for this one.

The couple should visit each set of parents individually. If you feel that your parents and your intended's parents will mix like oil and water, it's probably not a good idea to arrange a cozy "sixsome." You will probably have an opportunity to introduce everyone at a less stressful time, such as a party some time before the actual wedding.

The Pre-Nup

A pre-nuptial agreement is a contract a couple draws up that spells out what will happen to the assets, debts, income, and expenses that each partner brings to the marriage if the couple divorces or one spouse dies. In addition to how property will be distributed, the pre-nup may also protect one spouse from the other's debts or stipulate the level of support one will provide the other if the marriage ends. While it's not the most pleasant pre-wedding discussion a couple may have, absent this agreement, the disposition of assets is determined by the applicable laws of the state they are married or reside in.

The time to discuss a pre-nuptial arrangement is before you announce your engagement, pick out china, or look for a house in a good school district. It's a sensitive issue that easily can lead to insecurity on the part of one or both partners. Some discussions have become so inflammatory that they jettisoned the engagement—and each other— altogether. Since these discussions should be intensely private, it makes a lot of sense to weather whatever storms they may cause before wedding plans become public. Still, the pre-nup is a fact of life today, and no longer only the province of the very wealthy. Suggesting one does not necessarily mean that one partner or the other is having doubts about the success of the marriage.

Today pre-nups are widely used, especially when couples have children by former marriages they wish to protect. And as people are getting married later in life, it's not unusual for one or both parties to have accumulated assets worth protecting. The days when couples typically "started out" scrimping are not so commonplace as they used to be. A pre-nup is a balance of protection for your marital relationship and your property. It is a contract, and there are many variations. Check with a reputable attorney; and once you and your partner have agreed to have a pre-nup, let the attorney handle the gritty details—including who keeps Rover.

Above all, speak only to your future spouse and your attorney about your pre-nup. When asked by "well-meaning friends" if you have one, simply say that it is a very private matter and you don't discuss it with anyone but your spouse and your attorney. Conversely, refuse to discuss anyone else's pre-nup as well. It's intrusive and rude. You wouldn't want yours discussed, would you?

The Ring

There may or may not be an engagement ring. A ring or lack of it does not alter the fact that you are engaged.

In an ideal world, every bride-to-be is thrilled with the selection of her engagement ring and the couple lives happily ever after. If you think you live in an ideal world, you are not ready for marriage.

Suppose you receive a ring you dislike intensely, but it has been in his family since the Bronze Age, and his mother has her heart set on her little boy's bride wearing it.

> **Live and Learn**
>
> The tradition of giving diamond engagement rings began in Venice in the fifteenth century. One of the earliest and smallest diamond engagement rings was made for the two-year-old Princess Mary, daughter of Henry VIII of England, on her engagement to the dauphin of France in 1518.

Wear it. Smile. Do not change the setting. You can select a wide wedding band that will not comfortably accommodate the engagement ring. You can wear the engagement ring on your right hand for a while and eventually stop wearing it. After all, it's clumsy when you're at the computer. You'll think of something.

The same guidelines apply if your dearly beloved presents you with a terrible ring of his own choosing. (Nobody's perfect.) The day after the second wedding anniversary, you can start talking about having the ring reset.

Not every couple decides to go the formal engagement ring route. It is a nice idea, however, to cement your engagement with a permanent gift, and one that isn't overly practical, before the responsibilities of married life consume your resources. Some couples select jewelry other than rings as gifts for each other.

Parties

The bride's family, the groom's family, or close friends might decide to honor the couple with an engagement party. The form of the party can vary widely from a cocktail party to a barbecue. Traditionally, this is the first time the bride-to-be is seen wearing her engagement ring.

Invitations can be handwritten, printed, or extended by telephone. Don't mention "engagement" on the invitations. The purpose of the engagement party is to celebrate the good news, not to suggest that a gift is expected. You don't have to worry about the obligations intrinsic to a wedding invitation list. In fact, it isn't a common custom for the bride's family and best friends to give engagement presents.

Now that engagements are becoming shorter, engagement parties are becoming fewer, replaced by wedding showers.

Mind Your P's and Q's

Showers are also given for the groom. In fact, this practice is becoming almost as popular as the somewhat jaded concept of the bachelor party. The tradition of bachelor parties won't ever completely die out, but even these parties tend to be a bit healthier than parties in the past.

Showers

Bridesmaids or close friends of the bride usually give bridal showers. It is customary to ask the bride ahead of time what kind of shower she would like. Brides also should be very much aware that shower gifts are in addition to wedding gifts and constitute added expense. Thus it is only fair and kind to be just that—fair and kind—in suggesting the sort of gifts you would like. Kitchen gadget parties and garden parties can be creative, fun, and also easy on the budget.

No matter what, a shower invitation should never ask for money, and a host should never ask guests to contribute to the cost of the party. Showers should be small, intimate gatherings for friends, not fund-raisers.

Live and Learn

Congratulations are sometimes too fervidly put. When, for instance, the bride is a little past the bloom of youth and brightness, it is well for her friends and acquaintances not to be too gushingly insistent with their congratulations. To be so is rather to suggest that she has been successful against terrible odds.

—Mrs. Humphry, *Manners for Girls*, 1909

Although the bride should extend personal thanks for each gift as she opens it, sending handwritten thank-you notes is a gracious follow-up. A friend can unobtrusively take notes during the shower so that the bride will know for sure which gift came from which person.

Co-ed showers are more and more popular. They are usually held in the evening, at cocktail hour. Usually these showers have a theme, such as a kitchen gadget shower or a bar gadget shower. Lingerie showers still are women-only events.

Refreshments at co-ed showers are hors d'oeuvres and drinks. At all-women showers in the afternoon, light lunch or tea is served while the bride-to-be opens her gifts.

Announcements

Many couples announce their engagement in the newspaper. It is best to call your local paper and ask for its requirements. The paper might have a standard form for you to complete and return with a photograph. If the bride and groom are from different towns, contact both local newspapers. It also makes sense to send the announcement to college alumni offices.

If your newspaper doesn't have a form, write the announcement yourself. The bride's parents announce the engagement of their daughter. If the parents are divorced and wish to use both names, the announcement should read this way:

Mr. William Keates and Mrs. Maura Keates (or Mrs. Daniel Johns if she is remarried) announce the engagement of their daughter, Eileen, to Alan Barts, son of Dr. and Mrs. Edward Barts of Great Neck, Long Island.

Generally, if one of the parents is deceased, the surviving parent is the one mentioned in the invitation. But, as in most elements in this intensely personal tradition, variations are perfectly acceptable.

In the next paragraph, add information about where each person went to school, honors received, and current occupation. Add the wedding date at the end of the announcement. If you send a photograph, attach a caption to the back of it. Do not write on the back of the picture because it may interfere with the reproduction process. It is best to type the announcement, double-spaced.

There is no guarantee that the newspaper will run your announcement, but the smaller the paper, the better your chances. Send the announcement to your local community papers as well as the big-city daily to have the best chance of getting a clipping for your scrapbook. Some papers may not run a wedding announcement if they published a couple's engagement announcement, particularly if the wedding comes soon after the engagement.

Live and Learn

When acknowledging the news that a couple is engaged, tradition dictates that we congratulate the man and wish the woman every happiness. The thinking behind this practice is that the man is to be congratulated for winning his prize after a long and difficult chase. Congratulating the woman would imply that she had been pursuing the man. As charming a tradition as this is, most people would not recognize it anymore. What is most important here is wishing the engaged couple every happiness. Don't worry about who congratulates whom.

Breaking Up

If you break your engagement, call your friends and family and tell them. You do not owe anyone an explanation, and it is best not to delve into specifics or drift into character assassination, no matter how strong the temptation.

You must return any wedding gifts you've received. It is best to do so simply by mail. Include a note that says something like "While I am very grateful for your gift and good wishes, I must return it because we have cancelled our engagement."

If formal wedding invitations have already been sent, you will need to send a formal cancellation. Here's an example of one:

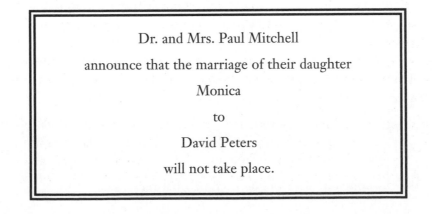

Dr. and Mrs. Paul Mitchell

announce that the marriage of their daughter

Monica

to

David Peters

will not take place.

If you have sent informal invitations, send each person who received one a brief, informal note:

> Dear Tom:
>
> This is to let you know that Henry and I have broken our engagement.
>
> Christine

Wedding Plans

When you begin serious planning for the wedding, some of the first questions to ask yourself should involve who will pay for what, whom you should invite, and what form the invitations should take.

Wedding Expenses

Let's start the wedding process with who pays for what. For many weddings, lots of people assume a share of the burden and thus have some say in the proceedings.

Traditionally, the bride's family pays for invitations, announcements, photographs at the wedding and the reception, flowers for the wedding party, the cost of the ceremony itself (flowers, canopy, music, cars, and so on), and all the reception expenses.

The groom is responsible for the marriage license, the bride's ring, his gift to the bride, the officiant's fee, gifts for his attendants, and the honeymoon. Sometimes the groom pays for the bride's bouquet and going-away corsage, the corsages for the mothers and grandmothers, and boutonnieres for his attendants and the fathers. The groom's family pays for the rehearsal dinner and hotel accommodations for the groom and his attendants.

But, tradition aside, the most practical and workable way to allocate wedding expenses is for the bride, the groom, and their families to sit down together and discuss the costs openly. This way, everyone will have the same picture of the event in his or her mind. Clear communication is essential from the start, especially about who should be billed for what as well as the billing and payment procedures.

Guest List

The wedding guest list dictates the cost and size of the wedding, so it is a good idea to agree on some outer limits before you begin. Usually the two families—the bride's and groom's—divide the number of guests equally between them.

Both families should determine their lists and then get together to combine the lists so that duplications can be eliminated. Be careful about assuming a certain number of no-shows. You could be in for some surprises. Friends from the past may consider your wedding an opportunity to renew acquaintances, and relatives or friends who live far away may decide to finally take that long trip they have been thinking about.

Invitations

Formal wedding invitations conform to a formula. They should be engraved on the top half of a piece of folded white or off-white paper. A loose piece of tissue paper protects the engraving, and the invitation is put into an inner envelope. The recipient's full name is written on the inner invitation in black ink by hand. This envelope then is put into another envelope of the same paper quality, and the outer envelope is addressed and stamped by hand.

The formula:

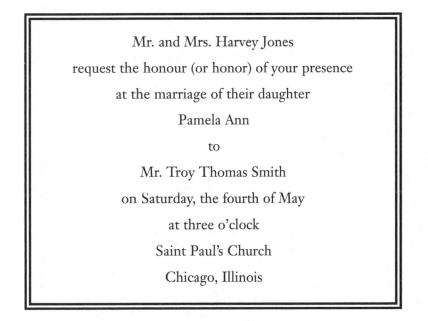

Mr. and Mrs. Harvey Jones

request the honour (or honor) of your presence

at the marriage of their daughter

Pamela Ann

to

Mr. Troy Thomas Smith

on Saturday, the fourth of May

at three o'clock

Saint Paul's Church

Chicago, Illinois

Although many people simply add "and guest" when they inscribe the inside envelope, it is a good idea to ask the person you are inviting whether you can send an individual invitation to the person who will be accompanying him or her.

A formal engraved invitation sends the message that your wedding will be formal. If your wedding is to be less formal, your invitation can send that message as well. You may, for example, choose to have the invitation printed rather than engraved, on colored stock. You might eliminate the extra envelope and alter the wording of the invitation to suit yourself.

If you and your intended are responsible for the entire wedding, you might want to send the invitations in your own name. Thus:

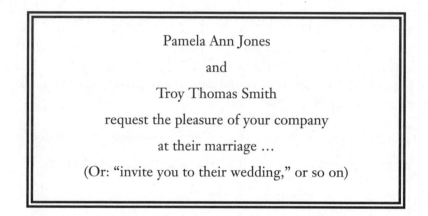

Pamela Ann Jones

and

Troy Thomas Smith

request the pleasure of your company

at their marriage …

(Or: "invite you to their wedding," or so on)

When the groom's family shares in the expense of the wedding, invitations are sent in the name of the groom's parents as well as the bride's:

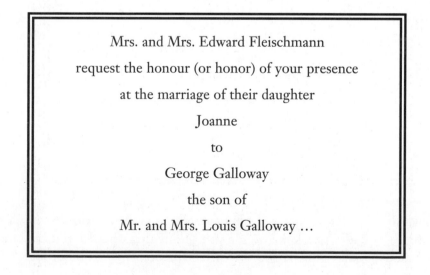

Mrs. and Mrs. Edward Fleischmann

request the honour (or honor) of your presence

at the marriage of their daughter

Joanne

to

George Galloway

the son of

Mr. and Mrs. Louis Galloway …

Mrs. and Mrs. Edward Fleischmann

and Mr. and Mrs. Louis Galloway …

request the honour (or honor) of your presence

at the marriage of their children

Joanne and George …

(Note: Middle names and initials are not necessary, but are considered more formal.)

When the bride and groom share some of the expense of the wedding, the invitation might say:

Barbara Tamms

and

Jonathan Kreck

join their parents

Susan and Wayne Tamms

and

Helen and Walter Kreck

in inviting you

to share their happiness

as they exchange marriage vows

Saturday, the fourth of May

Nineteen hundred and ninety-six

at three o'clock in the afternoon

Franklin Inn Club

422 South Camac Street

Philadelphia, Pennsylvania

If you are inviting all the wedding guests to the reception, you can include the words "and afterward at" following the wedding location on the invitation. Another option is to include a separate engraved or printed reception card with the wedding invitation. It should read as follows:

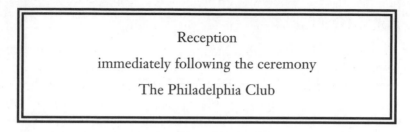

Reception

immediately following the ceremony

The Philadelphia Club

By all means, send maps with the invitations to those coming from a distance.

If you have fewer than 50 guests, you should write out your own invitations in the form of a note. The phrasing is up to you.

Replying to Invitations

Although there is a correct form to reply to formal wedding invitations, few people know about it, much less actually use it. However, it goes this way:

Mr. and Mrs. Peter Thompson

accept with pleasure

Mr. and Mrs. Warren Scott Tate's

kind invitation for

Saturday, the fourth of May

at three o'clock

at the Franklin Inn

(Or:)

regret they are unable to accept

Mr. and Mrs. Warren Scott Tate's …

Most invitations include a reply card, stamped and addressed by the host. In any case, the host would certainly appreciate a note from you saying that you will or will not attend. However, if you're invited to the ceremony, but not to the reception, a reply isn't necessary.

Wedding Announcements

After a small wedding, you may send engraved or printed wedding announcements to friends and acquaintances. After a large wedding, you may send announcements to those who were not invited, for example, to business and social acquaintances who are in your Rolodex, but never make it to your dinner table. The correct wording follows.

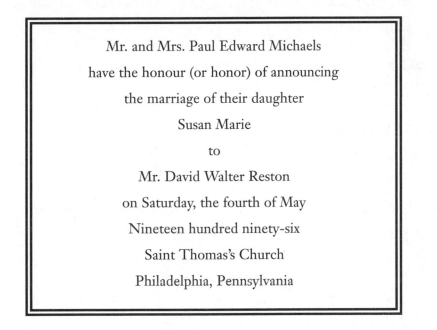

Mr. and Mrs. Paul Edward Michaels

have the honour (or honor) of announcing

the marriage of their daughter

Susan Marie

to

Mr. David Walter Reston

on Saturday, the fourth of May

Nineteen hundred ninety-six

Saint Thomas's Church

Philadelphia, Pennsylvania

The announcement does not need to mention where the wedding took place but should complement the style of the invitation in terms of paper stock and printing or engraving.

When couples plan their own weddings, they often send their own announcements. They are printed or engraved. The wording is

For the newspaper announcement, call to see whether a form is available. If not, give the following information:

- The bride's maiden name and the groom's name

- Hour, date, and place of the ceremony

- Name of the officiating person

- Names of people in the wedding party and their relationships to the bride and groom

- A description of the bride's dress and flowers and the bridesmaids' dresses

- Where the reception was held

- Names and occupations of the bride's parents

- Names of the bride's grandparents

- Where the bride went to school and college

- Where the bride is employed

- The same essential facts about the groom and his family

- Where the couple will live after the marriage

If the bride is keeping her family name, add this sentence to the announcement: "After the marriage, Ms. Michael will retain her family name." Or "After their marriage, Mr. Reston and Ms. Michael will use the surname Michael-Reston." Note that the use of hyphenated surnames is becoming less common these days.

You may send a photograph along with the announcement. The photograph may or may not get printed. Attach the caption to the back. Don't write on the back.

This chapter explained how people generally or traditionally prepare for a wedding. Nevertheless, you should plan and carry out your wedding in a way that you believe is appropriate. Remember, too, that your wedding is something that will always be a part of your memories and deserves a great deal of serious thought and careful preparation.

The Least You Need to Know

- The engaged couple must announce the news to each person's parents right away.

- Never reject someone's choice of an engagement ring. If you don't like it, figure out another way to deal with the problem.

- Generally, but not always, the bride's parents announce engagements and weddings.

- Both families must meet and decide in advance who will pay for what when it comes to the wedding.

- A well-defined and long-standing formula applies to formal wedding invitations, and it is not generally a good idea to deviate from it.

Chapter 30

The Big Day

In This Chapter

- ◆ The rehearsal
- ◆ Who's who
- ◆ What to wear
- ◆ The ceremony
- ◆ Kinds of weddings

So, the time has come. After all the planning and worrying about hundreds of details, the wedding is just a few days away. At this point things will happen fairly quickly, and you'll be grateful for all of the time and effort you and others have devoted to the preparations.

The big event actually begins a day or two before the wedding with the rehearsal and the rehearsal dinner.

The Rehearsal

Every great event, including a wedding, needs a rehearsal, a chance for all the participants to run through their roles and understand the big picture. In many cases the entire wedding party comes together for the first time at the rehearsal, which makes it an opportunity for family members and friends from both sides of the aisle to get to know one another.

The atmosphere at the rehearsal should be informal and cheerful. The rehearsal takes place where the wedding will occur so that the participants will feel more relaxed when they show up for the ceremony.

By tradition the bride asks one of her attendants to walk down the aisle in her place during the rehearsal, but otherwise, everyone goes through the exact routine he or she will perform on the wedding day. The officiant, usually a member of the clergy or a judge, will also either read or explain the remarks he or she will make at the ceremony. This is also a chance to get an idea from the officiant about the nature of his remarks. Anyone who will read a poem, piece of scripture, or other prose should practice doing so while you check out the sound system.

The Rehearsal Dinner

Traditionally, the participants attend the rehearsal dinner immediately following the wedding rehearsal. It's an opportunity for the two families to meet and get to know each other a little better before the wedding. In addition to the wedding party and the two families, the dinner sometimes includes out-of-town guests who have arrived early for the wedding.

The circumstances vary widely, but most often the parents of the groom host the dinner. When the groom's family is from out of town, the bride and her family should provide support by helping to choose the restaurant and making any other local arrangements. Sometimes a relative or even a close friend of the bride or the groom hosts the dinner.

Rehearsal dinners can be anything from black tie formal in a fancy hotel or restaurant to a picnic. When it's an informal occasion, invitations are telephoned, although written invitations are gracious, especially when the dinner is a formal occasion.

The rehearsal dinner is the time for the bride and groom to give their attendants their gifts. These modest gifts commemorate the wedding and thus often are engraved with the wedding date. Traditional gifts include bracelets and other jewelry for the bridesmaids and cuff links and silver shot glasses for the groomsmen.

The Cast of Characters

The bride, of course, is the star of the wedding. Traditionally, the groom's function is principally decorative. However, grooms are taking more active roles in their wedding planning than ever before. Here are the other participants with the roles they play:

◆ **The best man.** He assists the groom, escorts him to the church, and hands over the wedding ring at the appropriate moment. He safeguards the necessary money for church donations and other details, takes care of the groom's car, sees that he has his travel tickets, and so on. The best man also makes the first toast at the wedding reception. At the reception the best man may also read aloud any congratulatory telegrams that arrive for the couple.

◆ **Maid/matron of honor.** A maid of honor is unmarried, while a matron of honor is married. Whatever her status, she fusses over the bride as she prepares for the ceremony and helps her get ready to leave for her honeymoon. She holds the bride's bouquet during the ceremony and supervises the other bridesmaids and the child attendants.

◆ **Father of the bride.** He accompanies the bride to the church, walks her down the aisle, and hands her over to the groom at the altar. He also toasts the happy couple at the reception. If for any reason the father of the bride cannot do this function, a relative or close family friend will be chosen for these duties. If the bride's father is deceased and her mother has remarried, the mother's husband may play this role, providing he and the bride are on good terms. If there has been a divorce and a stepfather has raised the bride, she may still want her biological father to participate. These decisions are, of course, up to the bride, and she must follow her heart and her conscience.

◆ **Ushers.** These men greet the guests and help seat people for the ceremony. The usher offers his inside arm to escort the women down the aisle. Men follow behind the usher. If a group of women arrive at the same time, they can choose to wait while the usher escorts them one by one; or the usher can escort the woman he knows best or the most senior among them, and the others can seat themselves.

Live and Learn

According to the U.S. Census bureau, the median age for first marriages is about 27 for grooms and 25 for brides. In 1980, the median age was about 25 for grooms and 22 for brides. This means that the couples' tastes are more developed than at a younger age and the groom is more likely to express them in the wedding festivities.

Mind Your P's and Q's

The bride and groom must be fairly sure of a positive response when they ask people to be the maid/matron of honor and best man. These jobs involve a considerable commitment. And if you are asked to serve, remember that it is an honor to be asked and refusing can be very hurtful to the bride or groom or both.

What to Wear

Winter brides traditionally choose velvet, satin, brocade, or other heavy formal fabric. Spring brides favor taffeta and lace, and summer suggests chiffon, organdy, or cotton.

Tradition dictates that the bride's wedding dress be white or off-white. The number of nontraditional brides is growing at the moment, however, and brides are opting more and more for colored dresses and prints. Basically, a bride should feel comfortable and at ease in whatever she wears because she is the star of the show.

If the wedding is formal, the bride may wear a long veil reaching to her waist or a short face veil. Many brides opt to disregard the veil entirely in favor of a hat or simple flowers in the hair. When a groom wears a dark suit for his wedding, the bride sometimes opts for wearing a long white dress without train and veil.

The Expectant Bride

The pregnant bride can get away with wearing a simple, loose-fitting, long white dress if she's up to four months pregnant. However, if her condition is obvious, a long wedding dress with a train will seem ludicrous to many. A better choice might be a dressy white maternity dress, either long or short.

Bridesmaids

The bride chooses her attendants' dresses. However, because each attendant pays for her own dress, the bride must take cost into consideration.

Traditionally, all bridesmaids wear identical dresses. The maid/matron of honor wears either the same dress as the bridesmaids or a dress that complements those dresses but made in a slightly different style and/or color. To succeed in keeping the wedding party color-coordinated, many people choose to have the shoes dyed to match the dresses.

A small wedding may have only one attendant. The bride and her attendant should agree on the style and fabric of the attendant's dress. Although the bride might make some initial suggestions and give final approval (without being autocratic), the attendant should be able to choose her own dress.

Mind Your P's and Q's

One easy and risk-free fashion alternative for male members of an informal wedding is to wear navy blue blazers with gray trousers. Another attractive feature of this outfit is that it is already a part of many men's wardrobes.

The Groom

For traditional, formal daytime weddings, the men in the wedding party wear cutaway jackets, gray waistcoats, and dark striped trousers. For a more informal wedding, men wear gray sack coats, gray waistcoats, and dark striped trousers. Evening weddings (after 6 P.M.) are the most formal occasions. Traditionally, men wear white ties and tails. However, grooms are becoming somewhat more flamboyant and creative in their attire and now often stand out from their attendants just as the bride does from hers.

The Mothers

The mothers of the bride and groom do not have to dress similarly, particularly if they do not have the same tastes. No law, for example, says that both have to wear short or long dresses. They should consult with one another and the bride to be sure they don't clash, but they each should be comfortable in what they wear. Of course, they should not outshine the bride.

Guests

The time of day dictates the sort of attire guests wear.

For formal daytime weddings, women guests wear cocktail dresses or long skirts and festive blouses or sweaters. Men wear suits for formal daytime weddings, as well as for evening weddings. If an evening wedding is very formal, men wear dinner jackets and women wear dressy cocktail suits or dresses or long dresses.

Black is a fine color to wear at a wedding, although with so many other color choices, it seems pointless to court criticism. Traditionalists will argue that black is the color of mourning and thus has no place at a wedding. It is also fine to wear white or off-white to a wedding if you are a guest.

Presents

If you accept an invitation to a wedding, you're obliged to give a gift. If you do not attend, you do not have to give a gift, although it is gracious to give something modest when you decline if you are friends with the couple. There is a one-year "grace" period in giving wedding gifts. As long as you get it there before the couple's first anniversary, you're fine. Traditional gifts are silver, china, crystal, and items of lasting value. However, today's wedding gifts also include electronic equipment and practical items.

Send wedding gifts to the bride's home.

Bridal registries can be useful in making sure you are selecting something the bride and groom want and like. Personally, I avoid registries because I find them very impersonal.

The Wedding Ceremony

There are as many variations to the wedding ceremony as there are weddings. However, some elements are typical of all or most ceremonies. Of course, not everyone gets married in a church. However, going through what may be expected when it comes to entering and leaving the church, and approaching and withdrawing from the altar, will be helpful in thinking about arrangements in other circumstances.

Seating

At a traditional wedding, ushers escort guests to their seats, the bride's guests to the left and the groom's to the right. The mother of the bride is the last to be seated, and the wedding ceremony begins when she sits down. At small, informal weddings or ones that take place at home or outdoors, guests form a semicircle.

If no ushers are present, guests seat themselves, leaving the first few rows for the couple's families. There is no need to divide the ranks left and right in this case.

The Processional

In a formal wedding, the bride walks down the aisle on the arm of the man giving her away, usually her father (see "The Cast of Characters").

The bridesmaids lead the processional, followed by the maid or matron of honor, the flower girl or ring bearer, and the bride, in that order. The bride meets the groom, best man, and officiant at the altar. Generally, these three enter from a side door at the front.

After seating the guests, the ushers take their places in the processional, either walking down the aisle in pairs or accompanying the bridesmaids. After the ceremony, the ushers join the recessional, again walking in pairs or as escorts for the bridesmaids.

The Ceremony

In many weddings, the officiant asks, "Who gives this bride in marriage?" and the father says, "I do," or "Her mother and I do." However, if the bride objects to such sexist language, she may leave her father at the end of the aisle and walk the last few steps to the altar on her own. Or, sometimes, the bride and groom walk up the aisle together holding hands, particularly if they have been together for some time.

The Recessional

Traditionally, the bride takes the groom's right arm and walks away from the altar, followed by the flower girl and the maid of honor on the arm of the best man. If both a maid of honor and matron of honor are in attendance, one will be accompanied by an usher. (The matron of honor outranks the maid of honor in the wedding party hierarchy.) Next come the bridesmaids, usually accompanied by ushers. If not, they precede the ushers, walking single file from the altar.

At a small wedding with no recessional, the wedding ends with the groom kissing the bride. The officiant congratulates the couple, and then the immediate family does so. At this point an informal receiving line usually forms and guests give their good wishes to the couple.

The Receiving Line

The receiving line can form in the church vestibule or at the start of the reception. The receiving line always includes the bride and groom, the two mothers, and the matron or maid of honor. If there are both, the maid of honor can choose to be part of the line or not, since the matron of honor outranks her. Fathers and bridesmaids are optional.

Guests going through the receiving line shake hands with its members, wishing the couple every happiness, congratulating the groom, and telling the bride she is beautiful. Don't tarry for a chat. Give your name, state your relationship with the couple (if necessary), say what a wonderful wedding it was, and move along. Never go through a receiving line with a drink in your hand.

Kinds of Weddings

In some ways, all weddings are the same. In other ways, they may be profoundly different. Below are some examples of different sorts of weddings and some ideas about what to expect.

Civil Ceremonies

Civil ceremonies are usually small, although frequently a civil authority officiates at a large wedding in a public hall. In this case, follow the guidelines for a formal wedding, creating the stage by setting up rows of chairs on both sides of a central aisle.

When a civil ceremony takes place in a private home or judge's chambers, follow the guidelines for an informal wedding. If you go to a justice of the peace, dress in keeping with the dignity of the occasion, even though the ceremony might be short and rather impersonal.

The only people who absolutely must be present for a civil ceremony are the bride and groom, the civil official, and the legal witnesses, who need not even know the couple.

Beyond that, the couple may be attended by a bridesmaid or bridesmaids, best man, groomsmen, maid or matron of honor, someone to give the bride away, ushers, possibly child attendants (flower girls or ring bearers), friends, and relatives.

Roman Catholic Weddings

Roman Catholics are married in the presence of a priest. They may or may not have a nuptial Mass. The bride's father walks the bride down the aisle and "gives" her to the groom, who walks out a few steps to meet her. The father then assumes his seat in the front pew on the left.

If a nuptial Mass takes place, the bride and groom and the wedding party receive Communion, and the guests frequently do as well. Of course, guests who are not of the faith will remain in their pews during Communion. That little bench at your feet is a kneeler, used during prayer; it's not a footrest.

Family members or close friends often give scriptural readings.

Jewish Weddings

Jewish wedding ceremonies vary from Orthodox to Reform. However, some components of the wedding service are found in all Jewish services.

The *huppah*, or wedding canopy, covers the bride, groom, and rabbi during the ceremony. Originally, the *huppah* was the bridal chamber itself. In our times, the word symbolizes the couple's entering into the chamber.

In a traditional Jewish wedding ceremony, both the bride's mother and father give her away, not the father alone. The father is on one side, the mother on the other. Usually, both sets of parents stand just outside the canopy, not with the rest of the audience.

The wedding ring must be plain gold without any stones. The groom places it on the bride's finger as he says, "You are sanctified to me with this ring according to the religion of Moses and Israel."

He and the bride sip wine from the same glass over which blessings have been said. The groom steps on the wine glass, crushing it, to symbolize Jewish mourning for the destruction of the Temple in ancient Jerusalem. The wine glass is covered with cloth before it is crushed to prevent splinters and cuts.

Jewish weddings are forbidden on holy days, such as the Sabbath. However, the holy days end at sundown, and many Jewish couples have Saturday-night weddings.

Men cover their heads in the synagogue as a sign of respect for God. Guests are given skullcaps, called yarmulkes, for this purpose.

Islamic Weddings

Generally, Islamic weddings are not elaborate. The bride and groom exchange their vows in the mosque in the presence of family, friends, and the Imam, or religious leader. There are no restrictions as to color of clothing, but modest clothing is expected. Everyone removes their shoes before entering and places them on racks. Shoe removal is not a religious custom, but a sanitary one, since worshippers often pray touching the floor. At the end of the ceremony, those present often say, "salaam aleikum" (peace be with you) to one another.

After the ceremony, a reception is generally held in a hotel or hall. These receptions are very much like wedding receptions anywhere except that no alcohol is served and the food conforms to Islamic dietary laws.

Quaker Weddings

Quaker weddings are warm, personal, and intimate. No clergy preside at Quaker weddings because Quakers believe that the divine spirit is present in all of us, and that we all are ministers, in a sense.

Guests enter the meetinghouse and sit wherever they feel comfortable. When all are seated, one person will stand and explain what to expect during the service. There will then be a period of silence, perhaps lasting several minutes. When they are ready, the bride and groom stand and exchange their vows. They then sit down, and another period of silence ensues.

During this period of silence, those present may rise and give their blessings to the couple. When the blessings are finished, the same person who spoke at the beginning of the meeting will "break" the meeting by rising and shaking the hand of someone nearby.

After the wedding, those present are invited to sign the marriage certificate. You need not be a Quaker to sign the certificate.

The reception following the wedding will be considerably less elaborate than the usual wedding reception. Probably, it will also be more personal and homey.

Military Weddings

A bride or groom who is a member of the armed forces may opt to be married in uniform. When either or both are in full dress uniform, it automatically makes the wedding formal; thus formal civilian dress is the order of the day for a nonmilitary bride or groom.

Usually, the groom or bride's attendants are largely in uniform, although some of the ushers may be in civilian dress.

At the end of the ceremony, the ushers form the traditional arch of steel under which the bride and groom walk as they leave the ceremony. The saber or sword, as it is called in the Navy, is only worn by commissioned officers on active duty.

If the venue permits, the arch may be formed immediately after the bride and groom turn to face the assembled guests inside the building. In this case the head usher calls, "center face," and the ushers form two lines facing each other on the steps beneath the altar. The next command is "draw swords" or "arch sabers," and the ushers raise their swords, cutting edge facing up. The bride and groom pass under the arch.

The attendants then leave with the bride and groom. However, the attendants walk down the aisle and then leave through a side entrance to reassemble outside the building to form another arch. Other members in the wedding party wait just inside the building until the second arch is formed. Civilian ushers can choose to stand beside the military men forming the arch or not.

Same-Sex Weddings and Commitment Ceremonies

Gay couples who celebrate their commitment to each other often send formal invitations and invest as much energy into their ceremony as straight couples. They deserve to be honored as any other couple.

Often the couple dress alike for the ceremony—men might wear matching dark suits and women dress in the same color family and perhaps, style, carrying bouquets.

Guests who do not believe in the sanctity of these unions should attend and participate—to the degree to which they're comfortable—out of friendship. After all, a commitment is a commitment. Your friendship with the couple should be more important in this case than any disapproval you might harbor. Each of us has curried others' disapproval at one time or another; and we should be big enough to overlook disagreements to honor someone's lifetime commitment of love and respect.

Gift cards and letters of congratulations should wish for a long, happy, and abundant life with each other, and not use the terminology "as husband and wife."

Formal invitations to a commitment ceremony would list the two hosts in alphabetical order, on two separate lines.

Second Weddings and Stepfamilies

You may, of course, plan any sort of second wedding you please. What follows is the usual protocol for such events, and you may decide to follow it, amend it, or ignore it!

The service itself is generally limited to family and closest friends. The reception, on the other hand, may be as large and lavish as you wish. Those who eloped the first time may prefer an elaborate ceremony with all the trimmings the second time. Generally, however, couples dispense with the long white dress, the father "giving away" the bride, tossing the bouquet, and the presence of many bridesmaids.

Showers for second-time brides are not appropriate, and there is no rehearsal dinner. Wedding gifts are certainly in order, however. If you gave your friend a lavish gift for the first wedding, something more modest is now called for. You can send a gift even if you are not invited to the wedding. The gift should be accompanied by a note expressing congratulations and wishes for future happiness. The note should make no reference to the fact that this is a second (or third, etc.) marriage.

Stepparents, Stepchildren

When people with children remarry, many families face great emotional problems. The remarrying parent wants his or her children to attend the wedding, which may not sit well with the children's other parent. A parent's wedding may also present a crisis of conflicting loyalties for the children. The children may also see their stepsiblings as intruders who might invade their turf or steal their parent's affections. The new stepparent fears that he or she will never win the affection or even the respect of the new stepchildren.

In the best of worlds, the wedding comes off smoothly because of some emotional heroism on the part of those involved. The new spouse writes a letter from the heart to the former spouse saying how much it would mean to have the children at the wedding, expressing affection for the children and admiration for how they have been raised and pledging to do everything possible to keep peace and harmony in the family.

The former spouse tells the children they should attend the wedding with good grace (while planning a lavish resort visit or other indulgence during the time of the wedding for themselves). The children are convinced that the new siblings are not a threat and, in fact, will be a big plus in their lives. Everyone resolves not to speak out against other members of the now-extended family, especially to the children.

Renewing Wedding Vows

Traditionally, couples renewed their wedding vows after 25 years of marriage, or more. Today, that is very different. Some couples renew as quickly as after three years of marriage. This is a less formal occasion than the first wedding, and the couple stands at the altar rather than the bride walking down the aisle. Very often the original bridal party is present, and the immediate family attends.

It's best to talk with a clergyperson about this, since there really is no set protocol. The ceremony can take place as part of a regular church service or as a separate service. Sometimes the couple exchanges new wedding rings. When the ceremony is within a regular service, the couple wears whatever they normally would to their place of worship. If the occasion is a separate ceremony, they can decide what to wear according to the time of day and formality of the occasion. These decisions should be made with the clergyperson who will officiate.

Usually there is a gathering of some sort after the ceremony. It can be as lavish as a seated dinner in a hotel or as informal as cake and champagne immediately afterward at the church facility.

Bending the Rules

What happens when you make your own rules? Could be you end up with your perfect wedding.

Traditions exist because they fill a need in us for symbolism and ceremony. Yet, beauty is in the eye of the beholder.

Weddings always have been expressions of the couples' personality, taste, and values. Sometimes the time-honored traditions simply don't work. When that is the case, remember to honor yourselves and your commitment, and do what has meaning for you, as long as you are respectful and do not deliberately bash anyone's beliefs and values in so doing. It's up to your family and guests to open their minds and see things with your vision. The idea is to create an inclusive environment.

Having said that, what harm is there in asking a woman to serve as "best man?" or asking a "neutral" person to perform the ceremony rather than a clergyperson whose beliefs might conflict with your own? (My own sister asked a family friend who happened to be licensed to marry perform the ceremony, even though she was reared a Roman Catholic.) Or including your pets and children in your wedding?

None whatsoever.

All of the traditions, details, and variations in this chapter must never obscure the intrinsic truth of every wedding. It is a joyful occasion and a celebration of love. Everyone involved, from the bride and groom to the last guest, has an obligation to remember the reason for the wedding. Smile through the inevitable glitches. Put aside any criticisms or feelings of annoyance. Be helpful, be courteous, and most of all, be happy.

The Least You Need to Know

- Traditionally, the bride's family bears most of the cost of the wedding. The groom's family is responsible for the rehearsal dinner and other incidentals.

- If you attend a wedding, you must give a gift. If you are invited and do not attend, a gift is not necessary.

- Evening weddings are more formal than day weddings. If in doubt about what to wear, check with the mother of the bride or others who will be attending.

- The bride's friends and family sit to the left of the aisle; the groom's guests sit to the right.

- No two weddings are alike. They are made more interesting and more special through the influence of secular and religious traditions.

Index

X-Y-Z

Check Out These
Best-Sellers

978-1-59257-115-4
$16.95

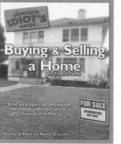

978-1-59257-458-2
$19.95

978-1-59257-451-3
$9.95

978-1-59257-485-8
$24.95

978-1-59257-480-3
$19.95

978-1-59257-469-8
$14.95

978-1-59257-439-1
$18.95

978-1-59257-483-4
$14.95

978-1-59257-389-9
$18.95

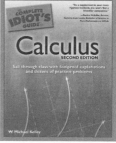

978-1-59257-471-1
$18.95

978-1-59257-437-7
$19.95

978-1-59257-463-6
$14.95

978-0-02-864244-4
$21.95

978-1-59257-335-6
$19.95

978-1-59257-491-9
$19.95

More than *450 titles* available at
booksellers and online retailers everywhere

www.idiotsguides.com

ALPHA